1995

The Ford Pinto Case

SUNY Series, Case Studies in Applied Ethics, Technology, and Society
John H. Fielder, editor

The Ford Pinto Case

A Study in Applied Ethics, Business, and Technology

Edited by

Douglas Birsch
and
John H. Fielder

STATE UNIVERSITY OF NEW YORK PRESS

Published by
State University of New York Press, Albany

For information, address State University of New York Press,
State University Plaza, Albany, NY 12246

Production by Cynthia Tenace Lassonde
Marketing by Fran Keneston

Library of Congress Cataloging-in-Publication Data

The Ford Pinto Case : a study in applied ethics, business, and society
  / Douglas Birsch and John Fielder, editors.
     p.   cm.
  Includes bibliographical references and index.
  ISBN 0-7914-2233-X (alk. paper.) — ISBN 0-7914-2234-8 (pbk. :
alk. paper)
  1. Business ethics—Case studies. 2. Social responsibility of
business—Case studies. 3. Ford Motor Company—Corrupt practices.
4. Pinto automobile.   I. Birsch, Douglas, 1951–   . II. Fielder,
John H., 1939–
Hf5387.F67   1994
338.4'76292222—dc20   94-838
                                                        CIP

10 9 8 7 6 5 4 3 2 1

For our parents
Edwin T. Birsch Jr., Patricia E. Birsch,
and Jack and Chris Fielder

Contents

PART V THE REGULATION OF BUSINESS

Preface

The Ford Pinto was a subcompact automobile manufactured by Ford Motor Company during the years 1971–1980. The Pinto's fuel system design and the decision to delay upgrading its integrity created a major controversy, which was heightened by the dramatic, criminal trial of Ford Motor Company in connection with the death by fire of three young women. To some people, the case is a classic example of corporate greed and lack of concern for consumers. For others, the case represents what can happen when a minor problem is blown out of proportion by media attention. Still another perspective holds that the Pinto case reveals the inability or unwillingness of the government to protect the driving public through regulatory agencies. All of these views have some merit, but a closer study of the Pinto case reveals a more difficult ethical terrain than this clear picture of heroes, villains, and victims. What we find in this case is a complex interplay of organizations, persons, policies, time and financial pressures, conflicts between engineering design and marketing strategies, and attempts to balance profit making and the protection of consumers. Every decision, policy, and institutional arrangement represents an intricate balancing of power, economics, and the public interest. We believe that a fair ethical assessment of the Pinto case must be based upon a knowledge of this intricate web of personal, institutional, economic, and political factors.

Having a responsible opinion on these matters requires an acquaintance with a wide range of materials dealing with various aspects of the case. In this book we have brought together the basic documents needed for reaching an informed judgment on the central ethical question in the Pinto case: did Ford Motor Company act ethically in designing the Pinto fuel system and in deciding not to upgrade the integrity of that system until 1978? In answering this question a number of other important questions arise. Did Ford decide not to fix a defective product in order to maximize profit? Did Ford use a cost-benefit analysis to make the decision not to upgrade the integrity of the Pinto fuel system? Is a cost-benefit analysis that places a monetary value on human life unethical? Should engineers at Ford have blown the whistle on a dangerous product that management had declined to improve? Is product liability an appropriate legal remedy to protect consumers from injury by defective products, and if so, what form should product liability take? Did government fail to adequately protect consumers in regard to the Pinto, and if so, what does that tell us about the effectiveness of the regulatory process? The attempt to answer these questions involves us in a complex and interesting story about an automobile and the people who were connected with it. It is a story that is relevant to all of us who drive or ride in cars.

Each of the previous questions is addressed in this book by articles and other relevant documents. The five parts of the book cover the case, cost-benefit analysis, whistle blowing, product liability, and government regulation. In addition, "Ethical Analysis of Case Studies" presents an overview of ethical concepts and some thoughts about the application of these ethical concepts to cases. It provides a vocabulary with which the ethical issues in the Pinto case can be more effectively discussed.

We believe that using a well-developed case to explore general business issues can be highly effective. It is extremely difficult to understand an issue like whistle blowing in general, unless one has seen the complexities involved in a real case where there was the potential to blow the whistle. We also believe that a well-developed case is essential to understanding specific business decisions or events because they are usually set in a complicated context. The Pinto decisions were set in the context of design, engineering, time, financial, and legal factors. One does not make the decision to alter a product, to blow the whistle on one's employer, or to fight against a piece of government regulation, in isolation. We would argue, for example, that an individual cannot make an intelligent decision about whether one or more of the Pinto engineers ought to have blown the whistle on Ford unless one really understands their situation. Hopefully, we have provided sufficient information concerning the case so that readers may draw their own conclusions about the various disputes based on their interpretation of the facts and their ethical positions.

Many people contributed to this book in a variety of ways. We wish to thank all those whose articles we have included, especially Mark Dowie since his article had such an enormous significance in the actual events. At Villanova University, we appreciate the efforts and support of John Immerwahr, Sandy Shupard, Mary Quilter,

Fr. Lawrence Gallen, Colleen Doyle, Dan Hipp, and John Bruni. At State University of New York Press, we were guided and supported by Carola Sautter, Cari Janice, Cindy Lassonde, Mary Beth Ray, and Fran Keneston. We would also like to thank Dan Guest, who did the diagrams in "Introduction: The Pinto Controversy" and David Wiedinmyer, who made a significant contribution to this project by preparing the index on short notice. Finally, we would like to thank our wives, Ellen Birsch and Pat Lawler, for their understanding and support.

Ethical Analysis of Case Studies

Being ethical has to do with meeting standards of conduct concerning the welfare of others and their right to make their own choices. An ethical person respects other's right to choose, takes their welfare into consideration, and cultivates habits of thought and action (virtues) that promote living an ethical life. Ethical issues in case studies raise questions about how to apply our ethical standards to new or complex situations. They pose difficult questions about right and wrong for which our unreflective ethical norms provide no clear answer. Ethical reflection attempts to articulate ethical standards, critically evaluate them, and apply them to a particular situation, taking into account all ethically relevant circumstances.

The Ford Pinto case raises many different kinds of ethical questions. The most obvious ones concern the choices of individuals within a corporation when faced with ethically significant decisions. We can also ask whether the actions of organizations, policies, and institutional arrangements reflect an adequate respect for the rights and welfare of persons affected by them.

There is general agreement among ethicists that there are two primary kinds of ethical considerations, those deriving from our status as beings who are able to reason and choose, and others based on our complex physical, social and emotional needs.[1] The former are emphasized in the ethical tradition of deontology, which focuses on the rights of autonomous human beings to make their own choices without undue interference from others. It is primarily concerned with respect for human choices rather than the good life and emphasizes respect for the rights of others to reason and choose for themselves.[2]

Human welfare has been the central idea of the other ethical tradition, that of consequentialism, which includes the various forms of utilitarianism. Here the emphasis is on how our actions affect the welfare of others by causing benefits and harms. Ethical life in this tradition emphasizes the good and bad effects (consequences) of ethical choices, policies, and institutions.

Many difficult ethical problems stem from conflicts between these two kind of ethical values. For example, should airline passengers be told that there has been a bomb threat on a particular flight? Doing so would respect their right to choose whether to take the risk of being killed if there is a bomb on board. But there are important negative consequences to the welfare of persons using the air travel system that such a policy of informing passengers would entail. Would terrorists be able to disrupt air travel at will? How many people would be deterred from taking a trip because of frivolous threats? Would the government's intelligence gathering methods be revealed? Even this brief example shows the complex interplay of individual freedom, different kinds of good and bad consequences, and complex factual conditions that is characteristic of case studies.

These two ethical considerations, human welfare and freedom to choose, are the foundations of our moral tradition. The familiar rules and principles of moral life, such as "Do not lie," are particular expressions of these fundamental ideas. Providing false information by lying interferes with a persons ability to make informed choices and it also may result in loss of goods or opportunities (welfare). Similar analyses can be provided for theft, invasion of privacy, confidentiality, and so forth.

There has been much philosophical debate about whether one of these ethical traditions is primary and/or implicitly includes the other. A number of ethical theories have been developed in response to this question, but there is no consensus concerning either their adequacy, usefulness for ethical evaluation of case studies, or the validity of the project of ethical theory itself.[3] Consequently, the material in this book does not assume any particular theoretical orientation other than the one outlined in this introduction. Readers who wish to analyze this case using a particular ethical theory are encouraged to do so, but we believe that this is not essential. Familiarity with ethical theory will undoubtedly bring additional insight into some aspects of the case, but so would a knowledge of law, organizational behavior, economics, or political science.

CASE STUDIES

The ethical analysis of case studies is concerned with making ethical judgments about actions, choices, policies and institutions in actual situations. The focus is on ethical evaluation that takes into account the complexity of all the ethically relevant circumstances. The analysis of case studies has many similarities to the legal tradition of common law, which is based on the interpretation of precedent cases rather than statutes. Those pursuing a career in law use both actual and hypothetical case studies in learning to apply legal standards of conduct to unusual, unforeseen and complicating circumstances of real life. Case analysis is often used in other professional programs, such as the Harvard Business School, because of its value in preparing students to deal with the kind of problems they will encounter in actual practice. It provides an opportunity to learn to apply management concepts and principles to the complex problems of business managers. Ethicists similarly apply ethical principles and concepts to actual situations, taking account of the ethically relevant circumstances.

The Ford Pinto case invites ethical evaluation in a wide range of areas. Did Ford design an adequately safe automobile? Were Ford's actions in responding to the design deficiencies ethical? Does the procedure through which automobiles are designed and engineered pay sufficient attention to safety? Should Ford engineers, who believed that the Pinto's fuel system was unsafe, have blown the whistle on Ford Motor Company? Is capitalism with government regulation adequate to ensure the level of safety that consumers have a right to expect? These are the kinds of questions the Pinto case raises: what kinds of conceptual tools can moral philosophy provide to answer them?

It is important to keep in mind that these questions can only be posed because we already have an ethical vocabulary in which we can ask ethical questions, propose answers, and debate them. We begin our ethical analysis already in possession of a set of shared ethical principles and concepts and with experience in using them. All of us start with the belief that it is generally wrong to lie, cheat, steal, invade people's privacy, inflict physical or emotional harm on them, prevent them from making their own life decisions, and so forth. We have had extensive experience in using these ideas to analyze ethical problems, make our own ethical judgments, and criticize the judgments of others. Making ethical judgments about persons, actions, policies, and institutions is an everyday feature of life.

While philosophers disagree about the role of ethical theory in analyzing case studies, they share a universal belief that ethical analysis can be strengthened by clarifying the important concepts we use in ethical analysis. This helps eliminate confusion, allows us to be more explicit about our analysis, and more accurately frame important points of disagreement. The remainder of this introduction sets out some of our basic ethical concepts and outlines their connections to the Ford Pinto case.

ETHICAL ANALYSIS: OBLIGATIONS AND RIGHTS

Ethical analysis of actual ethical problems is primarily a matter of articulating standards of ethical conduct and applying them in light of the particular circumstances of the case. It is essential to articulate the ethical requirements relevant for the evaluation of a particular individual or organizational action, policy, or institution. Two concepts that are of central importance for this task are obligations and rights.

Obligation is a concept that occurs in law, ethics, religion, and social life. It designates requirements of conduct that arise within a particular tradition or practice. Legal obligations arise from the framework of laws that govern our actions, and in a similar way religious traditions have specific requirements of conduct for their adherents. Membership in a community also creates social obligations to neighbors and others with whom we interact. Ethical obligations arise primarily from our participation in a community with shared norms of behavior. Whether we view those norms as having transcultural validity (as traditional ethical theories hold) or as the evolved values of western civilization (as some of the critics of ethical theory believe), these norms may be stated as obligations requiring certain kinds of conduct.

An obligation may usually be restated in terms of a right. For example, a teacher's obligation to protect the privacy of students' grades may be equivalently stated as the students' right to have the privacy of their grades protected. The ethical requirement can be stated from the point of view of those who act (their obligations) or those who are importantly affected by those acts (their rights). Respect for the rights of others means meeting the obligations those rights impose upon us. The language of rights is most closely associated with the deontological tradition of ethics, which emphasizes freedom of choice. Rights in this usage assert special protections against the interference of others or entitlements to certain basic goods.

POSITIVE AND NEGATIVE RIGHTS AND OBLIGATIONS

Most of the obligations we learned while growing up were negative, that is, they stipulated that one was not to do certain things: lie, cheat, steal, harm others and so forth. They were "do nots." These obligations can be stated as negative rights that require others not to interfere with us in certain ways, such as taking our possessions, causing us pain, or causing us to believe something false. These rights are primarily designed to protect us from the actions of others. It is the idea behind the familiar ethical principle that "your right to swing your fist ends where my nose begins."

While negative rights and obligations require that we refrain from certain actions, positive rights and obligations require that we perform certain actions. For example, parents are obligated to do many things to ensure that their childrens' needs are met. Proper diet, schooling, love, and nurturing are positive actions that parents owe their children. These obligations may be restated as positive rights, which are often called welfare rights. Children have a right to an adequate diet, and it is not only parents who have a corresponding obligation to see that they get it. Social and governmental institutions can powerfully affect the lives of children by making it easy or difficult for parents to meet their obligations to them. Organizations and institutions as well as individuals may be held ethically accountable for their roles in the ethical treatment of children.

The importance of this concept in automobile safety concerns the welfare rights of consumers. If they have a positive welfare right to safe products, then all those who have a role in providing those products have corresponding positive obligations to see that automobiles are safe. This will include not only individuals but also corporations and government agencies. All must meet ethical obligations if consumers have such a right. Much social criticism consists of showing that generally accepted positive rights to safety, health care, education, and so forth are not being respected by our current social arrangements.

TECHNOLOGY AS SOCIAL EXPERIMENTATION

An interesting way to discuss the ethical rights of consumers is to focus on the idea of technology as social experimentation.[4] Since it is impossible to foresee everything that could go wrong with something as sophisticated as an automobile, putting a new car on the market is a kind of social experiment. It is expected that some problems will emerge and that modifications will have to be made to correct them.

Automobile drivers and passengers are, in a sense, subjects taking part in an experiment. Automobiles are tested before being marketed, but the company must put them on the market and see how they work out when exposed to the varied conditions of daily driving and to different kinds of accidents. Viewing automobile drivers and passengers as participants in an experiment raises familiar questions about the rights of experimental subjects and implies that they are entitled to adequate safety provisions in the design of cars. This, in turn, means that individuals, organizations, and institutions have positive ethical obligations to respect the rights of automobile travelers with regard to safety.

SAFETY

Safety is defined as "of acceptable risk."[5] Risk is a combination of the probability and severity of harm. This captures our intuition that the most serious risks are those that involve both severe harm and a high probability that it will happen. This aspect of risk analysis can be carried out by experts who are trained to estimate the probability of occurrence and assess the kind of harms that would result.[6]

Whether or not something is safe depends upon whether the risk is "acceptable," and this is clearly not a technical question to be answered by experts. It is a social and political question in its application to automobile travel, for it is ultimately the public that should determine what kinds of risks are acceptable in driving cars. In the case of automobile travel, the public's agents, the Department of Transportation and its agency the National Highway Traffic Safety Administration, make decisions about safety. These decisions are certainly open to challenge. Some critics believe that automobile travel is not sufficiently safe, that the public has a right to more protection than has been provided in cases like the Ford Pinto.

PRESUMPTIVE RIGHTS AND OBLIGATIONS

Rights and obligations are generally regarded as "presumptive," meaning that they are assumed to be binding but may be set aside under certain conditions or "trumped" by more important rights and obligations. This is the familiar idea that ethical principles have exceptions. For example, although lying is assumed to be wrong, it is not difficult to imagine conditions under which it would be acceptable. Lying to the gestapo to protect Jews during World War II is morally right because the obligation to protect innocent lives is more important in that situation than the obligation to tell the truth. Both are *prima facie* obligations, but there seems to be no response that will fulfill both of them. When there is a conflict of obligations and there is no way to meet both, we have to decide which obligation should have priority. Many ethical disagreements concern issues where each side has a valid moral claim and the conflict concerns which is more important.

JUSTIFICATIONS, EXCUSES, AND SACRIFICE

Persons who defend their violation of the obligation to tell the truth (as in the example of lying to the gestapo to save Jews), argue that their actions are justified because they were not simply lying but were meeting an important obligation, that of preserving innocent lives. Since there was no way to meet both obligations, their violation of the less important one was morally justified. Such justifications will be accepted when we agree with the individual's ranking of the obligations.

A violation of a moral principle may also be excused. Suppose a friend promised to meet you for lunch, but on the way her car broke down. She has a good reason to claim that the failure to keep the promise is excused because of circumstances beyond her control. Of course, she could have abandoned the car, hailed a cab and kept the promise, but we would not require this amount of sacrifice of her other personal goals (e.g., to get the car fixed as soon as possible, to avoid extra expense, etc.) to keep this obligation. If she was the maid of honor or minister at your wedding however, the case would be different. Under either of these circumstances we would expect her to make more of an effort to attend because of the greater importance of the obligation. The greater the importance of the obligation, the greater the amount of sacrifice or risk taking is expected in order to meet it. The importance of an obligation and the amount of risk or loss that result from meeting it are key factors in determining what counts as an adequate excuse.

Whether we excuse the Pinto engineers for not demanding that the fuel system in the car be made safer depends partly on whether it was in their power to have safety modifications brought about. It also depends on the amount of risk taking and sacrifice we expect from them in this case. How much sacrifice can we expect from these engineers? Should we excuse them from their ethical obligation because the sacrifice needed to ensure greater safety would have been too great?

ROLE RESPONSIBILITIES

The most obvious place where ethical obligations apply is individual decisions. In a particular ethical problem we are not concerned simply with broad ethical principles (such as "Do not lie") that apply to all individuals, but with how those principles are applied in particular circumstances. An important feature of the circumstances in which ethical problems arise is the role a particular person has. The concept of role responsibility helps to clarify the obligations people have by deriving some of them from their roles.[7]

According to this approach, each role embodies a set of rights and obligations: ethical, social, and legal, connected to a social or organizational function. For example, a lifeguard has a greater ethical obligation to help persons who may be drowning than the vacationers walking along the beach. Similarly the lifeguard's role entails legal obligations concerning the upkeep of lifesaving equipment, which do not apply to others, and social requirements that arise in the community of lifeguards and persons associated with that role. Determining whether people acted ethically is often a matter of deciding what the person's relevant role obligations are, whether or not they were fulfilled, and whether there were any excusing or justifying conditions present.

In the Pinto case we may ask whether the Ford engineers and managers and the government employees of the NHTSA adequately fulfilled their role obligations. This question is complicated by the fact that the Ford employees had many other obligations besides those connected to safety, and that the people at the NHTSA investigated the Pinto although perhaps not as promptly as they should have. Role obligations may conflict with one another and there may be difficult questions about the time frame involved in fulfilling such obligations.

PROFESSIONAL OBLIGATIONS

An important subset of role obligations is professional obligations. These are obligations that apply to special kinds of careers that are called professions. Law, medicine, nursing, and engineering are typical examples of professions. They are characterized by a) the possession of specialized skills and knowledge that are b) obtained through extensive, formal education involving substantial theoretical content, and c) the service performed by the practitioner is essential to the community.[8] Because professionals possess essential specialized skills and knowledge not available to laypersons, the latter are relatively ignorant and dependent upon professionals for the services based on their specialized knowledge. Because of this unequal relationship, special ethical obligations apply to professionals that are designed to protect their vulnerable clients. In the Pinto case, professional engineers had knowledge of deficiencies in the fuel system, which were unknown to laypersons. Because that knowledge was of potential harm to the innocent (and ignorant) automobile drivers and passengers, the engineers had a professional obligation to take action to try to remove the harm.

The professional's understanding of those obligations is expressed in Codes of Ethics; e.g., one version of the Institute of Electrical and Electronic Engineering (IEEE) Code required that "Members shall, in fulfilling their responsibilities to the community: protect the safety, health, and, welfare of the public and speak out against abuses in these areas affecting the public interest." (Article IV, 1)

ORGANIZATIONAL ACTIONS

Ethical standards apply not only to individual decisions but also to organizational actions, policies, and institutional arrangements. Organizational actions, unlike individual ones, embody decisions made by groups of people acting within organizational roles and exercising organizational authority. These organizational decisions affect the rights and welfare of others. One set of ethical questions that arise here concerns the moral responsibility for organizational actions: Can individuals be held morally responsible for group decisions? Can corporations be held morally responsible for the acts of their employees? Can corporate employees be held morally responsible for corporate actions? Another question concerns whether organizational actions adequately embody respect for the rights and welfare of those who will be affected by them. As with individual decisions, much depends upon the specific character of the organizational action, its overall effects, the options available, and the constraints present.

In the Pinto case, the question of moral responsibility for the burn injuries and the lost lives is a complicated one. Can Ford Motor Company be held morally responsible, and if so, what exactly does it mean for a corporation to be morally responsible? Can individual Ford managers or engineers be held morally responsible for the fuel system problems? Should Lee Iacocca, the former president of Ford Motor Company, and the man ultimately in charge of the Pinto, be held morally responsible for the injuries and the lost lives? Organizational actions differ from individual choices in that the former are typically the result of interactions among individuals whose positions are defined by their roles in the organization. The resulting actions reflect both individual choices and the organization's history, culture, and structure, thus complicating the question of moral responsibility.[9]

POLICIES

Policies are larger patterns of organizational action. They can be evaluated according to whether or not they meet the obligations of the organization to those who will be affected by the policy. A policy may be explicitly spelled out in memos or other forms of organizational publication, such as personnel manuals, or they may be implicit, reflecting "how things are done around here" without being formally set out. Both represent organizational decisions about how to deal with a certain kind of issue and are subject to ethical evaluation. In the Ford Pinto case, it is important to look both at Ford's policies in connection with designing and building cars, and also at the policies of the NHTSA. Were the policies of the company and the regulatory agency adequate to ensure the degree of automobile safety to which the public was entitled?

INSTITUTIONAL ARRANGEMENTS

We may also direct ethical evaluation to the fundamental political arrangements in which the automobile industry functions. In the United States, the automobile manufacturers are corporations operating within a capitalist economic framework. Making sure that cars are safe is the responsibility of the Department of Transportation and the NHTSA. Political pressure is often put on government officials by members of Congress and representatives of the White House to protect the economic interests of their constituents. Critics have questioned the ability of safety organizations like the NHTSA to function when exposed to this political pressure. Some have charged that political pressure grounded in economic concerns prevents automobiles from being adequately safe. Those who believe that the capitalist system itself is the problem have more radical criticisms.

CONCLUSION

The ethical analysis of case studies demands both clarity about ethical concepts and familiarity with the actual circumstances in which we apply them. The Ford Pinto case is extremely complex and ethically interesting, involving high technology, government bureaucracies, powerful corporations, the individuals who work for them, various policies that attempt to meet sometimes conflicting values, and our basic institutional arrangements for insuring the safety of automobile travel. Because it touches so many different dimensions of contemporary commercial life, it generates a variety of difficult ethical questions. The ethical concepts, the information, and the analysis of ethical issues collected in this book will not answer all of them in a definitive way, but they will enable you to develop your own well-informed judgments about a difficult problem in contemporary life.

NOTES

1. See Louis Lombardi, *Moral Analysis*, (Albany, NY: SUNY Press, 1988) for an extended treatment of this issue.

2. See Jeffrey Stout, *Ethics After Babel* (Boston: Beacon Press, 1988), p. 286.

3. The debate about the role of ethical theory in philosophy is extensive. Good places to enter that literature are: Stanley G. Clarke and Evan Simpson, ed., *Anti-Theory in Ethics and Moral Conservatism*, (Albany, NY: State University of New York Press, 1989); Stuart Hampshire, *Morality and Conflict*, (Cambridge: Harvard University Press, 1983); and Albert Jonsen and Stephen Toulmin, *The Abuse of Casuistry*, (Berkeley: University of California Press, 1988).

4. This idea is developed in Mike W. Martin and Roland Schinzinger, *Ethics in Engineering*, (New York: McGraw-Hill, 1983), p. 55 ff.

5. William W. Lowrance, *Of Acceptable Risk*, (Los Altos, CA: William Kaufman, Inc., 1976), p. 8.

6. The public perception of risk is not always the same as that of the experts. See Paul Slovic, Baruch Fishchoff, and Sara Lichtenstein, "Facts and Fears: Understanding Perceived Risk," in *Societal Risk Assessment: How Safe is Safe Enough?* edited by Richard C. Schwing and Walter A. Albers (New York: Plenum Press, 1980).

7. See Norman F. Bowie and Ronald F. Duska, *Business Ethics*, second edition (Englewood Cliffs, NJ: Prentice-Hall, 1990), p. 4 ff. This idea is also developed in Louis Lombardi, *Moral Analysis.*

8. For a discussion of this issue as it applies to engineers, see D. Allan Firmage, *Modern Engineering Practice: Ethical, Professional, and Legal Aspects*, (New York: Garland STPM Press, 1980), p. 10–14.

9. For a view which holds that it makes no sense to apply concepts of moral responsibility to organizations, see Manuel G. Velasquez, "Why Corporations are Not Morally Responsible for Anything They Do," *Business and Professional Ethics Journal*, 2 (Spring 1983), p. 1–17.

Part I

THE PINTO CONTROVERSY

Introduction: The Pinto Controversy

SUMMARY OF THE CASE

The Ford Pinto appeared on the market in 1970, and sales of the car were good for the first few years. There were problems, however, with the early Pintos leaking fuel and catching on fire after relatively low-speed, rear-end collisions. The Pinto's gasoline tank was located behind the rear axle. In a rear-end collision of about twenty-eight miles per hour or more, the rear of the car would be crushed and the tank would be driven against the differential housing. The differential housing covers the differential, which is the large gear that transfers force from the driveshaft to the rear axle. In a rear-end collision, the gas tank could strike the bolts on the differential housing, causing the tank to split open and fuel to leak out. In addition, the filler pipe, which carries the fuel from the opening in the side of the car to the gas tank, could be torn loose and additional gasoline might leak from this area. The leaked fuel sometimes started fires, which led to fatalities or serious burns. In a gasoline fire, the gasoline vapor burns. When fuel leaks from the gas tank, the evaporating fumes may enter and surround the car. Any spark caused by the friction of metal hitting metal in the crash or from the electrical system can ignite the vapor and create an explosion.

Many victims of these Pinto fires or their relatives sued Ford in civil suits (tort cases), lawsuits where victims try to recover damages for the effects of wrongful or negligent actions. Ford tried to settle the cases out of court, but some of them led to trials that produced undesirable publicity for the company. The negative publicity connected to the Ford Pinto was greatly increased by the publication of an article in September of 1977 called "Pinto Madness." This essay, written by Mark Dowie, appeared in the magazine *Mother Jones*, and is the first selection in Part I. Dowie presents information about the case and offers a theory about why Ford did not respond quickly and effectively to the problems with the fuel system. Dowie's article helped bring the Pinto controversy to the general public. Ford Motor Company challenged the accuracy of "Pinto Madness," and Part I's second selection "Ford Rebuts Pinto Criticism and Says Article is Distorted" briefly presents Ford's response. In an eight-page statement, a company executive stated that the number of deaths and injuries resulting from Pinto fires was much lower than Dowie claimed and that the Pinto was not an unsafe car. (We were unable to obtain the original statement from Ford and therefore used this article from the *National Underwriter.*) After "Pinto Madness" was published, television and newspapers, especially the *Chicago Tribune*, took up the story and also criticized Ford. The accumulation of bad publicity led to a serious decline in the sales of the car.

The "Pinto Madness" article and the series by the *Chicago Tribune* were based, in part, on a set of internal Ford documents. These documents provided information on the design of the Pinto fuel system, on crash testing done to determining the safety of that system, on improvements suggested by Ford engineers, and on management's response to the fuel system problem. While we were not able to obtain permission to reprint these documents, we have included a selection discussing them from *Reckless Homicide?: Ford's Pinto Trial* by Lee Patrick Strobel. This selection, which is the third article in the book, provides the background to the controversy set out in "Pinto Madness" and Ford's response to it.

The fourth selection in the book, which we have titled "The Pinto Fuel System" is from *West's California Reporter* and provides two additional parts of the story: it describes the chain of command at Ford that supervised the development of the Pinto and summarizes the view of Harley Copp, a former Ford engineer and executive who testified against Ford in many civil cases.

On September 1, 1976, the portion of the National Highway Traffic Safety Administration's (NHTSA) Standard 301 related to rear-impact went into effect. This safety regulation limited the amount of fuel that could leak out of a car. Earlier Pintos would not have met this standard, but the 1977 Pinto was in compliance with it. A copy of this standard and a couple of the amendments to it have been included in the book as the fifth selection in Part I. Sections S5.5 and S6.2 set the standard for the amount of fuel that may leak from the fuel tank following a rear-end collision. Section S5.5 designates the amount of fuel that is allowed to leak: one ounce from impact until the motion of the car has ceased and one ounce a minute for five minutes afterwards. Section S6.2 establishes that the car has to be struck by a barrier moving at 30 mph, thus approximating a 30 mph vehicle-to-vehicle crash. The diagrams, included in the standard, are of a moving barrier. We included two of the amendments since they give some insight into the way the automobile companies negotiate with the NHTSA about federal standards.

In 1978, the NHTSA announced that it had made an initial determination that a safety defect existed in the fuel systems of 1971–1976 Ford Pintos and that it had scheduled public hearings for June. The sixth selection in Part I is the report on the Pinto from the Office of Defects Investigation Enforcement of the NHTSA. It includes the crash test results that substantiated the agency's allegation of a safety defect. These tests demonstrated that the Pinto was not as safe in a rear-end collision as the General Motors subcompact, the Vega. On June 9, 1978, Ford announced the recall of approximately one and a half million Pintos (model years 1971–1976) and 30,000 Mercury Bobcats to end public debate and concern over the matter. Two plastic shields were added to prevent the gas tank from being punctured by the differential housing, an improved sealing cap went on the tank, and a longer fuel-tank filler pipe was added. The estimated cost was somewhere between twenty and forty million dollars.

The voluntary recall set in motion events which would eventually end Ford's problems with the Pinto. There were still the remaining civil suits, with any more that might follow, but Ford was prepared to handle these cases. On September 13, 1978, however, an Indiana Grand Jury indicted Ford Motor Company for three felony counts of reckless homicide, resulting from an accident in which a van rear-ended a Pinto and three girls were burned to death. Witnesses claimed that it was a relatively low-speed collision. The prosecution charged that Ford had recklessly manufactured a lethal vehicle and kept it on the road despite obvious danger. The Indiana trial was a criminal trial, concerned with a violation of the law, instead of a civil trial. If Ford Motor Company were to have been found guilty, the corporation would have been fined up to $10,000 for each case of reckless homicide. On March 13, 1980, Ford was found innocent on all charges. Ford lawyers convinced the jury that the Pinto involved in the accident was stopped when it was hit by the van. Therefore, it was not a low-speed collision and hence the deaths of the driver and passengers were not a result of reckless homicide. This important victory for Ford established that, while there might have been ethical questions about Ford's actions, the company did not violate any laws. Because of two excellent books on the trial, *Reckless Homicide?: Ford's Pinto Trial* by Lee Patrick Strobel, and *Corporate Crime Under Attack: The Ford Pinto Case and Beyond* by Francis T. Cullen, William J. Maakestad, and Gray Cavender, and because we are more interested in ethical rather than legal issues, we have not explored the trial in our book.[1]

The last Ford Pinto was manufactured in 1980, and the car was phased out of the Ford line. Ford had manufactured about three million of these cars and a similar subcompact, the Mercury Bobcat. For most owners, the Pinto was economical transportation, but for some others it was instrumental in causing their deaths or serious injuries.

PINTO CONTROVERSIES: DESIGN AND PRODUCTION

There are a number of interesting and controversial issues connected to the Ford Pinto, which are made more difficult because of uncertainty about some of the facts of the case. The first controversy began around 1967 or 1968, and was whether or not Ford should build a subcompact. The president of Ford Motor Company, Semon Knudsen, opposed the idea of building a subcompact in the United States, but a Ford vice-president, Lee Iacocca, advised that they introduce a subcompact and build it domestically. Henry Ford II decided in favor of Iacocca, Knudsen resigned, and Iacocca later became president of Ford. Thus, from the very beginning, the building of a Ford subcompact was a very serious business decision with substantial consequences.

Lee Iacocca apparently took an active interest in the Pinto. According to Mark Dowie, Iacocca wanted the car on the market as soon as possible and ordered an accelerated production schedule. Dowie also claimed that Iacocca set rigid weight and price specifications for the car: 2000 pounds and $2000. Ford officials have denied that there were any strict limits set, and it is not possible to determine what was actually the case. While Iacocca was a member of Ford's product planning committee, it is unknown whether he had any direct effect on the the car's design. A *Chicago Tribune* article stated: "None of the documents obtained [internal Ford memos], however, shows any direct involvement by Iacocca in the design decision involving the car."[2]

The design work on the Pinto was begun in 1967. Dowie stated that the "normal" time frame for getting a car from the drawing board to the road is about 43 months. He believed that the Pinto schedule was set up for 25 months. Another source suggested that the total time was 38 months, but the actual figure cannot be determined from the available literature.[3] In either case, it was obviously to Ford's economic advantage to get the car into the showrooms as soon as possible and on the market at an inexpensive price. If Ford delayed, the foreign car makers, and perhaps General Motors with their new subcompact, the Chevrolet Vega, would gain market share. If the price was too high, the car would not be an attractive alternative to the competition. Therefore, even if there were no rigid specifications, we can assume that the design work on the Pinto was done in an atmosphere where time and price were important factors.

The major significance of a shorter production time is related to a manufacturing process called tooling, the building of the machines that will produce the car parts. Tooling normally begins after design, product development, and quality control are completed. The company usually builds and tests prototypes to make sure that all the parts work well together and that the car itself is satisfactory before starting to build the machines to make the car. Dowie charged that although Ford crash tests revealed the susceptibility of the fuel system to damage, the company did not alter the design before the car went into production because tooling had already begun, and therefore the design changes would have been too expensive.

PINTO CONTROVERSIES: PLACEMENT OF THE FUEL TANK

Another dispute concerns the placement of the fuel tank. Ford had two options to choose from: an over-the-axle tank, which had been used on the Ford Capri, and a behind-the-axle tank. (See Figures 1 and 2.) Placing the tank behind the axle was standard for the industry in regular sized cars and was also the standard for the Japanese subcompacts. Crash tests on the Ford Capri, however, had

FIGURE 1
This diagram shows the placement of the fuel tank in the Ford Pinto.

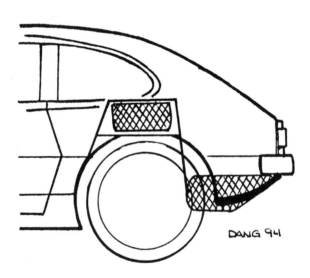

FIGURE 2
This diagram shows the actual placement of the fuel tank, as well as
the alternative placement above the rear axle.

shown that the over-the-axle tank performed very well in rear-end collisions. There were some drawbacks to the design, though, since it required a circuitous filler pipe, which was more likely to be dislodged in an accident. The tank also was closer to the passenger compartment and therefore might increase the threat of fire to the passengers. In addition, the higher placement of the tank raised the center of gravity of the car and might have adversely affected handling. Finally, the design led to reduced trunk space and could not be used on a hatchback or station wagon model. The behind-the-axle model was not as safe in rear-end collisions, but it did provide more trunk space and could be utilized in a hatchback or wagon. Ford decided to build the Pinto with the behind-the-axle gas tank. One claim is that the over-the-axle tank was rejected because of undesirable luggage space. Ford representatives later argued that this claim oversimplified the issue. There were also safety considerations in favor of the behind-the-axle model, and it was the industry standard. While Dowie considers the placement of the gas tank unethical, this matter is highly debatable. We should not forget that improvements to the behind-the-axle tank, mandated by Standard 301, led to a tank with this design, that people considered adequately safe.

PINTO CONTROVERSIES: FATALITIES

Another dispute in this case involves the number of people who were actually killed in low-speed, rear-end collisions involving Pintos. Dowie charged that there were somewhere between 500 and 900 fire-related deaths. Prior to the recall in 1978, Ford claimed that Pintos had been involved in 35 cases of rear-impact, fuel leakage fires; producing 23 burn injuries and 21 non-impact fatalities. Of the 29 resulting lawsuits, 8 cases had been settled out of court, 19 were pending, and 2 trials had been decided in favor of Ford. (These statistics are included in the NHTSA report in Part I.) The NHTSA's Investigation Report noted that the agency was aware of 38 cases of rear-end collisions and fires in Pintos that resulted in 27 fatalities and 24 cases of non-fatal burns. These 27 fatalities presumably included the 17 fatalities documented by the NHTSA's Fatal Accident Reporting System (FARS) over a two and a half year period from 1975 to the middle of 1977. Based on these FARS statistics, it would mean that there were about seven unnecessary deaths a year during that period. If the Ford numbers were accurate, there would have been an average of about three and one half. It is probable that both of these numbers are too low. Ford's count presumably is derived from lawsuits and it is possible that there were some cases where people did not sue. It also is possible that Ford under-reported the numbers for publicity reasons. The NHTSA's FARS numbers were based on police accident reports, which often did not report fires, or burn deaths that occurred after the crash, and which also did not always distinguish between impact and fire fatalities. Therefore, some fire deaths that were not specifically reported as such might not have been included. It is likely that the number of unnecessary deaths exceeded seven a year, but it is impossible to determine accurately how many deaths there were. Dowie's number of 500 to 900 fire-related deaths is too high, and Ford's number of 23 is too low.[4]

PINTO CONTROVERSIES: CRASH TESTING

It has been charged that Ford knew the fuel system design was defective because it had crash tested Ford Pintos in 1969, before the car was put into production and even before the tooling had begun. Ford denied crash testing Pintos prior to production. The reason for this dispute seems to be that, although subcompact cars were crash tested in 1969, these cars were not Pintos, but other subcompact models set up with Pinto-type fuel systems. In these tests, all the cars leaked fuel when crashed into a wall at 20 mph. The tests were fixed barrier tests, where the car crashes into a stationary wall, rather than moving barrier tests, where a barrier is towed into a stationary car. The moving barrier test causes less damage since the stationary car moves in the same direction as the wall when impacted, transfering some of the crash force into the motion of the car. In the fixed barrier test the car is moving into a fixed wall, and hence more force is absorbed by the car, causing more damage. If this 1969 crash test information is accurate, Ford had adequate knowledge to make design changes in the Pinto fuel system prior to tooling.

There were other crash tests performed on actual Pintos. A 1970 confidential Ford document "Final Test Report" provides the results from the crash test of a 1971 Pinto two-door sedan. The car impacted a fixed barrier at 21.5 mph (equivalent to a 28.3 mph moving barrier crash). The filler pipe was pulled out of the tank, causing fluid to leak. Also, a bolt on the differential housing punctured the gas tank, causing additional leakage.[5] Thus, in 1970, Ford knew that the Pinto represented a serious fire hazard following a low-speed, rear-end collision. Another Ford document written in 1972 shows six additional fixed barrier crash tests of 1971–1972 Pintos. The first test of a station wagon at 16.8 mph (equivalent to a 21.8 mph moving barrier crash) showed slight leakage from the tank, and the filler pipe was pulled out. The second test of a three-door or hatchback model at 15.5 mph (20 mph moving barrier crash) showed only slight leakage from the filler pipe at the tank inlet. The third test of a two-door model was done at 26.3 mph (34.7 mph moving barrier crash). The tank leaked from the filler pipe and was severely deformed, but did not leak further because a rubber bladder had been installed in the steel tank. The fourth test vehicle, also a two-door model, was crashed at 20.8 mph (27.4 mph moving barrier crash). It showed no leakage, but the car had been modified by the addition of two longitudinal side rails in the rear of the car. The fifth car, another two-door model, was crashed at 21 mph (27.9 mph moving barrier crash). Once again, a rubber bladder had been installed and only slight leakage occurred. Finally, the last test was an unmodified Pinto crashed at 21.5 mph (28.3 mph moving barrier crash). The filler pipe was pulled out of the tank, and the tank was punctured by the axle housing bolt. Consequently, the tests showed that the car was potentially unsafe following relatively low-speed, rear-end collisions.[6]

PINTO CONTROVERSIES: SAFETY AND THE FUEL SYSTEM

These crash tests provided the Ford engineers with sufficient information to have informed management that the car was potentially dangerous under certain conditions and that the car's safety could be significantly upgraded by the installation of a rubber bladder or longitudinal side rails. If Ford engineers had sufficient data to document the fuel system problem with the car, and if they had informed management of this problem, why did Ford choose not to upgrade the integrity of the fuel system prior to 1978? This question is the biggest controversy concerning the vehicle. Dowie charged that Ford did not recall the car because it used a cost-benefit analysis to determine that it was more profitable to pay the civil suits than to pay for the cost of fixing the automobile. A cost-benefit analysis is a management decision-making technique that weighs the economic costs and benefits of alternatives to provide a justification for carrying out the one that offers the greatest net benefit. The cost-benefit controversy is discussed in Part II of the book.

The final selection in Part I "Pinto Fires and Personal Ethics: A Script Analysis of Missed Opportunities" offers the view of a former

Ford employee concerning why the Pinto was not recalled at an earlier date to upgrade the fuel system. Dennis Gioia discusses his involvement in the early stages of the Pinto case, providing an account of the "...context and decision environment within which he failed to initiate an early recall of the defective vehicles."[7] He also offers an analysis of his missed opportunity in terms of the "script schema" or specialized cognitive framework that imposed a structure on the Pinto affair and led him to overlook key features of the case.

Presumably, there were Ford engineers working on the Pinto who thought that the integrity of the fuel system was inadequate and that the car was dangerous. We may assume that they had informed management of their concern, at least through the results of the crash testing. If management refused to order an upgrade of the fuel system, the engineers may have considered informing someone outside the company of the problem with the Pinto. Such an action would be an example of whistle blowing. Another controversy, discussed in Part III of the book, is whether the Pinto engineers should have blown the whistle on Ford Motor Company about the Pinto fuel system.

PINTO CONTROVERSIES: PRODUCT LIABILITY

The Ford Pinto case is usually labeled a product liability case. There are two controversies connected to the Ford Pinto and product liability. The first debate concerns the proper way to understand product liability. One view is that companies should be liable for injuries and deaths if there is improper conduct on the part of the company. Another view, called strict liability, claims that companies should be liable if the product is defective and unreasonably dangerous. The second view makes it easier for injured people or the relatives of those who have been killed to collect damages from the manufacturer. The second controversy relates to Ford and the Pinto specifically. Should Ford be held liable for the deaths and injuries caused by fuel fires and rear-end collisions involving Pintos? Part IV discusses both of these product liability controversies.

PINTO CONTROVERSIES: GOVERNMENT REGULATION

A final controversy connected to the Ford Pinto case involves government regulation. The NHTSA enacted Standard 301 to save lives, yet Ford and presumably the other automobile companies lobbied against government regulation because it would necessitate improvements and make the cars more expensive. Is it ethical for companies to lobby against regulations that would save lives? There are also interesting ethical questions connected to the priority that automobile companies give to safety. Is it unethical to put profits ahead of safety? The articles in Part V explore these controversies and other questions related to government regulation.

CONCLUSION

The selections in Part I provide the reader with a great deal of information about the case, including some essential documents. They also present a framework for the controversies connected to the Ford Pinto. An understanding of the material in Part I is important to get the most out of the other parts of the book. The incidents connected to the Ford Pinto involve the whole spectrum of business: engineering tests and decisions, management decision making, government regulation, civil court cases, a criminal court case, an enormous amount of money, satisfied customers, and other customers who died as a result of the way a product was designed. The articles in this book will provide many insights into the history of the car and the controversies mentioned earlier. By the end of the book, you should be able to draw your own conclusions about the various disputes. One thing to keep in mind as you read is that real-life business cases are enormously complicated, and there are rarely clear-cut villains or heroes.

NOTES

1. Lee Patrick Strobel, *Reckless Homicide?: Ford's Pinto Trial* (South Bend, Indiana: And Books, 1980) and Francis T. Cullen, William J. Maakestad, and Gray Cavender, *Corporate Crime Under Attack: The Ford Pinto Trial and Beyond* (Cincinnati, Ohio: Anderson Publishing Co., 1987).

2. *Chicago Tribune*, October 14, 1979, p. 18.

3. Lee Patrick Strobel, *Reckless Homicide*, p. 81.

4. In a phone conversation with one of the authors, Mark Dowie said that he derived his estimate of the fire related deaths from his interpretation of information received from "The President's Fire Commission." Based on the greater amount of information available today, he admitted that his number might be high, but insisted that Ford's number was too low. He agreed with our claim that no one will ever know exactly how many people died in Pinto fires caused by low-speed, rear-end collisions.

5. Lee Patrick Strobel, *Reckless Homicide,* p. 276.

6. Ibid., p. 278.

7. Dennis Gioia, "Pinto Fires and Personal Ethics: A Script Analysis of Missed Opportunities," *Journal of Business Ethics,* 11, (1992): 379.

1

Pinto Madness*

Illustration by Charley Brown

One evening in the mid-1960s, Arjay Miller was driving home from his office in Dearborn, Michigan, in the four-door Lincoln Continental that went with his job as president of the Ford Motor Company. On a crowded highway, another car struck his from the rear. The Continental spun around and burst into flames. Because he was wearing a shoulder-strap seat belt, Miller was unharmed by the crash, and because his doors didn't jam he escaped the gasoline-drenched, flaming wreck. But the accident made a vivid impression on him. Several months later, on July 15, 1965, he recounted it to a U.S. Senate subcommittee that was hearing testimony on auto safety legislation. "I still have burning in my mind the image of that gas tank on fire," Miller said. He went on to express an almost passionate interest in controlling fuel-fed fires in cars that crash or roll over. He spoke with excitement about the fabric gas tank Ford was testing at that very

---

* Reprinted with editorial changes by permission of the author. Copyright © 1977 by Mark Dowie.

moment. "If it proves out," he promised the senators, "it will be a feature you will see in our standard cars."

Almost seven years after Miller's testimony, a woman, whom for legal reasons we will call Sandra Gillespie, pulled onto a Minneapolis highway in her new Ford Pinto. Riding with her was a young boy, whom we'll call Robbie Carlton. As she entered a merge lane, Sandra Gillespie's car stalled. Another car rear-ended hers at an impact speed of 28 miles per hour. The Pinto's gas tank ruptured. Vapors from it mixed quickly with the air in the passenger compartment. A spark ignited the mixture and the car exploded in a ball of fire. Sandra died in agony a few hours later in an emergency hospital. Her passenger, 13-year-old Robbie Carlton, is still alive; he has just come home from another futile operation aimed at grafting a new ear and nose from skin on the few unscarred portions of his badly burned body. (This accident is real; the details are from police reports.)

Why did Sandra Gillespie's Ford Pinto catch fire so easily, seven years after Ford's Arjay Miller made his apparently sincere pronouncements—the same seven years that brought more safety improvements to cars than any other period in automotive history? An extensive investigation by *Mother Jones* over the past six months has found these answers:

- Fighting strong competition from Volkswagen for the lucrative small-car market, the Ford Motor Company rushed the Pinto into production in much less than the usual time.
- Ford engineers discovered in pre-production crash tests that rear-end collisions would rupture the Pinto's fuel system extremely easily.
- Because assembly-line machinery was already tooled when engineers found this defect, top Ford officials decided to manufacture the car anyway—exploding gas tank and all—*even though Ford owned the patent on a much safer gas tank.*
- For more than eight years afterwards, Ford successfully lobbied, with extraordinary vigor and some blatant lies, against a key government safety standard that would have forced the company to change the Pinto's fire-prone gas tank.

By conservative estimates Pinto crashes have caused 500 burn deaths to people who would not have been seriously injured if the car had not burst into flames. The figure could be as high as 900. Burning Pintos have become such an embarrassment to Ford that its advertising agency, J. Walter Thompson, dropped a line from the end of a radio spot that read "Pinto leaves you with that warm feeling."

Ford knows the Pinto is a firetrap, yet it has paid out millions to settle damage suits out of court, and it is prepared to spend millions more lobbying against safety standards. With a half million cars rolling off the assembly lines each year, Pinto is the biggest-selling subcompact in America, and the company's operating profit on the car is fantastic. Finally, in 1977, new Pinto models have incorporated a few minor alterations necessary to meet that federal standard Ford managed to hold off for eight years. Why did the company delay so long in making these minimal, inexpensive improvements?

- Ford waited eight years because its internal "cost-benefit analysis," *which places a dollar value on human life*, said it wasn't profitable to make the changes sooner.

Before we get to the question of how much Ford thinks your life is worth, let's trace the history of the death trap itself. Although this particular story is about the Pinto, the way in which Ford made its decision is typical of the U.S. auto industry generally. There are plenty of similar stories about other cars made by other companies. But this case is the worst of them all.

The next time you drive behind a Pinto (with over two million of them on the road, you shouldn't have much trouble finding one), take a look at the rear end. That long silvery object hanging down under the bumper is the gas tank. The tank begins about six inches forward of the bumper. In late models the bumper is designed to withstand a collision of only about five miles per hour. Earlier bumpers may as well not have been on the car for all the protection they offered the gas tank.

Mother Jones has studied hundreds of reports and documents on rear-end collisions involving Pintos. These reports conclusively reveal that if you ran into that Pinto you were following at over 30 miles per hour, the rear end of the car would buckle like an accordion, right up to the back seat. The tube leading to the gas-tank cap would be ripped away from the tank itself, and gas would immediately begin sloshing onto the road around the car. The buckled gas tank would be jammed up against the differential housing (that big bulge in the middle of your rear axle), which contains four sharp, protruding bolts likely to gash holes in the tank and spill still more gas. Now all you need is a spark from a cigarette, ignition, or scraping metal, and both cars would be engulfed in flames. If you gave that Pinto a really good whack—say at 40 mph—chances are excellent that its doors would jam and you would have to stand by and watch its trapped passengers burn to death.

This scenario is no news to Ford. Internal company documents in our possession show that Ford has crash-tested the Pinto at a top-secret site more than 40 times and that *every* test made at over 25 mph without special structural alteration of the car has resulted in a ruptured fuel tank. Despite this, Ford officials denied under oath having crash-tested the Pinto.

Eleven of these tests, averaging a 31-mph impact speed, came before Pintos started rolling out of the factories. Only three cars passed the test with unbroken fuel tanks. In one of them an inexpensive light-weight plastic baffle was placed between the front of the gas tank and the differential housing, so those four bolts would not perforate the tank. (Don't forget about that little piece of plastic, which costs one dollar and weighs one pound. It plays an important role in our story later on.) In another successful test, a piece of steel was placed between the tank and the bumper. In the third test car the gas tank was lined with a rubber bladder. But none of these protective alterations was used in the mass-produced Pinto.

In pre-production planning, engineers seriously considered using in the Pinto the same kind of gas tank Ford uses in the Capri. The Capri tank rides over the rear axle and differential housing. It has been so successful in over 50 crash tests that Ford used it in its Experimental Safety Vehicle, which withstood rear-end impacts of 60 mph. So why wasn't the Capri tank used in the Pinto? Or, why wasn't that plastic baffle placed between the tank and the axle—something that would have saved the life of Sandra Gillespie and hundreds like her? Why was a car known to be a serious fire hazard deliberately released to production in August of 1970?

Whether Ford should manufacture subcompacts at all was the subject of a bitter two-year debate at the company's Dearborn head-quarters. The principals in this corporate struggle were the then-president Semon "Bunky" Knudsen, whom Henry Ford II had hired away from General Motors, and Lee Iacocca, a spunky Young Turk who had risen fast within the company on the enormous success of the Mustang. Iacocca argued forcefully that Volkswagen and the Japanese were going to capture the entire American subcompact market unless Ford put out its own alternative to the VW Beetle.

Bunky Knudsen said, in effect: let them have the small-car market; Ford makes good money on medium and large models. But he lost the battle and later resigned. Iacocca became president and almost immediately began a rush program to produce the Pinto.

Like the Mustang, the Pinto became known in the company as "Lee's car." Lee Iacocca wanted that little car in the showrooms of America with the 1971 models. So he ordered his engineering vice president, Bob Alexander, to oversee what was probably the shortest production planning period in modern automotive history. The normal time span from conception to production of a new car model is about 43 months. The Pinto schedule was set at just under 25.

A quick glance at the bar chart on page 20 will show you what that speed-up meant. Design, styling, product planning, advance engineering and quality assurance all have flexible time frames, and engineers can pretty much carry these on simultaneously. Tooling, on the other hand, has a fixed time frame of about 18 months. Normally, an auto company doesn't begin tooling until the other processes are almost over: you don't want to make the machines that stamp and press and grind metal into the shape of car parts until you know all those parts will work well together. *But Iacocca's speed-up meant Pinto tooling went on at the same time as product development.* So when crash tests revealed a serious defect in the gas tank, it was too late. The tooling was well under way.

When it was discovered the gas tank was unsafe, did anyone go to Iacocca and tell him? "Hell no," replied an engineer who worked on the Pinto, a high company official for many years, who, unlike several others at Ford, maintains a necessarily clandestine concern for safety. "That person would have been fired. Safety wasn't a popular subject around Ford in those days. With Lee it was taboo. Whenever a problem was raised that meant a delay on the Pinto, Lee would chomp on his cigar, look out the window and say 'Read the product objectives and get back to work.'"

The product objectives are clearly stated in the Pinto "green book." This is a thick, top-secret manual in green covers containing a step-by-step production plan for the model, detailing the metallurgy, weight, strength and quality of every part in the car. The product objectives for the Pinto are repeated in an article by Ford executive F. G. Olsen published by the Society of Automotive Engineers. He lists these product objectives as follows:

1. TRUE SUBCOMPACT
   - Size
   - Weight

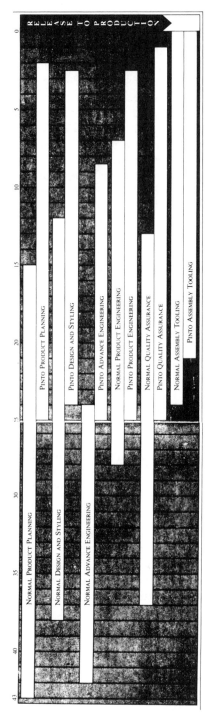

AUTOMOBILE PRE-PRODUCTION SCHEDULE

This chart shows how Ford sacrificed safety for profits. The key lines here are the two at the bottom. "Assembly tooling" means building the complex and expensive machinery that shapes the parts of the automobile. Because Ford rushed the Pinto into production in 25 months instead of the usual 43, this tooling was already under way when crash tests showed the Pinto had a dangerously inflammable gas tank.

2. LOW COST OF OWNERSHIP
   - Initial price
   - Fuel consumption
   - Reliability
   - Serviceability
3. CLEAR PRODUCT SUPERIORITY
   - Appearance
   - Comfort
   - Features
   - Ride and Handling
   - Performance

Safety, you will notice, is not there. It is not mentioned in the entire article. As Lee Iacocca was fond of saying, "Safety doesn't sell."

Heightening the anti-safety pressure on Pinto engineers was an important goal set by Iacocca known as "the limits of 2,000." The Pinto was not to weigh an ounce over 2,000 pounds and not to cost a cent over $2,000. "Iacocca enforced these limits with an iron hand," recalls the engineer quoted earlier. So, even when a crash test showed that that one-pound, one-dollar piece of plastic stopped the puncture of the gas tank, it was thrown out as extra cost and extra weight.

People shopping for subcompacts are watching every dollar. "You have to keep in mind," the engineer explained, "that the price elasticity on these subcompacts is extremely tight. You can price yourself right out of the market by adding $25 to the production cost of the model. And nobody understands that better than Iacocca."

Dr. Leslie Ball, the retired safety chief for the NASA manned space program and a founder of the International Society of Reliability Engineers, recently made a careful study of the Pinto. "The release to production of the Pinto was the most reprehensible decision in the history of American engineering," he said. Ball can name more than 40 European and Japanese models in the Pinto price and weight range with safer gas-tank positioning. Ironically, many of them, like the Ford Capri, contain a "saddle-type" gas tank riding over the back axle. *The patent on the saddle-type tank is owned by the Ford Motor Co.*

Los Angeles auto safety expert Byron Bloch has made an in-depth study of the Pinto fuel system (see diagram on page 22). "It's a catastrophic blunder," he says. "Ford made an extremely irresponsible decision when they placed such a weak tank in such a ridiculous location in such a soft rear end. It's almost designed to blow up—premeditated."

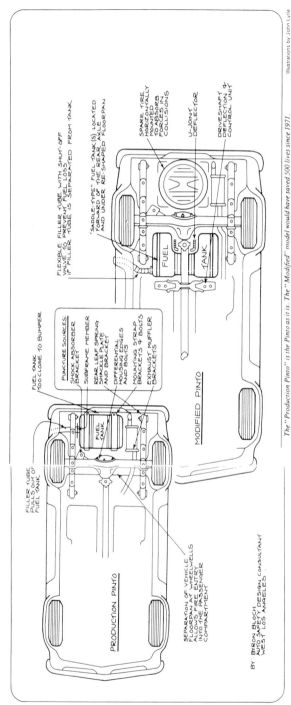

The "Production Pinto" is the Pinto as it is. The "Modified" model would have saved 500 lives since 1971.

A Ford engineer, who doesn't want his name used, comments: "This company is run by salesmen, not engineers; so the priority is styling, not safety." He goes on to tell a story about gas-tank safety at Ford:

Lou Tubben is one of the most popular engineers at Ford. He's a friendly, outgoing guy with a genuine concern for safety. By 1971 he had grown so concerned about gas-tank integrity that he asked his boss if he could prepare a presentation on safer tank design. Tubben and his boss had both worked on the Pinto and shared a concern for its safety. His boss gave him the go-ahead, scheduled a date for the presentation and invited all company engineers and key production planning personnel. When time came for the meeting, a grand total of two people showed up—Lou Tubben and his boss.

"So you see," continued the anonymous Ford engineer ironically, "there *are* a few of us here at Ford who are concerned about fire safety." He adds: "They are mostly engineers who read a lot of accident reports and look at pictures of burned people. But we don't talk about it much. It isn't a popular subject. I've never seen safety on the agenda of a product meeting and, except for a brief period in 1956, I can't remember seeing the word safety in an advertisement. I really don't think the company wants American consumers to start thinking too much about safety—for fear they might demand it, I suppose."

Asked about the Pinto gas tank, another Ford engineer admitted: "That's all true. But you miss the point entirely. You see, safety isn't the issue, trunk space is. You have no idea how stiff the competition is over trunk space. Do you realize that if we put a Capri-type tank in the Pinto you could only get one set of golf clubs in the trunk?"

Blame for Sandra Gillespie's death, Robbie Carlton's unrecognizable face and all the other injuries and deaths in Pintos since 1970 does not rest on the shoulders of Lee Iacocca alone. For, while he and his associates fought their battle against a safer Pinto in Dearborn, a larger war against safer cars raged in Washington. One skirmish in that war involved Ford's successful eight-year lobbying effort against Federal Motor Vehicle Safety Standard 301, the rear-end provisions of which would have forced Ford to redesign the Pinto.

But first some background:

During the early '60s, auto safety legislation became the *bête-noire* of American big business. The auto industry was the last great unregulated business, and if *it* couldn't reverse the tide of government regulation, the reasoning went, no one could.

People who know him cannot remember Henry Ford II taking a stronger stand than the one he took against the regulation of safety design. He spent weeks in Washington calling on members of Congress, holding press conferences and recruiting business cronies like W. B. Murphy of Campbell's Soup to join the anti-regulation battle. Displaying the sophistication for which today's American corporate leaders will be remembered, Murphy publicly called auto safety "a hula hoop, a fad that will pass." He was speaking to a special luncheon of the Business Council, an organization of 100 chief executives who gather periodically in Washington to provide "advice" and "counsel" to government. The target of their wrath in this instance was the Motor Vehicle Safety Bills introduced in both houses of Congress, largely in response to Ralph Nader's *Unsafe at Any Speed.*

By 1965, most pundits and lobbyists saw the handwriting on the wall and prepared to accept government "meddling" in the last bastion of free enterprise. Not Henry. With bulldog tenacity, he held out for defeat of the legislation to the very end, loyal to his grandfather's invention and to the company that makes it. But the Safety Act passed the House and Senate unanimously, and was signed into law by Lyndon Johnson in 1966.

While lobbying for and against legislation is pretty much a process of high-level back-slapping, press-conferencing and speech-making, fighting a regulatory agency is a much subtler matter. Henry headed home to lick his wounds in Grosse Pointe, Michigan, and a planeload of the Ford Motor Company's best brains flew to Washington to start the "education" of the new federal auto safety bureaucrats.

Their job was to implant the official industry ideology in the minds of the new officials regulating auto safety. Briefly summarized, that ideology states that auto accidents are caused not by *cars*, but by 1) people and 2) highway conditions.

This philosophy is rather like blaming a robbery on the victim. Well, what did you expect? You were carrying money, weren't you? It is an extraordinary experience to hear automotive "safety engineers" talk for hours without ever mentioning cars. They will advocate spending billions educating youngsters, punishing drunks and redesigning street signs. Listening to them, you can momentarily begin to think that it is easier to control 100 million drivers than a handful of manufacturers. They show movies about guardrail design and advocate the clear-cutting of trees 100 feet back from every highway in the nation. If a car is unsafe, they argue, it is because its owner doesn't properly drive it. Or, perhaps, maintain it.

In light of an annual death rate approaching 50,000, they are forced to admit that driving is hazardous. But the car is, in the words of Arjay Miller, "the safest link in the safety chain."

Before the Ford experts left Washington to return to drafting tables in Dearborn they did one other thing. They managed to informally reach an agreement with the major public servants who would be making auto safety decisions. This agreement was that "cost-benefit" would be an acceptable mode of analysis by Detroit and its new regulators. And, as we shall see, cost-benefit analysis quickly became the basis of Ford's argument against safer car design.

Cost-benefit analysis was used only occasionally in government until President Kennedy appointed Ford Motor Company President Robert McNamara to be Secretary of Defense. McNamara, originally an accountant, preached cost benefit with all the force of a Biblical zealot. Stated in its simplest terms, cost-benefit analysis says that if the cost is greater than the benefit, the project is not worth it—no matter what the benefit. Examine the cost of every action, decision, contract part or change, the doctrine says, then carefully evaluate the benefits (in dollars) to be certain that they exceed the cost before you begin a program or—and this is the crucial part for our story—pass a regulation.

As a management tool in a business in which profits matter over everything else, cost-benefit analysis makes a certain amount of sense. Serious problems come, however, when public officials who ought to have more than corporate profits at heart apply cost-benefit analysis to every conceivable decision. The inevitable result is that they must place a dollar value on human life.

Ever wonder what your life is worth in dollars? Perhaps $10 million? Ford has a better idea: $200,000.

Remember, Ford had gotten the federal regulators to agree to talk auto safety in terms of cost-benefit analysis. But in order to be able to argue that various safety costs were greater than their benefits, Ford needed to have a dollar value figure for the "benefit." Rather than be so uncouth as to come up with such a price tag itself, the auto industry pressured the National Highway Traffic Safety Administration to do so. And in a 1972 report the agency decided a human life was worth $200,725. (For its reasoning, see the box on page 26.) Inflationary forces have recently pushed the figure up to $278,000.

Furnished with this useful tool, Ford immediately went to work using it to prove why various safety improvements were too expensive to make.

WHAT'S YOUR LIFE WORTH?

Societal Cost Components for Fatalities,
1972 NHTSA Study

COMPONENT	1971 COSTS
FUTURE PRODUCTIVITY LOSSES	
Direct	$132,000
Indirect	41,300
MEDICAL COSTS	
Hospital	700
Other	425
PROPERTY DAMAGE	1,500
INSURANCE ADMINISTRATION	4,700
LEGAL AND COURT	3,000
EMPLOYER LOSSES	1,000
VICTIM'S PAIN AND SUFFERING	10,000
FUNERAL	900
ASSETS (Lost Consumption)	5,000
MISCELLANEOUS ACCIDENT COST	200

TOTAL PER FATALITY: $200,725

Here is a chart from a federal study showing how the
National Highway Traffic Safety Administration has calculated the value of a human life. The estimate was arrived
at under pressure from the auto industry. The Ford Motor
Company has used it in cost-benefit analyses arguing why
certain safety measures are not "worth" the savings in
human lives. The calculation above is a breakdown of the
estimated cost to society every time someone is killed in
a car accident. We were not able to find anyone, either in
the government or at Ford, who could explain how the
$10,000 for "pain and suffering" has been arrived at.

Nowhere did the company argue harder that it should make no changes than in the area of rupture-prone fuel tanks. Not long after the government arrived at the $200,725-per-life figure, it surfaced, rounded off to a cleaner $200,000, in an internal Ford memorandum. This cost-benefit analysis argued that Ford should not make an $11-per-car improvement that would prevent 180 fiery deaths a year. (This minor change would have prevented gas tanks from breaking so easily both in rear-end collisions, like Sandra Gillespie's, and in rollover accidents, where the same thing tends to happen.)

Ford's cost-benefit table (see the box on page 28) is buried in a seven-page company memorandum entitled "Fatalities Associated with Crash-Induced Fuel Leakage and Fires." The memo argues that there is no financial benefit in complying with proposed safety standards that would admittedly result in fewer auto fires, fewer burn deaths and fewer burn injuries. Naturally, memoranda that speak so casually of "burn deaths" and "burn injuries" are not released to the public. They are very effective, however, with Department of Transportation officials indoctrinated in McNamarian cost-benefit analysis.

All Ford had to do was convince men like John Volpe, Claude Brinegar and William Coleman (successive Secretaries of Transportation during the Nixon-Ford years) that certain safety standards would add so much to the price of cars that fewer people would buy them. This could damage the auto industry, which was still believed to be the bulwark of the American economy. "Compliance to these standards," Henry Ford II prophesied at more than one press conference, "will shut down the industry."

The Nixon Transportation Secretaries were the kind of regulatory officials big business dreams of. They understood and loved capitalism and thought like businessmen. Yet, best of all, they came into office uninformed on technical automotive matters. And you could talk "burn injuries" and "burn deaths" with these guys, and they didn't seem to envision children crying at funerals and people hiding in their homes with melted faces. Their minds appeared to have leapt right to the bottom line—more safety meant higher prices, higher prices meant lower sales and lower sales meant lower profits.

So when J. C. Echold, Director of Automotive Safety (which means chief anti-safety lobbyist) for Ford wrote to the Department of Transportation—which he still does frequently, at great length—he felt secure attaching a memorandum that in effect says it is acceptable to kill 180 people and burn another 180 every year, *even though we have the technology that could save their lives for $11 a car.*

$11 VS. A BURN DEATH

Benefits and Costs Relating to Fuel Leakage Associated with the Static Rollover Test Portion of FMVSS 208

Benefits

Savings: 180 burn deaths, 180 serious burn injuries, 2,100 burned vehicles.

Unit Cost: $200,000 per death, $67,000 per injury, $700 per vehicle.

Total Benefit: 180 × ($200,000) + 180 × ($67,000) + 2,100 × ($700) = **$49.5 million.**

Costs

Sales: 11 million cars, 1.5 million light trucks.

Unit Cost: $11 per car, $11 per truck.

Total Cost: 11,000,000 × ($11) + 1,500,000 × ($11) = **$137 million.**

—*from Ford Motor Company internal memorandum: "Fatalities Associated with Crash-Induced Fuel Leakage and Fires."*

Furthermore, Echold attached this memo, confident, evidently, that the Secretary would question neither his low death/injury statistics nor his high cost estimates. But it turns out, on closer examination, that both these findings were misleadng.

First, note that Ford's table shows an equal number of burn deaths and burn injuries. This is false. All independent experts estimate that for each person who dies by an auto fire, many more are left with charred hands, faces and limbs. Andrew McGuire of the Northern California Burn Center estimates the ratio of burn injuries to deaths at ten to one instead of the one to one Ford shows here. Even though Ford values a burn at only a piddling $67,000 instead of the $200,000 price of a life, the true ratio obviously throws the company's calculations way off.

The other side of the equation, the alleged $11 cost of a fire-prevention device, is also a misleading estimation. One document that was *not* sent to Washington by Ford was a 'Confidential" cost analysis *Mother Jones* has managed to obtain, showing that crash fires could be largely prevented for considerably *less* than $11 a car. The cheapest method involves placing a heavy rubber bladder inside the gas tank to keep the fuel from spilling if the tank ruptures. Goodyear had developed the bladder and had demonstrated it to the automotive industry. We have in our possession crash-test reports showing that the Goodyear bladder worked well. On December 2, 1970 (*two years before* Echold sent his cost-benefit memo to Washington), Ford Motor Company ran a rear-end crash test on a car with the rubber bladder in the gas tank. The tank ruptured, but no fuel leaked. On January 15, 1971, Ford again tested the bladder and again it worked. The total purchase and installation cost of the bladder would have been $5.08 per car. That $5.08 could have saved the lives of Sandra Gillespie and several hundred others.

When a federal regulatory agency like the National Highway Traffic Safety Administration (NHTSA) decides to issue a new standard, the law usually requires it to invite all interested parties to respond before the standard is enforced—a reasonable enough custom on the surface. However, the auto industry has taken advantage of this process and has used it to delay lifesaving emission and safety standards for years. In the case of the standard that would have corrected that fragile Pinto fuel tank, the delay was for an incredible eight years.

The particular regulation involved here was Federal Motor Vehicle Safety Standard 301. Ford picked portions of Standard 301 for strong opposition way back in 1968 when the Pinto was still in the blueprint stage. The intent of 301, and the 300 series that followed it, was to protect drivers and passengers *after* a crash occurs. Without question the worst post-crash hazard is fire. So Standard 301 originally proposed that all cars should be able to withstand a fixed barrier impact of 20 mph (that is, running into a wall at that speed) without losing fuel.

When the standard was proposed, Ford engineers pulled their crash-test results out of their files. The front ends of most cars were no problem-with minor alterations they could stand the impact without losing fuel. "We were already working on the front end," Ford engineer Dick Kimble admitted. "We knew we could meet the test on the front end." But with the Pinto particularly, a 20-mph rear-end standard meant redesigning the entire rear end of the car. With the Pinto scheduled for production in August of 1970, and with $200 million worth of tools in place, adoption of this standard would have created a minor financial disaster. So Standard 301 was targeted for delay, and, with some assistance from its industry associates, Ford succeeded beyond its wildest expectations: the standard was not adopted until the 1977 model year. Here is how it happened:

There are several main techniques in the art of combating a government safety standard: a) make your arguments in succession, so the feds can be working on disproving only one at a time; b) claim that the real problem is not X but Y (we already saw one instance of this in "the problem is not cars but people"); c) no matter how ridiculous each argument is, accompany it with thousands of pages of highly technical assertions it will take the government months or, preferably, years to test. Ford's large and active Washington office brought these techniques to new heights and became the envy of the lobbyists' trade.

The Ford people started arguing against Standard 301 way back in 1968 with a strong attack of technique b). Fire, they said, was not the real problem. Sure, cars catch fire and people burn occasionally. But statistically auto fires are such a minor problem that NHTSA should really concern itself with other matters.

Strange as it may seem, the Department of Transportation (NHTSA's parent agency) didn't know whether or not this was true. So it contracted with several independent research groups to study auto fires. The studies took months, which was just what Ford wanted.

The completed studies, however, showed auto fires to be more of a problem than Transportation officials ever dreamed of. Robert Nathan and Associates, a Washington research firm, found that 400,000 cars were burning up every year, burning more than 3,000 people to death. Furthermore, auto fires were increasing five times as fast as building fires. Another study showed that 35 per cent of all fire deaths in the U.S. occurred in automobiles. Forty per cent of all fire department calls in the 1960s were to vehicle fires—a public cost of $350 million a year, a figure that, incidentally, never shows up in cost-benefit analyses.

Another study was done by the Highway Traffic Research Institute in Ann Arbor, Michigan, a safety think-tank funded primarily by the auto industry (the giveaway there is the words "highway traffic" rather than "automobile" in the group's name). It concluded that 40 per cent of the lives lost in fuel-fed fires could be saved if the manufacturers complied with proposed Standard 301. Finally, a third report was prepared for NHTSA by consultant Eugene Trisko entitled "A National Survey of Motor Vehicle Fires." His report indicates that the Ford Motor Company makes 24 per cent of the cars on the American road, yet these cars account for 42 per cent of the collision-ruptured fuel tanks.

Ford lobbyists then used technique a)—bringing up a new argument. Their line then became: yes, perhaps burn accidents do happen, but rear-end collisions are relatively rare (note the echo of technique b) here as well). Thus Standard 301 was not needed. This set the NHTSA off on a new round of analyzing accident reports. The government's findings finally were that rear-end collisions were seven and a half times more likely to result in fuel spills than were front-end collisions. So much for that argument.

By now it was 1972; NHTSA had been researching and analyzing for four years to answer Ford's objections. During that time, nearly 9,000 people burned to death in flaming wrecks. Tens of thousands more were badly burned and scarred for life. And the four-year delay meant that well over 10 million new unsafe vehicles went on the road, vehicles that will be crashing, leaking fuel and incinerating people well into the 1980s.

Ford now had to enter its third round of battling the new regulations. On the "the problem is not X but Y" principle, the company had to look around for something new to get itself off the hook. One might have thought that, faced with all the latest statistics on the horrifying number of deaths in flaming accidents, Ford would find the task difficult. But the company's rhetoric was brilliant. The problem was not burns, but...impact! Most of the people killed in these fiery accidents, claimed Ford, would have died whether the car burned or not. They were killed by the kinetic force of the impact, not the fire.

And so once again, as in some giant underwater tennis game, the ball bounced into the government's court and the absurdly pro-industry NHTSA began another slow-motion response. Once again it began a time-consuming round of test crashes and embarked on a study of accidents. The latter, however, revealed that a large and growing number of corpses taken from burned cars involved in rear-end crashes contained no cuts, bruises or broken bones. They clearly would have survived the accident unharmed if the cars had not caught fire. This pattern was confirmed in careful rear-end crash tests performed by the Insurance Institute for Highway Safety. A University of Miami study found an inordinate number of Pintos burning on rear-end impact and concluded that this demonstrated "a clear and present hazard to all Pinto owners."

Pressure on NHTSA from Ralph Nader and consumer groups began mounting. The industry-agency collusion was so obvious that Senator Joseph Montoya (D-N.M.) introduced legislation about Standard 301. NHTSA waffled some more and again announced its intentions to promulgate a rear-end collision standard.

Waiting, as it normally does, until the last day allowed for response, Ford filed with NHTSA a gargantuan batch of letters, studies and charts now arguing that the federal testing criteria were unfair. Ford also argued that design changes required to meet the standard would take 43 months, which seemed like a rather long time in light of the fact that the entire Pinto was designed in about two years. Specifically, new complaints about the standard involved the weight of the test vehicle, whether or not the brakes should be engaged at the moment of impact and the claim that the standard should only apply to cars, not trucks or buses. Perhaps the most amusing argument was that the engine should not be idling during crash tests, the rationale being that an idling engine meant that the gas tank had to contain gasoline and that the hot lights needed to film the crash might ignite the gasoline and cause a fire.

Some of these complaints were accepted, others rejected. But they all required examination and testing by a weak-kneed NHTSA, meaning more of those 18-month studies the industry loves so much. So the complaints served their real purpose—delay; all told, an eight-year delay, while Ford manufactured more than three million profitable, dangerously incendiary Pintos. To justify this delay, Henry Ford II called more press conferences to predict the demise of American civilization. "If we can't meet the standards when they are published," he warned, "we will have to close down. And if we have to close down some production because we don't meet standards we're in for real trouble in this country."

While government bureaucrats dragged their feet on lifesaving Standard 301, a different kind of expert was taking a close look at the Pinto—the "recon man." "Recon" stands for reconstruction; recon men reconstruct accidents for police departments, insurance companies and lawyers who want to know exactly who or what caused an accident. It didn't take many rear-end Pinto accidents to demonstrate the weakness of the car. Recon men began encouraging lawyers to look beyond one driver or another to the manufacturer in their search for fault, particularly in the growing number of accidents where passengers were uninjured by collision but were badly burned by fire.

Pinto lawsuits began mounting fast against Ford. Says John Versace, executive safety engineer at Ford's Safety Research Center, "Ulcers are running pretty high among the engineers who worked on the Pinto. Every lawyer in the country seems to want to take their depositions." (The Safety Research Center is an impressive glass and concrete building standing by itself about a mile from Ford World Headquarters in Dearborn. Looking at it, one imagines its large staff protects consumers from burned and broken limbs. Not so. The Center is the technical support arm of Jack Echold's 14-person anti-regulatory lobbying team in World Headquarters.)

When the Pinto liability suits began, Ford strategy was to go to a jury. Confident it could hide the Pinto crash tests, Ford thought that juries of solid American registered voters would buy the industry doctrine that drivers, not cars, cause accidents. It didn't work. It seems that juries are much quicker to see the truth than bureaucracies, a fact that gives one confidence in democracy. Juries began ruling against the company, granting million-dollar awards to plaintiffs.

"We'll never go to a jury again," says Al Slechter in Ford's Washington office. "Not in a fire case. Juries are just too sentimental. They see those charred remains and forget the evidence. No sir, we'll settle."

Settlement involves less cash, smaller legal fees and less publicity, but it is an indication of the weakness of their case. Nevertheless, Ford has been settling when it is clear that the company can't pin the blame on the driver of the other car. But, since the company carries $2 million deductible product liability insurance, these settlements have a direct impact on the bottom line. They must therefore be considered a factor in determining the net operating profit on the Pinto. It's impossible to get a straight answer from Ford on the profitability of the Pinto and the impact of lawsuit settlements on it—even when you have a curious and mildly irate shareholder call to inquire, as we did. However, financial officer Charles Matthews did admit that the company establishes a reserve for large dollar settlements. He would not divulge the amount of the reserve and had no explanation for its absence from the annual report.

Until recently, it was clear that, whatever the cost of these settlements, it was not enough to seriously cut into the Pinto's enormous profits. The cost of retooling Pinto assembly lines and of equipping each car with a safety gadget like that $5.08 Goodyear bladder was, company accountants calculated, greater than that of paying out millions to survivors like Robbie Carlton or to widows and widowers of victims like Sandra Gillespie. The bottom line ruled, and inflammable Pintos kept rolling out of the factories.

In 1977, however, an incredibly sluggish government has at last instituted Standard 301. Now Pintos will have to have rupture-proof gas tanks. Or will they?

To everyone's surprise, the 1977 Pinto recently passed a rear-end crash test in Phoenix, Arizona, for NHTSA. The agency was so convinced the Pinto would fail that it was the first car tested. Amazingly, it did not burst into flame.

"We have had so many Ford failures in the past," explained agency engineer Tom Grubbs, "I felt sure the Pinto would fail."

How did it pass?

Remember that one-dollar, one-pound plastic baffle that was on one of the three modified Pintos that passed the pre-production crash tests nearly ten years ago? Well, it is a standard feature on the 1977 Pinto. In the Phoenix test it protected the gas tank from being perforated by those four bolts on the differential housing.

We asked Grubbs if he noticed any other substantial alterations in the rear-end structure of the car. "No," he replied. "the [plastic baffle] seems to be the only noticeable change over the 1976 model."

But was it'? What Tom Grubbs and the Department of Transportation didn't know when they tested the car was that it was manufactured in St. Thomas, Ontario. Ontario? The significance of that becomes clear when you learn that Canada has for years had extremely strict rear-end collision standards.

Tom Irwin is the business manager of Charlie Rossi Ford, the Scottsdale, Arizona, dealership that sold the Pinto to Tom Grubbs. He refused to explain why he was selling Fords made in Canada when there is a huge Pinto assembly plant much closer by in California. "I know why you're asking that question, and I'm not going to answer it," he blurted out. "You'll have to ask the company."

But Ford's regional office in Phoenix has "no explanation" for the presence of Canadian cars in their local dealerships. Farther up the line in Dearborn, Ford people claim there is absolutely no difference between American and Canadian Pintos. They say cars are shipped back and forth across the border as a matter of course. But they were hard pressed to explain why some Canadian Pintos were shipped all the way to Scottsdale, Arizona. Significantly, one engineer at the St. Thomas plant did admit that the existence of strict rear-end collision standards in Canada "might encourage us to pay a little more attention to quality control on that part of the car."

The Department of Transportation is considering buying an American Pinto and running the test again. For now, it will only say that the situation is under investigation.

Whether the new American Pinto fails or passes the test, Standard 301 will never force the company to test or recall the more than two million pre-1977 Pintos still on the highway. Seventy or more people will burn to death in those cars every year for many years to come. If the past is any indication, Ford will continue to accept the deaths.

According to safety expert Byron Bloch, the older cars could quite easily be retrofitted with gas tanks containing fuel cells. "These improved tanks would add at least 10 mph improved safety performance to the rear end," he estimated, "but it would cost Ford $20 to $30 a car, so they won't do it unless they are forced to." Dr. Kenneth Saczalski, safety engineer with the Office of Naval Research in Washington, agrees. "The Defense Department has developed virtually fail-safe fuel systems and retrofitted them into existing vehicles. We have shown them to the auto industry and they have ignored them."

Unfortunately, the Pinto is not an isolated case of corporate malpractice in the auto industry. Neither is Ford a lone sinner. There probably isn't a car on the road without a safety hazard known to its manufacturer. And though Ford may have the best auto lobbyists in Washington, it is not alone. The anti-emission control lobby and the anti-safety lobby usually work in chorus form, presenting a well-harmonized message from the country's richest industry, spoken through the voices of individual companies—the Motor Vehicle Manufacturers Association, the Business Council and the U.S. Chamber of Commerce.

Furthermore, cost-valuing human life is not used by Ford alone. Ford was just the only company careless enough to let such an embarrassing calculation slip into public records. The process of willfully trading lives for profits is built into corporate capitalism. Commodore Vanderbilt publicly scorned George Westinghouse and his "foolish" air brakes while people died by the hundreds in accidents on Vanderbilt's railroads.

The original draft of the Motor Vehicle Safety Act provided for criminal sanctions against a manufacturer who willfully placed an unsafe car on the market. Early in the proceedings the auto industry lobbied the provision out of the bill. Since then, there have been those damage settlements, of course, but the only government punishment meted out to auto companies for non-compliance to standards has been a minuscule fine, usually $5,000 to $10,000. One wonders how long the Ford Motor Company would continue to market lethal cars were Henry Ford II and Lee Iacocca serving 20-year terms in Leavenworth for consumer homicide.

2

Ford Rebuts Pinto Criticism and Says Article is Distorted*

Allegations that Ford Pintos have faulty fuel tanks which make them firetraps and cause the death of some 70 people each year is pure exaggeration, a spokesman for the automaker said last week.

In an eight-page statement released nearly a month after a highly publicized news conference held by the magazine *Mother Jones* (NU, Aug. 19), Vice President Herbert L. Misch said statistical evidence "totally discredits the opinions of the alleged safety experts quoted by Mother Jones."

In the article, author Mark Dowie wrote "by conservative estimates, Pinto crashes were responsible for 500 burn deaths to people who would not have been seriously injured if the car had not burst into flames." Mr. Dowie added that the "figure could be as high as 900."

Mr. Misch, however, claimed the article contained "half-truths and distortions."

---

* Reprinted with the permission from *National Underwriter* © 1994, The National Underwriter Company (*The National Underwriter*, September 9, 1977)

CITES STATISTICS

He said nationwide accident statistics maintained by the National Highway Traffic Safety Administration show that in 1975, for example, "there were 848 deaths associated with passenger-car accidents in which fires also occurred in some parts of the vehicles. Only 12 of these 848 reported fatalities involved occupants of Pintos, including two who had been ejected from their cars. In 1976, the number of occupant fatalities in fire-associated passenger-car accidents in which Pintos were involved was 11 out of 942."

Mr. Misch, referring to further "distortions," said "it is true, for example, that early model Pintos did not pass rear-impact tests at 20 mph. It is not true, however, that these test results mean the early Pintos were unsafe compared with the range of other cars of that era, or on any basis of rational judgment."

According to Mr. Misch, some of Ford's tests on 1971 Pintos were conducted "to learn what revisions would be required to make our cars meet rear-impact requirements prepared by the Federal government for future cars."

The truth, he said, is that "in every model year the Pinto has been tested and met, or surpassed, the Federal fuel-system-integrity standard applicable to it."

Mr. Misch further said that in 1976, while Pintos accounted for about 2 percent of all cars in operation, their involvement rate in fire-associated fatality reports was only 1.17 percent.

"This is evidence with substance—objective statistics on how the Pinto performs in real-world accidents—and it totally discredits the opinions of the alleged safety experts quoted by Mother Jones."

Mr. Dowie also charged in the article that Ford lobbied for eight years to prevent the implementation of a Federal safety standard for fuel-integrity in rear impacts, and opposed such standards on grounds their implementation would have cost $11 per vehicle.

The facts, according to Mr. Misch, are that as early as March 18, 1968, Ford recommended an "early adoption of a Federal fuel-integrity standard incorporating rear moving-barrier impact requirements at 20 miles per hour, and reiterated to the government its support for such a standard on two other occasions during the next two and a half years."

What Ford did oppose, Mr. Misch admitted, were "certain excessive testing requirements involving 20- or 30-mile-per-hour rear crashes into a massive, fixed barrier and a post-crash rollover test which we viewed as imposing wastefully expensive costs. We suggested that, considering the total spectrum of safety improvement, this might be an unwise allocation of resources for a single type of hazard. In the end, a rollover requirement was retained in the final standards, and a 30-mile-per-hour rear impact by a 4,000 pound barrier was specified."

Mr. Misch also contested Mr. Dowie's assertion that a plastic fuel tank baffle had been tested and found effective in preventing fuel tank punctures prior to introduction of the first Pinto in the fall of 1970, but was discarded by Ford.

Ford tests report, said Mr. Misch, that "the fuel tank baffle in question was first tested in 1974. And the stopped Pinto involved in the collision described in the article appears to be the same car that Ford investigation revealed was struck so severely by a vehicle weighing more than 3,900 pounds that the fuel tank was massively crushed by the impact forces that demolished the car.

"It appears," Mr. Misch said, "the author has misinterpreted the Ford test reports on which he says his article was based."

The government's data show that "the performance of the Pinto's fuel tank system in actual accidents appears to be superior to that which might be expected of cars of its size and weight."

3

The Pinto Documents*

When the scathing *Mother Jones* article was published in 1977, it largely based its conclusions on a core of significant internal Ford documents which the magazine had obtained. Those documents provided a revealing, shocking glimpse inside Ford Motor Company. But since then, a flurry of civil litigation had pried loose new documents which put the Pinto controversy into sharper focus and provided important additional evidence concerning Ford's conduct.

Most of these recent documents had never been made public. One reason was that when Ford was sued in a civil case involving a fire in a Pinto or some other Ford model, it sought and usually obtained a court order sealing the case file from public view. These "protective orders" meant that if Ford was forced into disclosing some of its internal documents during that case, the lawyer for the plaintiff could

---

* Reprinted, with editorial changes, from *Reckless Homicide?: Ford's Pinto Trial*, by Lee Patrick Strobel, Copyright © 1980 by Lee Strobel, by permission of And Books, South Bend, Indiana.

see them but they would be kept secret from everyone else unless they were ever successfully introduced into evidence at a trial.

Ford often obtained these protective orders by claiming the documents contained "trade secrets" which must be kept away from other automakers for competitive reasons. Lawyers fighting Ford, though, contended that Ford's true motive was "to prevent highly incriminating documents from becoming generally known." Ford's record of disclosure of documents during civil cases has been stained with dishonesty. Courts have censured Ford for deliberately withholding and secreting documents, providing false answers under oath about documents, and other misconduct.

The documents, some of which were veterans of the *Mother Jones* article but more than a dozen of which contained important new material never before published, formed the basis of a series of widely reprinted articles in *The Chicago Tribune* in October, 1979. The documents proved to be so much in demand that one private attorney unsuccessfully offered $5,000 in cash for just one of them he wanted to use against Ford in a civil trial.

Since publication of *The Tribune* series, a few more internal Ford documents have been obtained which disclose even more evidence concerning the Pinto controversy. The details of these documents, such as the so-called "Pricor Report," have never been published before this book, [*Reckless Homicide?: Ford's Pinto Trial*] although statements made in court indicate Kiely had the documents and intended to use them as part of the criminal case against Ford. [Terrence Kiely was a DePaul University professor who helped with the prosecution of Ford.]

Kiely, who had little technical background, had to meet with several engineers so he could understand the significance of the technical jargon in the Pinto Papers.

For instance, there were three different kinds of crash tests involving Pintos. One was a car-to-car test in which a free-standing Pinto would be smashed from behind by another car to determine the amount of damage sustained by the Pinto at a certain speed. This sort of crash gave an accurate idea of what would happen in an actual highway collision.

The second was a moving-barrier test in which a 4,000 pound wall was moved into the back of a free-standing Pinto. Because the wall was flat, it could not duplicate an actual highway crash involving another vehicle. However, this kind of test resulted in damage which was close to what a car would suffer in a car-to-car collision at the same speed.

The third was a fixed-barrier test in which a Pinto would be towed rearward into a stationary cement wall. A fixed-barrier test caused much more damage to a car than a moving-barrier test at the same speed. For instance, the amount of damage sustained by a car in a 20 mile-per-hour fixed-barrier crash would be the same as a car in a moving-barrier crash at 28 miles per hour.

To Cosentino and Kiely, the Ford documents they obtained told a story which went back to June, 1967, when Ford, using the code-name "G-Car," began working on plans to build an American-made subcompact to compete against the popular imports which dominated the small-car market. [Michael A. Cosentino was the Elkhart County state's attorney who prosecuted the Pinto trial.] According to Cosentino's information, this was a rushed project in which corporate executives rigidly enforced an edict that the car must weigh under 2,000 pounds and cost under $2,000 when it was introduced.

An early question in the car's design stage, of course, was where to safely put the gas tank, which had the explosive power of dozens of sticks of dynamite when it was full. To see how other small cars handled the problem, Ford in 1967 bought a Rover, an English-built subcompact which featured its gas tank in a location above the car's rear axle. Ford engineers smashed the Rover from behind with a moving-barrier at 30 miles per hour and, according to the test report, "there was no deformation, puncture, or leakage of the fuel tank." A rousing success for the over-the-axle design.

Ford engineers at that time were already familiar with how to move the gas tank away from the rear of the car. According to records from the U.S. Patent Office, Ford was granted a patent in 1961 for a "saddle-type" tank which could fit above and mostly forward of the car's rear axle. The patent pointed out that this design would remove the tank "from possible puncture or damage as a result of the vehicle dropping into holes or hitting obstructions."

Not long after Ford's successful Rover test, researchers at the University of California at Los Angeles announced the results of a detailed engineering study on how cars should be designed to protect passengers from fire in high-speed, rear-end crashes. Ford helped finance the study with a research grant and donated some of the cars that were crash-tested.

The study concluded that "much progress can be made" in cutting down the risk of gas spillage and subsequent fire in rear-end crashes by using "relatively inexpensive design considerations relating to fuel tanks and related fuel system."

The study also concluded that "fuel tanks should *not* be located directly adjacent to the rear bumper or behind the rear wheels adjacent to the fender sheet-metal as this location exposes them to rupture at very low speeds of impact."

Instead of putting the tank at the car's rear, the study said that "an improved location" appeared to be *above the rear axle*, as in the Rover tested by Ford. "This location is least often compromised in collision of all types," the researchers said. The reason was that this would put the tank away from the back of the vehicle where crushing occurs in rear-end crashes.

The study warned that care must be taken in designing the filler pipe so that it would not be yanked out of the tank during a crash, exposing a hole through which gasoline could gush. In a summary of the UCLA study published in a journal for automotive engineers, the researchers said that a design in which the filler pipe was rigidly attached to the car's body at the gas-cap end, and then merely inserted into the gas tank, could cause the pipe to pull out during rear-end crashes as low as 20 miles per hour because the tank would be shoved forward.

After the study was released, Ford engineers tried designing the future Pinto—now code-named the "Phoenix"—with its gas tank located over the axle as in the Rover. In a report dated January 21, 1969, Ford engineers in the "product development group" evaluated this design.

The conclusion: "Due to the undesirable luggage space attained...it was decided to continue with the strap-on tank arrangement." This meant abandoning the over-the-axle location in favor of putting the tank at the car's rear. Apparently, the over-the-axle design resulted in a luggage compartment which would be limited in its ability to carry long objects, such as golf clubs.

The same memo also illustrated how concerned the engineers were to slice off pennies from the car's cost to stay as far below the $2,000 price limit as possible. They proudly reported under "significant accomplishments" that the use of a certain type of control lever would shave 18 cents off the cost of an alternative lever. They reported that another 50 cents per car could be shaved by redesigning the car's floor, and another $1.84 per car could be eliminated by relocating the headlight dimmer switch.

Six months later, Ford engineers took a Japanese Toyota and modified its rear-end so it would be similar to the proposed Pinto. This involved not only putting the gas tank at the rear of the car, but also eliminating any rear frame which would strengthen the car against excessive crushing. The car was rammed from behind by a moving barrier at 21 miles per hour. The results: The tank was severely deformed and ruptured, resulting in gas spilling out.

It was about this time that Ford, after several years of planning, introduced in Europe its Capri model, compact car similar in shape to the Pinto but with its gas tank located over the axle. The Capri, largely the creation of Harley Copp, was launched with a major advertising blitz which bragged that its gas tank was "safely cradled between the rear wheels and protected on all sides."

In mid-1969—more than a year before the Pinto was introduced—Ford engineers took three Capris and modified their rear-ends to be similar to the proposed Pinto. This meant moving the gas tank from the over-the-axle position and placing it at the car's rear.

When one of them was backed into a wall at 17.8 miles per hour, the welds on the gas tank split open, the tank was damaged when it hit the axle, the filler pipe pulled out, and the tank fell out of the car, resulting in massive gas spillage. The welds on the car's floor also pulled apart, which could let gasoline spill inside the car.

In two other tests in which the car was rear-ended by moving barriers at 21 miles per hour, gas leaked either from the filler pipe pulling out or because sharp objects punctured the fuel tank.

Nevertheless, the Pinto was put on sale on September 11, 1970, with its gas tank located at the car's rear just six inches away from the largely ornamental bumper. Sharp bolts on the differential housing were situated three inches from the front of the tank in the exact path the tank would be pushed in a rear-end crash. Other sharp metal edges also were dangerously located just inches away from the tank.

In addition, the filler pipe was rigidly attached to the car's body at the gas cap end and then only loosely inserted into the gas tank to a depth of 2.6 inches, the sort of design which UCLA researchers warned earlier would cause the pipe to pull out in low-speed crashes. Unlike Ford's own Capri, the Pinto had no added rear frame to strengthen against excessive crushing when the car was hit from behind.

The Pinto was billed as "the carefree little American car" and boasted a pricetag of $1,919—about $170 less than the price announced for its soon-to-be-released competitor, the Chevrolet Vega, and within $80 of the big-selling Volkswagen Beetle.

Embarrassingly, within six months there would be two recalls of the Pinto—one because of a tendancy of the engine compartment to burst into flames when the car was started, and the other because the accelerator pedal sometimes got stuck.

One of the most significant experimental crash tests occurred less than a month after the Pinto appeared in showrooms. On October 9, 1970, Ford engineers took a Capri—with its over-the-axle gas tank design—and subjected it to a 31 mile-per-hour rear crash into a cement wall. This test, which was the equivalent of about a 45 mile-per-hour car-to-car crash, was a tremendous success—"No leakage was observed from the fuel tank or lines."

There was a dramatic contrast between this impressive result and the next one conducted at Ford's Dearborn testing facility. This time engineers took a standard Pinto and crashed it backwards into a concrete wall at 21 miles per hour, which would be equal to a car-to-car crash of about 31 miles per hour.

In a report marked "confidential," engineer H. P. Snider said that the Pinto's soft rear-end crushed up 18 inches in 91 milliseconds. He said: "The filler pipe was pulled out of the fuel tank and fluid discharged through the outlet. Additional leakage occurred through a puncture in the upper right front surface of the fuel tank which was caused by contact between the fuel tank and a bolt on the differential housing."

In addition, there were two more punctures of the tank from nearby sharp metal objects and both passenger doors jammed shut, which would have prevented any quick escape or rescue in an actual crash.

This pattern of devastation and hazardous gasoline spillage was repeated in other Pinto tests conducted in the following months, at even lower speeds. When a Pinto was rear-ended by a moving barrier at 19.5 miles per hour on December 15, 1970, the filler pipe pulled out, causing gas to escape, and the left door jammed shut.

When the Pinto went on sale, the federal government had no standards concerning how safe a car must be from gas leakage in rear-end crashes. However, within days of the Pinto's introduction, the government announced strict proposals that cars must be able to withstand a 20 mile-per-hour fixed-barrier crash without gasoline leakage as of 1972. This would be equal to about a 30 mile-per-hour car-to-car crash. And by 1973, cars would have to be able to survive a 30 mile-per-hour fixed-barrier rear-crash, which would be equal to about a 44 mile-per-hour car-to-car collision.

Automakers panicked because they knew that cars like the Pinto would fall far short of meeting those requirements. Ford's response was to join other automakers in an aggressive lobbying campaign in an attempt to block the proposals from ever becoming law. In an internal Ford memo dated November 10, 1970, Ford officials developed some lesser safety standards which they believed "the Department of Transportation can be expected to buy."

This opposition by Ford came even though its own crash test of the Capri demonstrated it knew how to build cars safe enough to pass even the government's most stringent proposed standard.

Apparently believing its lobbying would be successful in eliminating the government proposals, Ford then adopted its own internal standard for rear-end crashes. In a policy-setting memo from key corporate executives dated November 20, 1970, Ford adopted a requirement that its cars must pass a 20 mile-per-hour moving-barrier rear-end crash without gasoline leakage starting with the 1973 models. This was less than half as stringent as the government's proposal for that year.

The same memo added that for the Pinto even to meet this lesser requirement by 1973, its filler pipe would have to be fixed so that it wouldn't pull out as easily and the car's structure would have to be beefed up.

At the same time, Ford assigned engineers to develop ways of making the Pinto substantially safer from the risk of fire in rear-end crashes, just in case the strict government proposals or similar standards did become law.

It was only 12 days after the Pinto's introduction when Ford engineers spelled out in an internal memo what would be necessary to greatly improve the Pinto's ability to withstand rear-end collisions without gas leakage and to comply with even the government's strictest proposals:

"This will probably require repackaging of the fuel tanks in a *protected area* such as above the rear axle." The memo added: "Currently there are no plans for (future) models to repackage the fuel tanks."

In an internal memo two months later, Ford engineers reiterated that an over-the-axle gas tank design would be among the necessary changes to significantly improve the Pinto's safety from fire in rear-end crashes. "Fuel tanks must be repackaged to afford maximum protection from impact at any angle," the memo said. Engineers even submitted a diagram showing precisely how the tank could be placed over the axle in the Pinto and listed some pros and cons of the change.

On February 9, 1971, in a study titled, "Confidential Cost Engineering Report," Ford engineers concluded that the cost of an over-the-axle tank design, including a protective sheet metal barrier, would be $9.95 for the average car. This figure was not broken down according to different models.

In another approach to making the Pinto safer, engineers tried installing a heavy rubber bladder, reinforced with nylon, inside the metal gas tank. In a 20 mile-per-hour rear crash into a cement wall—equal to a 30 mile-per-hour car-to-car collision—the gas tank ruptured as it had in all Pinto tests at that speed. But the inner bladder kept any gasoline from spilling out. The engineers tried the bladder again in a 26 mile-per-hour crash into a cement wall, and again the bladder successfully retained the gas even though the metal tank was punctured in several places.

"The bladder tank provides a substantial improvement in crashworthiness when compared against a conventional steel tank in which any rupture leads to fuel spillage," said a memo dated January, 1971.

The memo said that the Goodyear Tire & Rubber Co. gave a preliminary price estimage of $6 per bladder, although engineers were skeptical of this figure and said that developmental problems would have to be ironed out.

The following month, the Advanced Chassis Engineering Department reported that the bladder would greatly improve the Pinto's safety in rear-end crashes, but recommended further testing only "in the event that future legislation should require the. . . liner."

Another alternative was a "tank-in-tank" system in which polyurethane foam was added between an inner and outer metal fuel tank shell. According to a confidential cost study in February, 1971, this design would help to significantly boost rear-end safety from fire at a cost of $5.08 per car. Figures were not given for individual Ford models.

It was only two months after the Pinto went on sale when engineers first raised the idea of adding a shield to the car to protect the gas tank from being punctured by sharp bolts on the differential housing. The idea was repeated in another internal memo three months later.

When engineers obtained price estimates, they found the "material cost" for a rugged nylon shield would be 44 cents apiece or 22 cents each for an ultra-high molecular polyethylene shield. "Both materials appear to have the potential of stopping fuel tank penetration by the differential housing at a reasonable cost," said a memo dated March 20, 1974.

The memo added that a shield made of polyethylene "is likely to offer better fuel tank protection for a lower cost than any other plastic material and. . .will simplify vehicle installation."

In the Grimshaw trial, Copp testified that the design cost of a shield for the Pinto would have been $2.35 per car or the axle could have been made smooth for a design cost of $2.10 per car. A design cost is the price of direct material and labor.

A 30-page study of gas tank safety for Ford's "light cars" was issued just five months after the Pinto's introduction. Called the "Pricor Report" after its author, Ford engineer A. J. Pricor, the analysis involved nine experimental crash tests of several light-car models, including the Pinto. Its conclusion listed several concrete recommendations for how to make the car substantially safer from fuel leakage and fire in rear-end crashes.

Among its conclusions was that by positioning the spare tire properly, it would absorb up to 10 percent of the energy in a rear-end crash and cushion the gas tank from deformation.

The Capri was an example of how Ford designers had used this system successfully. In a memo dated October 27, 1970, Ford engineers concluded Capri's ability to withstand the equivalent of a 45 mile-per-hour car-to-car crash was based not only on its over-the-axle tank design, but also on the "favorable location of the spare tire which carried the impact force directly into the rear axle."

However, engineers did not position the Pinto's spare tire in a manner which would protect the gas tank when the car was hit from behind.

Also, the Pricor study concluded that the "desirable fuel tank location" appeared to be 13 to 17 inches away from the rear bumper— not six inches as in the Pinto.

In addition, the report stated that small cars should have "body rails" installed on both sides. These are steel rails which run lengthwise in the car and attach to the rear to absorb some of the impact during a rear-end crash. Pricor said these were "necessary to absorb and control vehicle collapse on a predictable basis" and were effective in "preventing surrounding sheet metal from total collapse."

Early in 1971, Ford engineers installed two side rails on a Pinto to see what would happen when it was crashed backward into a cement wall at 21 miles per hour. This was the same speed—equal to a 31 mile-per-hour car-to-car crash—at which Pintos without rails demonstrated a history of massive damage and extensive spilling of gas.

The result was that the Pinto with the side rails crushed considerably less than the standard Pinto and there was no leakage from the tank or filler pipe.

The Pricor analysis did not provide any cost estimate for side rails. However, during his Grimshaw testimony, Copp said the design cost of adding rails to both sides of the Pinto would have been $2.40 per car.

Ford management, though, decided against putting any side rails on the Pinto until the 1973 model, at which time only one rail was added instead of two, providing much less protection than Pricor recommended. A second rail was added starting in the 1974 Pinto, but an internal memo dated April 26, 1972, described those rails of being of a type "which is poor, undesirable for energy absorption."

Pricor also warned that the type of filler pipe used in the Pinto "invites fuel leakage" and that an alternate design like that used in the Capri would be the "most desirable" system. Other memos written during this time period also cited the necessity of improving the filler pipe to make the Pinto safer. And a memo dated October, 1970, from Ford's, "product development group" included a diagram of a design "which would eliminate filler neck leakage."

Still other memos reported during the autumn of 1970 that "heavier gauge tank metal" could contribute to improving the Pinto's ability to withstand gas spillage in rear-end crashes.

In the spring of 1971, Ford engineers were coming to believe that a "flak suit" would be the answer to making the Pinto significantly safer from gas leakage in rear-end crashes if some structural improvements were also made. A flak suit was like a rubber tire that fit around the tank to cushion it from impact and prevent puncture. Another 1971 memo said the flak suit design "has merit in high-energy situations and should be considered as an alternative."

A "confidential" memo dated April 22, 1971, said that the design cost of the flak suit or the bladder would be $8 per car. But the same memo said that based on this amount, executives recommended that the company "defer adoption of the flak suit or bladder on all affected cars until 1976 to realize a design cost savings of $20.9 million compared to incorporation in 1974."

They said they hoped that in the meantime "cost reductions can be achieved or the need for the flak suit or bladder eliminated after further engineering development."

During this time, Ford and other automakers continued to lobby vigorously against the stringent government safety proposals. In the end, they were successful. The strict fixed-barrier proposals were abandoned.

It was at a meeting in the fall of 1971—a year after the Pinto appeared in showrooms—that a committee of high-ranking Ford executives got together to decide whether any of the various improvements would be adopted to make the Pinto safer from gas spillage and the risk of fire in rear-end crashes.

In an October 26, 1971 memo labeled "confidential," the decision was disclosed: There would be no additional improvements for the 1973 and later models of the Pinto until "required by law."

It wasn't until six years later—after 1,513,339 Pinto sedans were built and sold—when the government finally imposed its first safety requirement designed to protect against gas leakage and fire risk in rear-end crashes. The standard was that all 1977 cars must be able to withstand a 30 mile-per-hour moving-barrier crash in the rear without gas leakage, a regulation which was considerably weaker than the earlier proposal which had aroused the ire of the auto industry.

To make the 1977 Pinto capable of passing the test, Ford dusted off some of its old ideas and added a polyethylene shield to prevent puncturing of the gas tank; improved the filler pipe so it wouldn't pull out so easily; and added some rear-ended strength by making the bumper stronger.

The shield and improved filler pipe were, of course, the same changes made to improve the 1971–76 Pintos and 1975–76 Mercury Bobcats in the recall which was announced in 1978 after the government determined that those cars were prone to spill gas when hit from behind.

Among the most controversial documents obtained by Kiely and Cosentino was a "cost-benefit" study which Ford developed as part of its campaign against plans by the government to adopt regulations concerning auto safety.

A cost-benefit analysis is a business tool used to determine whether the cost of a project would justify the dollar value of the benefits which would be derived. If the price of achieving the benefit is greater than the value of the benefit itself, the project is viewed as not being financially worthwhile.

According to the *Mother Jones* article, the auto industry pressured NHTSA into setting a price tag on human lives and suffering, and then the automakers plugged those figures into cost-benefit equations in order to argue why safety improvements were too expensive to be worthwhile.

One of these Ford cost-benefit studies, originally excerpted in the *Mother Jones* article, concluded that it would not be worth the cost of making an $11 improvement per car in order to save 180 people from burning to death and another 180 from suffering serious burn injuries each year.

On the "benefit" side of the equation, Ford calculated that making the improvement would result in the saving of those 180 lives and 180 serious injuries. Ford then translated this human suffering into dollars according to NHTSA's figures—$200,000 for the life of a burn victim; $67,000 for each serious burn injury; and $700 for each fire-ravaged vehicle. Ford referred to dead and injured persons as "units."

When all of this was added up, the "total benefit" of making the safety improvement and eliminating the death and pain was calculated to be $49.5 million.

This was balanced against the cost of making the $11 improvement to 1.5 million light trucks and 11 million cars throughout the auto industry, for a "total cost" of $137 million.

"Thus," the report concluded, "the cost is almost three times the benefits, even using a number of highly favorable benefit assumptions."

The study added that NHTSA's dollar figures for lives and injuries (Ford called it a "casualty-to-dollar conversion") were higher than some other sources "and their use does not signify that Ford accepts or concurs in the values."

Ford officials submitted this analysis to NHTSA in 1973 as part of its campaign against the government's plans to adopt a regulation concerning how safe cars must be from fire risk in crashes in which the vehicle rolls over.

Ford executives indignantly responded to disclosure of this study by saying they only used NHTSA's own figures and had been asked by the government to perform the study. They contended the analysis was never intended for the purpose of making engineering decisions and never affected the design of the Pinto or any other car.

However, an associate administrator of NHTSA insisted that the dollar figures were developed for other purposes and "were never intended to be used in such a cost-benefit analysis." He said the figures were created to estimate the loss to society when a person dies, based largely on lost productivity, so the agency could study what traffic fatalities cost the nation.

When Ford submitted this study to the government, it said the analysis concerned the proposed rollover safety requirement but added that "analyses of other portions of the proposed regulation would also be expected to yield poor benefit-to-cost ratios."

Yet shortly after this was submitted, a Ford executive completed another cost-benefit study concerning another portion of the proposed law that dealt with limiting fuel leakage in side and rear crashes. And, as it turned out, the results were quite different from the rollover proposal.

In this instance, the study concluded there was some financial sense in spending $8 per car throughout the industry for safety improvements which would save 370 lives and 370 serious injuries a year from fiery side and rear crashes.

The "benefit" of saving those lives and injuries was calculated at $102 million, based on the same formula of each life being worth $200,000 and each serious burn injury being valued at $67,000. On the other side of the equation, the "cost" of making the $8 improvement was estimated to total $100 million.

"Thus, the costs are comparable to the most generously estimated benefits, indicating marginal cost-effectiveness." the study concluded.

This analysis, then, tended to justify in dollar terms the side and rear impact portions of the government's proposed safety regulations. However, Ford never submitted this study to the government.

At that time, Ford was not opposing the proposed side and rear impact requirements, which included the later-adopted standard that cars must be able to withstand a 30 mile-per-hour moving-barrier rear-end crash as of the 1977 model year. Yet this study confirmed that at least as far back as 1973, Ford management was aware that it would be relatively inexpensive per vehicle to achieve this degree of added safety.

4

The Pinto Fuel System*

DESIGN OF THE PINTO FUEL SYSTEM

In 1968, Ford began designing a new subcompact automobile which ultimately became the Pinto. Mr. Iacocco, then a Ford Vice President, conceived the project and was its moving force. Ford's objective was to build a car at or below 2,000 pounds to sell for no more than $2,000.

Ordinarily marketing surveys and preliminary engineering studies precede the styling of a new automobile line. Pinto, however, was a rush project, so that styling preceded engineering and dictated engineering design to a greater degree than usual. Among the engineering decisions dictated by styling was the placement of the fuel tank. It was then the preferred practice in Europe and Japan to locate the gas tank over the rear axle in subcompacts because a small

---

* Reprinted, with editorial changes, by permission of West's Publishing Company from *West's California Reporter*.

vehicle has less "crush space" between the rear axle and the bumper than larger cars. The Pinto's styling, however, required the tank to be placed behind the rear axle leaving only 9 or 10 inches of "crush space"—far less than in any other American automobile or Ford overseas subcompact. In addition, the Pinto was designed so that its bumper was little more than a chrome strip, less substantial than the bumper of any other American car produced then or later. The Pinto's rear structure also lacked reinforcing members known as "hat sections" (two longitudinal side members) and horizontal cross-members running between them such as were found in cars of larger unitized construction and in all automobiles produced by Ford's overseas operations. The absence of the reinforcing members rendered the Pinto less crush resistant than other vehicles. Finally, the differential housing selected for the Pinto had an exposed flange and a line of exposed bolt heads. These protrusions were sufficient to puncture a gas tank driven forward against the differential upon rear impact.

CRASH TESTS

During the development of the Pinto, prototypes were built and tested. Some were "mechanical prototypes" which duplicated mechanical features of the design but not its appearance while others, referred to as "engineering prototypes," were true duplicates of the design car. These prototypes as well as two production Pintos were crash tested by Ford to determine, among other things, the integrity of the fuel system in rear-end accidents. Ford also conducted the tests to see if the Pinto as designed would meet a proposed federal regulation requiring all automobiles manufactured in 1972 to be able to withstand a 20-mile-per-hour fixed barrier impact without significant fuel spillage and all automobiles manufactured after January 1, 1973, to withstand a 30-mile-per-hour fixed barrier impact without significant fuel spillage.

The crash tests revealed that the Pinto's fuel system as designed could not meet the 20-mile-per-hour proposed standard. Mechanical prototypes struck from the rear with a moving barrier at 21 miles per hour caused the fuel tank to be driven forward and to be punctured, causing fuel leakage in excess of the standard prescribed by the proposed regulation. A production Pinto crash tested at 21 miles per hour into a fixed barrier caused the fuel neck to be torn from the gas tank and the tank to be punctured by a bolt head on the differential housing. In at least one test, spilled fuel entered the driver's compartment through gaps resulting from the separation of the seams joining the real wheel wells to the floor pan. The seam separation was occasioned by the lack of reinforcement in the rear structure and insufficient welds of the wheel wells to the floor pan.

Tests conducted by Ford on other vehicles, including modified or reinforced mechanical Pinto prototypes, proved safe at speeds at which the Pinto failed. Where rubber bladders had been installed in the tank, crash tests into fixed barriers at 21 miles per hour withstood leakage from punctures in the gas tank. Vehicles with fuel tanks installed above rather than behind the rear axle passed the fuel system integrity test at 31-mile-per-hour fixed barrier. A Pinto with two longitudinal hat sections added to firm up the rear structure passed a 20-mile-per-hour rear impact fixed barrier test with no fuel leakage.

THE COST TO REMEDY DESIGN DEFICIENCIES

When a prototype failed the fuel system integrity test, the standard of care for engineers in the industry was to redesign and retest it. The vulnerability of the production Pinto's fuel tank at speeds of 20- and 30-miles-per-hour fixed barrier tests could have been remedied by inexpensive "fixes," but Ford produced and sold the Pinto to the public without doing anything to remedy the defects. Design changes that would have enhanced the integrity of the fuel tank system at relatively little cost per car included the following: Longitudinal side members and cross members at $2.40 and $1.80, respectively; a single shock absorbent "flak suit" to protect the tank at $4; a tank within a tank and placement of the tank over the axle at $5.08 to $5.79; a nylon bladder within the tank at $5.25 to $8; placement of the tank over the axle surrounded with a protective barrier at a cost of $9.95 per car; substitution of a rear axle with a smooth differential housing at a cost of $2.10; imposition of a protective shield between the differential housing and the tank at $2.35; improvement and reinforcement of the bumper at $2.60; addition of eight inches of crush space a cost of $6.40. Equipping the car with a reinforced rear structure, smooth axle, improved bumper and additional crush space at a total cost of $15.30 would have made the fuel tank safe in a 34- to 38-mile-per-hour rear-end collision by a vehicle the size of the Ford Galaxie. If, in addition to the foregoing, a bladder or tank within a tank were used or if the tank were protected with a shield, it would have been safe in a 40- to 45-mile-per-hour rear impact. If the tank had been located over the rear axle, it would have been safe in a rear impact at 50 miles per hour or more.

MANAGEMENT'S DECISION TO GO FORWARD WITH KNOWLEDGE OF DEFECTS

The idea for the Pinto, as has been noted, was conceived by Mr. Iacocco, then Executive Vice President of Ford. The feasibility study was conducted under the supervision of Mr. Robert Alexander, Vice President of Car Engineering. Ford's Product Planning Committee, whose members included Mr. Iacocca, Mr. Robert Alexander, and Mr. Harold MacDonald, Ford's Group Vice President of Car Engineering, approved the Pinto's concept and made the decision to go forward with the project. During the course of the project, regular product review meetings were held which were chaired by Mr. MacDonald and attended by Mr. Alexander. As the project approached actual production, the engineers responsible for the components of the project "signed off" to their immediate supervisors who in turn "signed off" to their superiors and so on up the chain of command until the entire project was approved for public release by Vice Presidents Alexander and MacDonald and ultimately by Mr. Iacocca. The Pinto crash tests results had been forwarded up the chain of command to the ultimate decision-makers and were known to the Ford officials who decided to go forward with production.

Harley Copp, a former Ford engineer and executive in charge of the crash testing program, testified that the highest level of Ford's management made the decision to go forward with the production of the Pinto, knowing that the gas tank was vulnerable to puncture and rupture at low rear impact speeds creating a significant risk of death or injury from fire and knowing that "fixes" were feasible at nominal cost. He testified that management's decision was based on the cost savings which would inure from omitting or delaying the "fixes."

Mr. Copp's testimony concerning management's awareness of the crash tests results and the vulnerability of the Pinto fuel system was corroborated by other evidence. At an April 1971 product review meeting chaired by Mr. MacDonald, those present received and discussed a report (Exhibit 125) prepared by Ford engineers pertaining to the financial impact of a proposed federal standard on fuel system integrity and the cost saving which would accrue from deferring even minimal "fixes."[1] The report refers to crash tests of the integrity of the fuel system of Ford vehicles and design changes needed to meet anticipated federal standards. Also in evidence was a September 23, 1970, report (Exhibit 124) by Ford's "Chassis Design Office" concerning a program "to establish a corporate [Ford] position and reply to the government" on the proposed federal fuel system integrity standard which included zero fuel spillage at 20 miles per hour fixed barrier crash by January 1, 1972, and 30 miles per hour by January 1, 1973. The report states in part: "The 20 and 30 mph rear fixed barrier crashes will probably require repackaging the fuel tanks in a protected area such as above the rear axle. This is based on moving barrier crash tests of a Chevelle and a Ford at 30 mph and other Ford products at 20 mph.

Currently there are no plans for forward models to repackage the fuel tanks. Tests must be conducted to prove that repackaged tanks will live without significantly strengthening rear structure for added protection." The report also notes that the Pinto was the "[s]mallest car line with most difficulty in achieving compliance." It is reasonable to infer that the report was prepared for and known to Ford officials in policy-making positions.

The fact that two of the crash tests were run at the request of the Ford Chassis and Vehicle Engineering Department for the specific purpose of demonstrating the advisability of moving the fuel tank over the axle as a possible "fix" further corroborated Mr. Copp's testimony that management knew the results of the crash tests. Mr. Kennedy, who succeeded Mr. Copp as the engineer in charge of Ford's crash testing program, admitted that the test results had been forwarded up the chain of command to his superiors.

Finally, Mr. Copp testified to conversations in late 1968 or early 1969 with the chief assistant research engineer in charge of cost-weight evaluation of the Pinto, and to a later conversation with the chief chassis engineer who was then in charge of crash testing the early prototype. In these conversations, both men expressed concern about the integrity of the Pinto's fuel system and complained about management's unwillingness to deviate from the design if the change would cost money.

NOTES

1. The "Fuel System Integrity Program Financial Review" report included the following:

"PRODUCT ASSUMPTIONS

"To meet 20 mph movable barrier requirements in 1973, fuel filler neck modifications to provide breakaway capability and minor upgrading of structure are required.

"To meet 30 mph movable barrier requirements, original fuel system integrity program assumptions provided for relocation of the fuel tanks to over the axle on all car lines beginning in 1974. Major tearup of rear and center floor pans, added rear end structure, and new fuel tanks were believed necessary for all car lines. These engineering assumptions were developed from limited vehicle crash test data and design and development work.

"Since these original assumptions, seven vehicle crash tests have been run, which now indicate fuel tank relocation is probably not required. Although still based heavily on judgment, Chassis Engineering currently estimates that the 30 mph movable barrier requirement is achievable with a reduced level of rear end tearup.

"In addition to added rear-end structure, Chassis Engineering believes that other rubber 'flak' suits (similar to a tire carcass), or alternatively, a bladder lining within the fuel tank may be required on all cars with flat fuel tanks located under the luggage compartment floor (all cars, except Ford/Mercury/Lincoln and Torino/Montego station wagons). Although further crash tests may show that added structure alone is adequate to meet the 30 mph movable barrier requirement, provisions for flak suits or bladders must be provided. The design cost of a single flak suit, located between the fuel tank and the axle, is currently estimated at $(4) per vehicle. If two flak suits (second located at the rear of the fuel tank), or a bladder are required, the design cost is estimated at $(8) per vehicle. Based on these estimates, it is recommended that the addition of the flak suit/bladder be delayed on all affected cars until 1976. However, package provision for both the flak suits and the bladder should be included when other changes are made to incorporate 30 mph moveable barrier capability. A design cost savings $10.9 million (1974–1975) can be realized by this delay. Although a design cost provision of $(8) per affected vehicle has been made in 1976 program levels to cover contingencies, it is hoped that cost reductions can be achieved, or the need for any flak suit or bladder eliminated after further engineering development.

"Current assumptions indicate that fuel system integrity modifications and 1973 bumper improvement requirements are nearly independent. However, bumper requirements for 1974 and beyond may require additional rear end structure which could benefit fuel system integrity programs."

5

Motor Vehicle Safety Standard, Part 571; S 301

Fuel System Integrity

S1. Scope. This standard specifies requirements for the integrity of motor vehicle fuel systems.

S2. Purpose. The purpose of this standard is to reduce deaths and injuries occurring from fires that result from fuel spillage during and after motor vehicle crashes.

S3. Application. This standard applies to passenger cars, and to multipurpose passenger vehicles, trucks, and buses that have a GVWR of 10,000 pounds or less and use fuel with a boiling point above 32° F., and to school buses that have a GVWR greater than 10,000 pounds and use fuel with a boiling point above 32° F.

S4. Definition. "Fuel spillage" means the fall, flow, or run of fuel from the vehicle but does not include wetness resulting from capillary action.

S5. General requirements.

S5.1 Passenger cars. Each passenger car manufactured from September 1, 1975, to August 31, 1976, shall meet the requirements of S6.1 in a perpendicular impact only, and S6.4. Each passenger car manufactured on or after September 1, 1976, shall meet all the requirements of S6, except S6.5.

S5.2 Vehicies with GVWR of 6,000 pounds or less. Each multipurpose passenger vehicle, truck, and bus with a GVWR of 6,000 pounds or less manufactured from September 1, 1976, to August 31, 1977, shall meet all the requirements of S6.1 in a perpendicular impact only, S6.2, and S6.4. Each of these types of vehicles manufactured on or after September 1, 1977, shall meet the requirements of S6, except S6.5.

S5.3 Vehicies with GVWR of more then 6,000 pounds but not more than 10,000 pounds. Each multipurpose passenger vehicle, truck, and bus with a GVWR of more than 6,000 pounds but not more than 10,000 pounds manufactured from September 1, 1976, to August 31, 1977, shall meet the requirements of S6.1 in a perpendicular impact only. Each vehicle manufactured on or after September 1, 1977, shall meet all the requirements of S6, except S6.5

S5.4 School buses with a GVWR greater than 10,000 pounds. Each school bus with a GVWR greater than 10,000 pounds manufactured on or after April 1, 1977, shall meet the requirements of S6.5.

S5.5 Fuel spillage: Barrier crash. Fuel spillage in any fixed or moving barrier crash test shall not exceed 1 ounce by weight from impact until motion of the vehicle has ceased, and shall not exceed a total of 5 ounces by weight in the 5-minute period following cessation of motion. For the subsequent 25-minute period (for vehicles manufactured before September 1, 1976, other than school buses with a GVWR greater than 10,000 pounds: the subsequent 10-minute period), fuel spillage during any 1-minute interval shall not exceed 1 ounce by weight.

S5.6 Fuel spillage: Rollover. Fuel spillage in any rollover test, from the onset of rotational motion, shall not exceed a total of 5 ounces by weight for the first 5 minutes of testing at each successive 90° increment. For the remaining testing period, at each increment of 90° fuel spillage during any 1-minute interval shall not exceed 1 ounce by weight.

S6. Test requirements. Each vehicle with a GVWR of 10,000 pounds or less shall be capable of meeting the requirements of any applicable barrier crash test followed by a static rollover, without alteration of the vehicle during the test sequence. A particular vehicle need not meet further requirements after having been subjected to a single barrier crash test and a static rollover test.

S6.1 Frontal barrier crash. When the vehicle traveling longitudinally forward at any speed up to and including 30 mph impacts a fixed collision barrier that is perpendicular to the line of travel of the vehicle, or at any angle up to 30° in either direction from the perpendicular to the line of travel of the vehicle, with 50th-percentile test dummies as specified in Part 572 of this chapter at each front outboard designated seating position and at any other position whose protection system is required to be tested by a dummy under the provisions of Standard No. 208, under the applicable conditions of S7, fuel spillage shall not exceed the limits of S5.5. (Effective: October 15, 1975)

S6.2 Rear moving barrier crash. When the vehicle is impacted from the rear by a barrier moving at 30 mph, with test dummies as specified in Part 572 of this chapter at each front board designated seating position, under the applicable conditions of S7, fuel spillage shall not exceed the limits of S5.5.

S6.3 Lateral moving barrier crash. When the vehicle is impacted laterally on either side by a barrier moving at 20 mph with 50th-percentile test dummies as specified in Part 572 of this chapter at positions required for testing to Standard No. 208, under the applicable conditions of S7, fuel spillage shall not exceed the limits of S5.5.

S6.4 Static rollover. When the vehicle is rotated on its longitudinal axis to each successive increment of 90°, following an impact crash of S6.1, S6.2, or S6.3, fuel spillage shall not exceed the limits of S5.6.

S6.5 Moving contoured barrier crash. When the moving contoured barrier assembly traveling longitudinally forward at any speed up to and including 30 mph impacts the test vehicle (school bus with a GVWR exceeding 10,000 pounds) at any point and angle, under the applicable conditions of S7.1 and S7.5, fuel spillage shall not exceed the limits of S5.5.

S7. Test conditions. The requirements of S5 and S6 shall be met under the following conditions. Where a range of conditions is specified, the vehicle must be capable of meeting the requirements at all points within the range.

S7.1 General test conditions. The following conditions apply to all tests:

S7.1.1 The fuel tank is filled to any level from 90 to 95 percent of capacity with Stoddard solvent, having the physical and chemical properties of type 1 solvent, Table I ASTM Standard D484–71, "Standard Specifications for Hydrocarbon Dry Cleaning Solvents."

S7.1.2 The fuel system other than the fuel tank is filled with Stoddard solvent to its normal operating level.

S7.1.3 In meeting the requirements of S6.1 through S6.3, if the vehicle has an electrically driven fuel pump that normally runs when the vehicle's electrical system is activated, it is operating at the time of the barrier crash.

S7.1.4 The parking brake is disengaged and the transmission is in neutral, except that in meeting the requirements of S6.5 the parking brake is set.

S7.1.5 Tires are inflated to manufacturer's specifications.

S7.1.6 The vehicle, including test devices and instrumentation, is loaded as follows:

(a) Except as specified in S7.1.1, a passenger car is loaded to its unloaded vehicle weight plus its rated cargo and luggage capacity weight, secured in the luggage area, plus the necessary test dummies as specified in S6, restrained only by means that are installed in the vehicle for protection at its seating position.

(b) Except as specified in S7.1.1, a multipurpose passenger vehicle, truck, or bus with a GVWR of 10,000 pounds or less is loaded to its unloaded vehicle weight, plus the necessary test dummies, as specified in S6, plus 300 pounds of its rated cargo and luggage capacity weight, whichever is less, secured to the vehicle and distributed so that the weight on each axle as measured at the tire-ground interface is in proportion to its GAWR. If the weight on any axle, when the vehicle is loaded to unloaded vehicle weight plus dummy weight, exceeds the axle's proportional share of the test weight, the remaining weight shall be placed so that the weight on that axle remains the same. Each dummy shall be restrained only by means that are installed in the vehicle for protection at its seating position.

(c) Except as specified in S7.1.1, a school bus with a GVWR greater than 10,000 pounds is loaded to its unloaded vehicle weight plus 120 pounds of unsecured weight at each designated seating position.

S7.2 Lateral moving barrier crash test conditions. The lateral moving barrier crash test conditions are those specified in S8.2 of Standard No. 208, 49 CFR 571.208.

S7.3 Rear moving barrier test conditions. The rear moving barrier test conditions are those specified in S8.2 of Standard No. 208, 49 CFR 571.208, except for the positioning of the barrier and the vehicle. The barrier and test vehicle are positioned so that at impact—

(a) The vehicle is at rest in its normal attitude;

(b) The barrier is traveling at 30 mph with its face perpendicular to the longitudinal center line of the vehicle; and

(c) A vertical plane through the geometric center of the barrier impact surface and perpendicular to that surface coincides with the longitudinal centerline of the vehicle.

S7.4 Static rollover test conditions. The vehicle is rotated about its longitudinal axis, with the axis kept horizontal, to each successive increment of 90°, 180°, and 270° at a uniform rate, with 90° of rotation taking place in any time interval from 1 to 3 minutes. After reaching each 90° increment the vehicle is held in that position for 5 minutes.

S7.5 Moving contoured barrier test conditions. The following conditions apply to the moving contoured barrier crash test:

S7.5.1 The moving barrier, which is mounted on a carriage as specified in Figure 1, is of rigid construction, symmetrical about a vertical longitudinal plane. The contoured impact surface, which is 24.75 inches high and 78 inches wide, conforms to the dimensions shown in Figure 2, and is attached to the carriage as shown in that figure. The ground clearance to the lower edge of the impact surface is 5.25 ± 0.5 inches. The wheelbase is 120 ± 2 inches.

S7.5.2 The moving contoured barrier, including the impact surface, supporting structure, and carriage, weighs 4,000 ± 50 pounds with the weight distributed so that 900 ± 25 pounds is at each rear wheel and 1100 ± 25 pounds is at each front wheel. The center of gravity is located 54.0 ± 1.5 inches rearward of the front wheel axis,

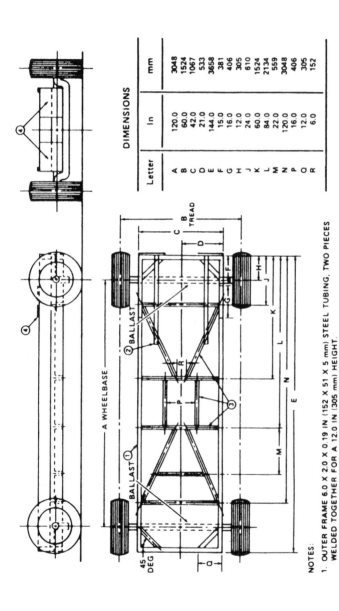

NOTES:

1. OUTER FRAME 6.0 X 2.0 X 0.19 IN (152 X 51 X 5 mm) STEEL TUBING, TWO PIECES WELDED TOGETHER FOR A 12.0 IN (305 mm) HEIGHT.

2. BALLAST TIE DOWNS.

3. ALL INNER REINFORCEMENTS AND FRAME GUSSETS OF 4.0 X 2.0 X 0.19 IN (102 X 51 X 5 mm) STEEL TUBING.

4. REINFORCE AREAS FOR BOLTING ON FACE PLATES.

FIGURE 1

Common Carriage for Moving Barriers

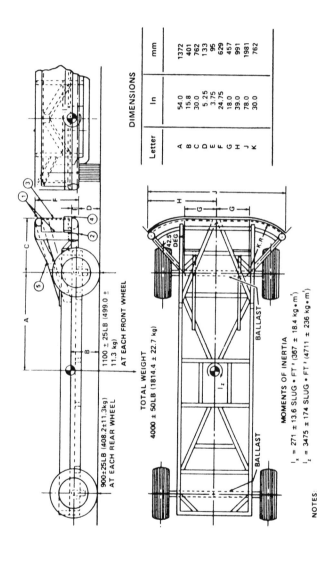

DIMENSIONS

Letter	In	mm
A	54.0	1372
B	15.8	401
C	30.0	762
D	5.25	133
E	3.75	95
F	24.75	629
G	18.0	457
H	39.0	991
J	78.0	1981
K	30.0	762

900±25LB (408.2±11.3kg)
AT EACH REAR WHEEL

1100 ± 25LB (499.0 ± 11.3 kg)
AT EACH FRONT WHEEL

TOTAL WEIGHT
4000 ± 50LB (1814.4 ± 22.7 kg)

MOMENTS OF INERTIA

I_x = 271 ± 13.6 SLUG • FT² (367 ± 18.4 kg•m²)

I_z = 3475 ± 174 SLUG • FT² (4711 ± 236 kg•m²)

42.5 DEG

BALLAST

BALLAST

NOTES:

1. UPPER FRAME 4.0 IN DIA X 0.25 IN WALL (102 mm DIA X 6 mm WALL) STEEL TUBING (THREE SIDES).

2. LOWER FRAME 6.0 IN DIA X 0.50 IN WALL (152 mm DIA X 13 mm WALL) STEEL TUBING.

3. FACE PLATE 0.75 IN (19 mm) THICK COLD ROLLED STEEL.

4. LEADING EDGE 1.0 X 4.0 IN (25 X 102 mm) STEEL BAND, SHARP EDGES BROKEN

5. ALL INNER REINFORCEMENTS 4.0 X 2.0 X 0.19 IN (102 X 51 X 5 mm) STEEL TUBING.

FIGURE 2
Common Carriage with Contoured Impact Surface Attached
Part 571; S 301–3

in the vertical longitudinal plane of symmetry, 15.8 inches above the ground. The moment of inertia about the center of gravity is:

$$I_x = 271 \pm 13.6 \text{ slug ft}^2$$
$$I_z = 3475 \pm 174 \text{ slug ft}^3$$

S7.5.3 The moving contoured barrier has a solid nonsteerable front axle and fixed rear axle attached directly to the frame rails with no spring or other type of suspension system on any wheel. (The moving barrier assembly is equipped with a braking device capable of stopping its motion.)

S7.5.4 The moving barrier assembly is equipped with G78–15 pneumatic tires with a tread width of 6.0 ± 1 inch, inflated to 24 psi.

S7.5.5 The concrete surface upon which the vehicle is tested is level, rigid, and of uniform construction, with a skid number of 75 when measured in accordance with American Society of Testing and Materials Method E-274–65T at 40 mph, omitting water delivery as specified in paragraph 7.1 of that method.

S7.5.8 The barrier assembly is released from the guidance mechanism immediately prior to impact with the vehicle.

38 F.R. 22397
August 20, 1973

40 F.R. 48352
October 15, 1975

PREAMBLE TO AMENDMENT TO
MOTOR VEHICLE SAFETY STANDARD NO. 301
Fuel System Integrity
(Docket No. 70–20; Notice 2)

This notice amends Motor Vehicle Safety Standard No. 301 on fuel system integrity to specify static rollover requirements applicable to passenger cars on September 1, 1975, and to extend applicability of the standard to multipurpose passenger vehicles, trucks, and buses with a GVWR of 10,000 pounds or less on September 1,1976.

The NHTSA proposed amending 49 CFR 571.301, *Fuel Tanks, Fuel Tank Filler Pipes, and Fuel Tank Connections,* on August 29, 1970, (35 F.R. 13799). Under the proposal the standard would be extended to all vehicles with a GVWR of 10,000 pounds or less. No fuel spillage would be permitted during the standard's tests. As proposed, these would include a spike stop from 60 mph, and a 30 mph frontal barrier crash. Additional tests for vehicles with a GVWR of 6,000 pounds or less would include a rear-end collision with a fixed barrier at 30 mph, and a static rollover test following the frontal barrier crash. With respect to the proposal: the frontal impact and static rollover tests are adopted but with an allowance of fuel spillage of 1 ounce per minute; the spike stop test is not adopted; and the rear-end fixed barrier collision test is being reproposed in a separate rule making action published today to substitute a moving barrier.

The proposal that there be zero fuel spillage was almost universally opposed for cost/benefit reasons. The NHTSA has concluded that the requirement adopted, limiting fuel spillage to 1 ounce per minute, will have much the same effect as a zero-loss requirement. The standard will effectively require motor vehicles to be designed for complete fuel containment, since any spillage allowed by design in the aftermath of testing could well exceed the limit of the standard. At the same time, the 1-ounce allowance would eliminate concern over a few drops of spillage that in a functioning system may be unavoidable.

Fuel loss will be measured for a 15-minute period for both impact and rollover tests.

The NHTSA proposed a panic-braking stop from 60 mph to demonstrate fuel system integrity. Many commented that this appeared superfluous, increasing testing costs with no performance improvements, since the proposed front and rear impact tests represented considerably higher deceleration loadings than could be achieved in braking. The NHTSA concurs, and has not adopted the panic stop test. The frontal barrier crash at 30 mph has been retained for passenger cars, and extended to multipurpose passenger vehicles, trucks, and buses with a GVWR of 10,000 pounds or less as of September 1, 1976.

The static rollover test was adopted as proposed. It applies to passenger cars as of September 1, 1971, and to multipurpose passenger vehicles, trucks, and buses with a GVWR of 6,000 pounds or less, as of September 1, 1976. The rollover test follows the front barrier crash, and consists of a vehicle being rotated on its longitudinal axis at successive increments of 90°. A condition of the test is that rotation between increments occurs in not less than 1 minute and not more than 3 minutes. After reaching a 90° increment, the vehicle is held in that position for 5 minutes.

The proposed rear-end crash test incorporated a fixed collision barrier. Manufacturers generally favored a moving barrier impact as a closer simulation of real world conditions. The NHTSA concurs and is not adopting a rear end fixed barrier test. Instead, it is proposing a rear-end moving barrier collision test as part of the notice of proposed rulemaking published today.

Under the proposal the vehicle would be loaded to its GVWR with the fuel tank filled to any level between 90 and 100 percent of capacity. Many commenters objected on the grounds that full loading of a vehicle represents an unrealistic condition in terms of actual crash experience. The NHTSA does not agree. Although full loading of a vehicle is not the condition most frequently encountered, it certainly occurs frequently enough that the vehicle should be designed to give basic protection in that condition. The vehicle test weight condition has been adopted as proposed. It should be noted that, in the parallel notice of proposed rulemaking issued today, vehicles would be tested under the weight conditions specified in Standard No. 208, effective September 1, 1975.

In consideration of the foregoing, 49 CFR Part 571.301, Motor Vehicle Safety Standard No. 301, is amended...

Effective date: September 1, 1975. Because of the necessity to allow manufacturers sufficient production leadtime it is found for good cause shown that an effective date later than 1 year after issuance of this rule is in the public interest.

(Sec. 103, 119, Pub. L. 89–563, 80 Stat. 718, 15 U.S.C. 1392, 1407; delegation of authority at 49 CFR 1.51.)

Issued on August 15, 1973.

James B. Gregory
Administrator

38 F.R. 22397
August 20,1973

PREAMBLE TO AMENDMENT TO
MOTOR VEHICLE SAFETY STANDARD NO. 301
Fuel System Integrity
(Docket No. 73–20; Notice 2)

The purpose of this notice is to amend Federal Motor Vehicle Safety Standard No. 301, *Fuel System Integrity*, to upgrade substantially the requirements of the standard by specifying a rear moving barrier crash, a lateral moving barrier crash, and a frontal barrier crash including impacts at any angle up to 30° in either direction from the perpendicular.

A notice of proposed rulemaking published August 20, 1973 (38 F.R. 22417) proposed the imposition of additional testing requirements designed to ameliorate the dangers associated with fuel spillage following motor vehicle accidents. In an amendment to Standard No. 301, published on the same day as the proposal, a frontal barrier crash and a static rollover test were specified. In order to ensure the safety of fuel systems in any possible collision situation, the NHTSA finds it essential to incorporate additional proposed test requirements into the present standard and to make these requirements applicable to all vehicle types with a GVWR of 10,000 pounds or less.

Comments in response to the proposal were received from 29 commenters. Any suggestions for changes of the proposal not specifically mentioned herein are denied, on the basis of all the information presently available to this agency. A number of the issues raised in the comments have been dealt with by the agency in its response to the petitions for reconsideration of the final rule issued on August 20, 1973. In its notice responding to the petitions, the NHTSA considered objections to the use of actual fuel during testing, the specified fuel fill level, the application of the standard to vehicles using diesel fuel, the fuel spillage measuring requirement, and the allegedly more stringent loading requirements applicable to passenger cars. The type of fuel subject to the standard was also clarified.

Objections were registered by 13 commenters to the proposed inclusion of a dynamic rollover test in the fuel system integrity standard. As proposed, the requirement calls for a measurement of the fuel loss while the vehicle is in motion. Commenters pointed out the exceptional difficulty in measuring or even ascertaining a leakage when the vehicle is rolling over at 30 mph. The NHTSA has decided that the objections have merit, and has deleted the dynamic rollover test. The results of the dynamic rollover do not provide sufficiently unique data with regard to the fuel system's integrity to justify the cost of developing techniques for accurately measuring spillage during such a test, and of conducting the test itself. The NHTSA has concluded that the severity of the other required tests, when conducted in the specified sequence, is sufficient to assure the level of fuel system integrity intended by the agency.

Triumph Motors objected to the use of a 4,000-pound barrier during the moving barrier impacts, asserting that such large barriers discriminate against small vehicles. Triumph requested that the weight of the barrier be the curb weight of the vehicle being tested in order to alleviate the burden on small vehicles. The NHTSA has concluded that no justification exists for this change. The moving barrier is intended to represent another vehicle with which the test vehicle must collide. The use of a 4,000-pound moving barrier is entirely reasonable since vehicles in use are often over 4,000 pounds in weight and a small vehicle is as likely to collide with vehicle of that size as one smaller. The NHTSA considers it important that vehicle fuel systems be designed in such a way as to withstand impacts from vehicles they are exposed to on the road, regardless of the differences in their sizes.

Jeep and American Motors objected to the effective dates of the proposed requirements and asked that they be extended. Jeep favors an effective date not earlier than September 1, 1979, and American Motors favors a September 1, 1978, effective date. The NHTSA denies these requests. It has found that the time period provided for development of conforming fuel systems is reasonable and should be strictly adhered to considering the urgent need for strong and resilient fuel systems.

Several commenters expressed concern over the impact of the prescribed testing procedures on manufacturers of low-volume specialty vehicles. The NHTSA appreciates the expense of conducting crash tests on low-production vehicles, realizing that the burden on the manufacturer is related to the number of vehicles he manufactures. However, there are means by which the small-volume manufacturer can minimize the costs of testing. He can concentrate test efforts on the vehicle(s) in his line that he finds most difficult to produce in conformity with the standard. These manufacturers should also be aware that an exemption from application of the standard is available where fewer than 10,000 vehicles per year are produced and compliance would subject him to substantial financial hardship.

In responding to the petitions for reconsideration of the amendment to Standard No. 301, published August 20, 1973, the NHTSA revised the fuel system loading requirement to specify Stoddard solvent as the fuel to be used during testing. In accordance with that amendment, the proposed requirement that the engine be idling during the testing sequence is deleted. However, electrically driven fuel pumps that normally run when the electrical system in the vehicle is activated shall be operating during the barrier crash tests.

In order to fulfill the intention expressed in the preamble to the proposal, that simultaneous testing under Standards Nos. 208 and 301 be possible, language has been added to subparagraph S7.1.5 of Standard No. 301 specifying the same method of restraint as that required in Standard No. 208. In its response to petitions for reconsideration of Standard No. 301 (39 F.R. 10586) the NHTSA amended the standard by requiring that each dummy be restrained during testing only by means that are installed in the vehicle for protection at its seating position and that require no action by the vehicle occupant.

Suggestions by several commenters that the application of certain crash tests should be limited to passenger cars in order to maintain complete conformance to the requirements of Standard No. 208 are found to be without merit. Enabling simultaneous testing under several standards, although desirable, is not the most important objective of the safety standards. The NHTSA is aware of the burden of testing costs, and therefore has sought to ease that burden where possible by structuring certain of its standards to allow concurrent testing for compliance. It must be emphasized, however, that the testing requirements specified in a standard are geared toward a particular safety need. Application of the tests proposed for Standard No. 301 to all vehicle types with a 10,000 pounds or less is vital to the accomplishment of the degree of fuel system integrity necessary to protect the occupants of vehicles involved in accidents.

No major objections were raised concerning the proposed angular frontal barrier crash, lateral barrier crash, or rear moving barrier crash. On the basis of all information available to this agency, it has been determined that these proposed crash test should be adopted as proposed.

In consideration of the foregoing, 49 CFR 571.301, Motor Vehicle Safety Standard No. 301, is amended to read as set forth below.

Effective date: September 1, 1975, with additional requirements effective September 1, 1976, and September 1, 1977, as indicated.

(Secs. 103, 119, Pub. L. 89–563, 80 Stat. 718, 15 U.S.C. 1392, 1407; delegation of authority at 49 CFR 1.51.)

Issued on March 18, 1974.

James B. Gregory
Administrator
39 F.R. 10588
March 21, 1974

6

Investigation Report, Phase I: Alleged Fuel Tank
and Filler Neck Damage in Rear-End Collision of
Subcompact Passenger Cars

1971–1976 FORD PINTO
1975–1976 MERCURY BOBCAT

OFFICE OF DEFECTS INVESTIGATION
ENFORCEMENT
NATIONAL HIGHWAY TRAFFIC SAFETY ADMINISTRATION

MAY 1978

A PORTION OF THIS REPORT HAS BEEN WITHHELD
FROM THE PUBLIC FILE PURSUANT TO 5 U.S.C.
552(b) (4).

TABLE OF CONTENTS

I. BACKGROUND

A. *Basis for Investigation*

A formal defect investigation case was initiated on September 13, 1977, based upon allegations that the design and location of the fuel tank in the Ford Pinto make it highly susceptible to damage on rear impact at low to moderate closing speeds.

On August 10, 1977, a press conference was held in Washington, D.C., to announce the release of an article entitled, "Pinto Madness", which was published in the September/October issue of *Mother Jones* magazine. The article made several allegations concerning the safety of the Pinto fuel tank. The most significant of these charges as related to the National Highway Traffic Safety Administration's (NHTSA) defect investigation are as follows:

1. That the Pinto fuel tank is designed and located so that in rear-impact collisions at low to moderate speeds, it is displaced forward until it impacts the differential housing on the rear axle, resulting in tank cuts and/or puncture. The leakage of gasoline thus presents a significant fire hazard.
2. That the Ford Motor Company had knowledge of this "defect" during the developmental phase of the Pinto through its own test programs, but concluded that it was more cost-effective to produce the vehicle without modifications which would have corrected the problem but added to the production cost.

Investigation was initiated to determine whether the alleged problem constitutes a safety-related defect within the meaning of the National Traffic and Motor Vehicle Safety Act of 1966.

B. *Description and Function*

The Pinto fuel tank is of sheet metal construction and is attached to the undercarriage of the vehicle by means of two metal straps. In addition, the fuel filler tube extends into the top left side of the tank in a sliding fit through a gasketed opening. At its other end the fuel filler tube is affixed to the inner side of the left rear quarter panel by means of a bracket which is firmly attached to the quarter panel surface.

The fuel tank is the resevoir that holds the supply of gasoline required for engine operation. In the Pinto and Bobcat of model years in question, the tank capacity is approximately 11 gallons.

C. *Analysis of the Alleged Problem*

MODE:

Allegedly, rear impact of the Pinto by another vehicle at low to moderate closing speed displaces the fuel tank forward until it is cut or punctured by the differential housing, or its bolts. Fuel tank filler necks pull out of the tank as well. The resulting fuel spillage may then be ignited, creating a fire hazard of obvious significance.

SYMPTOMS:

There are no symptoms to indicate the existence of the alleged safety hazard. The alleged problem addresses the rear impact crashworthiness of the Pinto and Bobcat which is exhibited only under collision conditions.

D. *Investigative Inputs and Actions*

Following public release of the article, "Pinto Madness", the NHTSA initiated, on August 11, 1977, a preliminary evaluation of the alleged safety defect, and on September 13, a formal defect investigation case. The following activities were undertaken in these efforts.

1. The author of the magazine article, Mark Dowie, was asked to make available to the NHTSA, documentation and evidence upon which his article was based.
2. Consumer letters, including Congressional inquiries on behalf of constituents, were received and appropriately processed.
3. The National Center for Statistics and Analysis conducted a search of the Fatal Accident Reporting System (FARS) files, to compile relevant fatal accident statistics and data.
4. The Ford Motor Company was requested to provide various technical and legal data concerning the matter.
5. Contact was established and maintained with the Canadian Ministry of Transport (CMOT), which also initiated an investigation of the "Pinto Madness" charges.

6. A test program of staged vehicle-to-vehicle rear-end collisions was developed and a contract awarded for the performance of these tests.

The details of the aforementioned sources of information, as well as NHTSA actions taken and the findings which resulted, are detailed in subsequent sections of this report.

II. PROBLEMS ALLEGED

A. *Reports From Consumers*

Since public release of the *Mother Jones* article, the NHTSA has received over 900 inquires from the public concerning this matter. The defect investigation case file contains 54 letters and telephone contacts, including 18 Congressional inquiries on behalf of constituents. The Office of Public Affairs and Consumer Participation has received approximately 540 inquiries from Pinto and other vehicle owners concerning this matter, in addition to an estimated 30 inquiries from the media, and several inquiries from various consumer groups. The Auto Safety Hotline reported that an estimated 250 telephone inquiries have been received with no further contacts made with these consumers. In addition, over 40 telephone contacts have been made by ODI Staff personnel with various consumers, media representatives and with NHTSA representatives in Regional Offices. These contacts were generally non-contributory to the investigation in terms of furnishing factual data, and are not documented in the record.

Of the consumer letters and other inquires, only one involved an actual report of a fire occurrence in a Pinto vehicle upon rear-end impact, not previously reported to the NHTSA through other sources. This particular instance involved a parked Pinto sedan of unknown model year which was rear-ended by a 1969 Pontiac Firebird in a residential area. The incident resulted in fire damage to both the Pinto and other real property, but no bodily injuries and/or fatalities were sustained.

B. *Reports From Ford Motor Company (Ford)*

In response to the NHTSA's requests, Ford provided information concerning the number and nature of known incidents in which rear impact of a Pinto vehicle reportedly caused fuel tank damage, fuel system leakage or fire occurrence. This information disclosed the following:

Total Number Rear Impact/Fuel Leakage/Fire cases reported:	35
Lawsuits/Liability Claims:	29
Total Number injuries, including fatalities, reported in all vehicles:	107
Total Number injuries, including fatalities, sustained by Pinto occupants:	57
Total Number fatalities reported:	26
Number fatalities sustained by Pinto occupants:	25
Lawsuits/Liability Claims:	29
(Cases involving fires/burn injuries or claims of defective/ dangerous fuel tank/negligence in fuel system design)	
Number burn injuries:	23
Number fatalities reported (non-impact):	21
Number cases settled out of court or by judgment against Ford/defendants:	8
Number cases pending trial:	19
Cases settled in favor of Ford/under investigation:	2

C. *Reports From Canadian Ministry of Transport (CMOT)*

Since the initiation of this defect investigation case, two incidents have been reported to the NHTSA by the CMOT, involving rear-impact collisions of Ford Pintos which resulted in fires. These incidents resulted in one fatality, and two impact/burn injury cases.

D. *Summary of Problem Reports*

In total, the NHTSA is aware of 38 cases in which rear-end collisions of Pinto vehicles have resulted in fuel tank damage, fuel system leakage and/or ensuing fire. These cases have resulted in a total of 27 fatalities sustained by Pinto occupants, of which one is reported to have resulted from impact injuries. In addition, 24 occupants of these Pinto vehicles have sustained non-fatal burn injuries.

III. TECHNICAL DATA

The following technical data acquired from Ford and other sources has relevance to the design, materials, construction or performance aspect of the fuel tank installed in the 1971–1976 Pinto and 1975–1976 Bobcat.

1. The Pinto two-door sedan was introduced for sale in the United States on September 11, 1970, as a 1971 model year vehicle. A 1971 model year Pinto three-door version was introduced in February 1971. The station wagon model was introduced as a 1972 model year vehicle on March 17, 1972.

2. Production statistics for the pre-1977 Pinto are as follows:

Model Year	2-Door Sedan	3-Door Sedan	Station Wagon	Totals
1971	267,694	59,173	0	326,867
1972	171,616	187,657	96,221	455,494
1973	109,080	141,440	204,514	455,034
1974	120,911	159,999	217,351	498,261
1975	58,697	63,129	83,137	204,963
1976	86,842	87,101	99,138	273,081
Totals	814,840	698,499	700,361	2,213,700

3. Based upon R.L. Polk and Company statistics of vehicle registration as of July 1, 1976, it is estimated that 1.9 million Pintos of 1971–1976 model years are currently in use. These Pinto vehicles accounted for 2.0% of all registered cars as of July 1, 1976.

4. The 1971–1976 Pinto fuel tank is of sheet steel construction and is attached to the vehicle's rear undercarriage by two metal straps, with mounting brackets. The tank is located aft of the rear axle which, in the Pinto, may be one of two types; 6 3/4-inch ring gear with integral carrier, or 8-inch ring gear with removeable carrier. The rear differential cover on the 8-inch axle is welded on, and employs no mechanical fasteners. The 6 3/4-inch axle differential cover is attached by eight 5/16-18x0.62 hex head locking screws. The differential cover dome protrudes further aft than do the the screw heads, as follows:

	Height of Fastener Head Relative to Adjacent Cover	Distance of Fastener Head *Forward* of Cover Dome Surface
S.O.P. 1971–	.314/.246	1.954/1.827
Approx. 3/71– Model Year 1977	.313/.293	1.907/1.827

The outer edge of the differential cover dome also protrudes aft approximately 1/8-inch, the apparent result of the dome forming process.

In answering NHTSA questions, Ford provided information concerning nominal distances from the forward surface of the fuel tank to the aft surface of the differential cover. While the true distance from the fuel tank body to the nearest point on the rear axle varies from one model year to another and from sedan to station wagon models, the 1971–1976 Pinto with the 6 3/4-inch axle maintained this distance at approximately 3 inches. In the 1977 model year, this distance was increased by a minimum of 1 inch. It was also disclosed that the left shock absorber is located approximately equidistant from the fuel tank as the rear axle.

In this investigation, the fuel filler neck is considered to be an integral part of the tank. The filler neck is firmly attached by a flange with mounting screws, to the inner side of the left rear quarter panel. At its other end, the filler neck extends into the fuel tank through a gasketed opening in the left side of the tank.

Ford initiated 82 post-introduction engineering changes in the Pinto fuel tank, fuel filler neck, and associated hardware utilized for attaching the fuel tank to the vehicle underbody. Review of these data disclosed the following changes with potential relevance to the rear-impact crash performance of the fuel tank.

- 1973 Station Wagon filler pipe—length of fuel filler pipe reduced by 0.50 inches at tank attachment end. Initiated at Job #1.
- 1977 Sedan and Station Wagon fuel tank shield—plastic shield added between fuel tank and straps. Initiated at Job #1.

- 1977 Sedan filler pipe assembly—filler pipe assembly lengthened to reduce fuel capacity by 1.3 gallons and vehicle weight by 8 pounds.
- Other engineering changes involved various items including tank capacity, filler pipe flange and seals, and tank straps and brackets.

5. According to Ford, *Mercury Bobcat* vehicles ". . .utilize essentially the same structures as Pintos of contemporary manufacture and their fuel systems and related components are identical to those employed in such Pintos."

Production statistics for the pre-1977 Mercury Bobcat are as follows:

Model Year	3-Door Runabout	Station Wagon	Totals
1975	14,605	17,851	32,456
1976	20,212	21,207	41,419
Totals	34,817	39,058	73,875

6. Prior to initial introduction of the Pinto for sale, Ford performed four rear impact barrier crash tests which included ". . .assessment of the post-impact condition of the fuel tank and/or filler pipe." These tests were reportedly conducted on ". . .experimental vehicles equipped with differing rear structure and fuel system designs proposed from time to time for incorporation in the Pinto. . ." Ford further reported that ". . .none of the tested vehicles employed structure or fuel system designs representative of structures and fuel systems incorporated in the Pinto as introduced in September 1970." These tests were conducted May 1969 through November 1969, utilizing a vehicle identified as a "Special Maverick."

Following initial introduction of the Pinto for sale, Ford continued a program of rear barrier impact tests on Pintos which included assessment of the post impact condition of the fuel tank and/or filler pipe. Reports of 55 rear barrier crash tests conducted ". . .on both production vehicles and vehicles with experimental components and/or modified structures. . ." were provided, including tests of Mercury Bobcats. While these tests were reportedly performed, in part, in connection with

proposed NHTSA rulemaking activities, three items developed
a history of consistent results:

a. At impact speeds as low as 21.5 miles per hour with a fixed
    barrier (Crash Test No. 1616), the fuel tank was punctured
    by contact with the differential housing and/or its bolts, or
    with some other underbody structure.
b. Under similar test conditions as (a), above, the fuel filler
    neck was pulled out of the tank completely.
c. Again, under similar test conditions as (a), above, structural
    and/or sheet metal damage to the vehicle was sufficient to
    jam one, or both of the passenger doors closed.

Among the experimental and other modifications studied in
these tests were:

- Use of rubber bladder with locally reinforced textured nylon
  patches in "puncture prone areas", installed inside steel tank
- Modification of filler pipe attachment to the left rear quarter
  panel and fuel tank to prevent pull-out during impact.
- Installation of plastic shields on the fuel tank immediately
  aft of the differential housing.
- Modified exhaust system with muffler located behind the
  rear axle.
- Fuel tank made of molded polyethylene.
- Increased length of fuel filler neck extending inside the tank.
- Modified rear underbody structure and reinforced rear
  quarter panels.

Review of the test reports in question suggested that Ford had
studied several alternative solutions to the numerous
instances in which fuel tank deformation, damage or leakage
occurred during or after impact.

IV. MAJOR NHTSA INVESTIGATIVE ACTIONS

A. *Examination of Accident Statistics*

A search of the NHTSA's Fatal Accident Reporting System
(FARS) file was conducted by the National Center for
Statistics and Analysis, Research and Development. Search of
the automated FARS file provided information on fatal

accidents for approximately 2 1/2 years of data collection. A purpose of the search was to determine whether Pintos had been involved in rear-end fatal crashes with fires.

In terms of the purely quantitative data, the following tabulations specifically applicable to the Pinto were disclosed by the FARS examination (covering 1975, 1976 and approximately half of 1977):

- Total Number Fatal Pinto Accidents Due to All Causes, 1975–1977   1,626
- Total Number Pinto Occupant Fatalities in Accidents Due to All Causes, 1975–1977   1,417
- Total Number Fatal Pinto Accidents with Fire, 1975–1977   33
- Total Number Pinto Occupant, Fatalities in Accidents with Fire, 1975–1977   41
- Total Number Fatal Pinto Accidents with Rear End Collision, 1975–1977   95
- Total Number Pinto Occupant Fatalities in Accidents with Rear End Collision, 1975–1977   72
- Total Number Fatal Pinto Accidents with Rear End Collision and Fire, 1975–1977   11
- Total Number Pinto Occupant Fatalities in Accidents Rear End Collision and Fire, 1975–1977   17

The data show that rear-end collisions of Pinto vehicles have resulted in fires and fatalities. This fact is substantiated by the historical details of various litigation cases.

These data were recognized to be subject to qualifications and amplifications. Basically pertinent among these are the following:

- Make/model information in FARS comes from two sources: vehicle registration data and automated decoding of the Vehicle Identification Number. Therefore, a particular car was identified where *either one* of these two sources indicated it to be the make/model in question.
- Fire/explosion is not a standard data element on most police reporting forms, unless a non-collision fire caused an accident. Thus, FARS coding of fire is due primarily to its specific mention, if any, in the officer's accident description. In addition, FARS data do not indicate the origin of the fire.

- If a death due to burns occurred sometime after the crash, it is less likely that it would be reported on the officer's accident report.
- FARS does not record the cause of death, only its fact; it does not distinguish between deaths due to impact and those caused by the fire.
- The FARS cases examined disclosed limited availability of data necessary to establish accurate pre-impact closing speeds.

B. NHTSA Crash Test Program

On September 30, 1977, a Request for Proposals was issued in order to select a contractor to perform a series of staged vehicle-to-vehicle crash tests at moderate speeds. The program was designed to generate data and to document the results of specified rear impact collisions under actual driving conditions. The stationary vehicles were specified as Pintos, Chevrolet Vegas, and full size sedans, with the moving vehicles to be identical full size sedans. The program required that the fuel tanks of the stationary vehicles be filled to at least 95% of rated capacity, and that the engines of both stationary and moving vehicles be running and at normal operating temperature at the time of impact. In addition, the brake lights were illuminated on the stationary vehicle at impact. Other test variables included:

- Speed and attitude of the moving vehicle
- Illumination of headlights on the moving vehicle
- Angle and parallelism of vehicles at impact

The contract was awarded to Dynamic Science, Incorporated, in Phoenix, Arizona, and testing commenced on February 1, 1978. As orginally designed, the test program involved 6 Pintos, 6 Vegas, and 3 full size vehicles for use as stationary cars. The program was subsequently amended to include 4 Pintos of 1974–1976 model years and 2 Pinto Station Wagons. Other changes in test requirements were made as the program progressed: these are identified in the matrix of test results attached as Figure 2, to this report. In its final form, the program entailed:

11 Full size vehicles/Pinto tests
 1 Pinto/fixed barrier test (tank filled with Stoddard solvent)
 5 Full size vehicle/Vega tests
 1 Vega/fixed barrier test (tank filled with Stoddard solvent)
 <u>1</u> Full size vehicle/Full size vehicle test
19 Total tests

The results of the tests are summarized in Figure 1. Therein, it is noted that in two Pinto tests with the full size vehicle travelling at 35 miles per hour, fires resulted. In similar tests at 30 miles per hour, significant leakage of the Pinto fuel tanks resulted without fire. A significant finding in the test program was the fact that the design of the Pinto fuel filler pipe resulted in its being completely dislodged from the tank in some cases. Impacts sufficient to result in puncture/tearing of the fuel tank generally resulted in leakage of fuel in a *pouring* fashion. Separation of the filler neck from the tank provided a fuel spillage mechanism in a wide *dispersion* fashion.

No fires were produced by the tests involving Vegas and full size vehicles as stationary cars.

All of the tests were documented by high-speed and normal speed color motion pictures, as well as by still photography following impacts.

V. OTHER NHTSA ACTIONS

The following are other actions taken by the NHTSA.

A. *Media and Consumer Groups*

On August 11, 1977, the first of several letters was sent to Mr. Mark Dowie, author of the *Mother Jones* article, requesting that he make available to the NHTSA, documentation and evidence upon which his article was based.

Because of the sensitivity and widespread media attention given to the *Mother Jones* article, as well as to the settlements of two related lawsuits during the course of this investigation, specific requests to various media and consumer organizations for information were generally not made. Efforts were expended, however, in cooperating with the media and consumer groups to advise them of the nature, scope and status of the NHTSA's investigation. Included among the organizations contacted were the Center for Auto Safety, ABC-TV Evening News, and various television stations and newspapers.

B. *Records Checks*

1. Vehicle Owner Letter File

   The NHTSA's motor vehicle owner letter file, initiated in September 1966, contains all letters and telephone contacts received from all sources reporting defects and other problems with motor vehicles. At present, approximately 2,500 documents enter this file each month.

   All letters received by the NHTSA in specific reference to this investigation were noted in Section II.A., of this report.

2. NHTSA Motor Vehicle Defect Recall Campaign Log

   The log contains the make, model, year and a brief description of the defect for all safety defect recall campaigns reported to the NHTSA by manufacturers in accordance with the Act of 1966.

   A check of the Campaign Log disclosed that at least 17 previous recalls have been conducted for correction of various specific problems that could allow fuel leakage from the fuel tank/filler neck/cap. Of note is Campaign No. 77V048, in which General Motors recalled 128,700 1968–1970 Opel Kadetts for correction of an uncovered tail-light mounting bolt which could puncture the fuel tank in low speed right rear impacts.

   In Campaign No. 77V114, the Ford Motor Company recalled 642 1977 Pintos for replacement of an erroneously installed U-nut on the inboard rear attachment of the rear bumper isolator. The edge of the U-bolt could possibly contact and puncture the fuel tank.

3. Technical Reference Library

   A search of the Technical Reference Library filed was conducted for information and publications relevant to this investigation. This search disclosed that previously cited Pinto recall campaign (77V114), as well as three others which could involve possible fuel leakage and fire potential.

A review of all Pinto Standards Enforcement Tests disclosed that a 1976 Pinto Pony MPG failed to meet the requirements of FMVSS 301, Fuel Systems Integrity.

4. Canadian Ministry of Transport (CMOT)

On September 30, 1977, a 1974 Pinto was involved in a rear impact, fatal fire accident in Windsor, Ontario, Canada. The Pinto was impacted by a 1976 Chevrolet Impala in a braking attitude and forced into the rear of a 1976 Mercury Monarch. The fuel tank of the Pinto was punctured or torn in several locations, the filler neck pulled out completely, and the vehicle was completely engulfed by fire. One of the two Pinto occupants sustained fatal injuries.

The CMOT acquired possession of the Pinto and performed a thorough inspection of the vehicle on November 29 and 30. This inspection was attended by NHTSA and Ford representatives.

On February 24, 1978, the CMOT reported the occurrence of a rear impact with fire incident involving a 1973 Pinto. The single Pinto occupant was attempting engine repairs when the vehicle was struck by a 1976 Plymouth Volare reportedly travelling at 35 miles per hour. A report of the incident, with photographs taken within seconds after the collision by a nearby pedestrian, was furnished to the NHTSA on March 30, 1978.

VI. OBSERVATIONS

The fuel tank and filler pipe assembly installed in the 1971–1976 Ford Pinto is subject to damage which results in fuel spillage and fire potential in rear impact collisions by other vehicles at moderate closing speeds.

When impacted from the rear by other vehicles at moderate closing speeds, the Pinto fuel tank may be punctured, cut or torn, by contact with the rear axle differential housing assembly, the left shock absorber and/or its lower bracket, or by other vehicle rear underbody components.

In nine staged collision tests of 1971–1976 Pinto 2-door sedans and 3-door runabouts impacted by 1971 Chevrolet Impalas at closing speeds of 30 and 35 miles per hour, two tests resulted in fires. In all of the remaining seven tests, fuel tank damage occurred with fuel leakage rates ranging from 6 to 700 ounces per minute, with an average rate in excess of 240 ounces per minute.

In one test of a 1972 Pinto towed rearward into a fixed barrier at 21.5 miles per hour, the fuel tank sustained damage and the filler pipe pulled out of the tank. Fuel leakage was measured to exceed 12 ounces per minute.

In tests of 1 ea., 1972 and 1976 Pinto station wagons, no significant fuel leakage rates were measured. Similarly, no punctures or tears of the fuel tanks were caused, and the fuel filler pipes did not completely pull out of the tanks.

Data from the Ford Motor Company indicates that at least 35 rear-end collisions of 1971–1976 Pintos have occurred in the United States, in which fuel tank damage and/or fuel leakage and/or fires have resulted. These incidents have resulted in at least 25 fatalities and 23 cases of non-fatal burn injuries.

Data from the Fatal Accident Reporting System disclosed that from January 1975 through approximately June 1977, 33 fatal Pinto accidents occurred that involved fire, and resulted in 41 Pinto occupant fatalities. During this same period of time, 11 fatal accidents occurred in which Pintos were impacted from the rear and fires resulted; 17 Pinto occupants sustained fatal injuries in these cases.

Since initiation of this investigation, two cases have occurred in Canada Involving rear impact of Pintos which resulted in fuel tank fires. These occurrences resulted in 1 fatality and 1 burn injury case.

In the history of product liability actions filed against Ford and other co-defendants involving rear impact of Pintos with fuel tank damage/fuel leakage/fire occurrences, nine cases have been settled. Of these, the plaintiffs have compensated in 8 cases, either by jury awards or out of court settlements.

VII. CONCLUSIONS

Based upon the information either developed or acquired during this investigation, the following conclusions have been reached:

1. 1971–1976 Ford Pintos have experienced moderate speed, rear-end collisions that have resulted in fuel tank damage, fuel

leakage, and fire occurrences that have resulted in fatalities and non-fatal burn injuries.

2. Rear-end collision of Pinto vehicles can result in puncture and other damage of the fuel tank and filler neck, creating substantial fuel leakage, and in the presence of external ignition sources fires can result.

3. The dynamics of fuel spillage are such that when impacted by a full size vehicle, the 1971–1976 Pinto exhibits a "fire threshold" at closing speeds between 30 and 35 miles per hour.

4. Relevant product liability litigation and previous recall campaigns further establish that fuel leakage is a significant hazard to motor vehicle safety, including such leakage which results from the crashworthiness characteristics of the vehicle.

5. The fuel tank design and structural characteristis of the 1975–1976 Mercury Bobcat which render it identical to contemporary Pinto vehicles, also render it subject to like consequences in rear impact collisions.

FIGURE 1
Fuel Tank Integrity Collision Tests Results

DATE	TEST NO.	MATRIX NO.	STATIONARY VEHICLE	STRIKING VEHICLE	TEST CONDITIONS	RESULTS
2/1	1	7	1971 Pinto	1971 Chev. Impala	34.88 mph, in-line	FIRE
2/2	2	10	1971 Vega	"	35.27 mph, in-line	Filler pipe and tank leakage less than 1 ounce, total
2/15	3	8	1972 Pinto	"	35.27 mph, in-line, 0.4g	FIRE
2/15	4	11	1971 Vega	"	34.78 mph, in-line, 0.4g	Leakage greater then 7 oz./min.
2/16	5	9	1972 Pinto	"	29.01 mph, offset, normal attitude	Filler pipe and tank leakage greater than 6 oz./min.
2/17	6	12	1971 Vega	"	35.09 mph, offset, 0.7 g	No leakage
2/20	7	2	1971 Pinto	"	29.91 mph, in-line, 0.7g	Filler pipe leakage greater than 100 oz./min.
2/21	8	5	1871 Vega	"	40.74 mph, in-line, 0.7g	Leakage greater than 19.5 oz./min.
2/23	9	1	1971 Pinto	"	29.91 mph, Angle 15°, L/R, 0.6g	Filler pipe and tank leakage greater than 10.2 oz./min.
2/24	10	4	1972 Vega	"	35.24 mph, Angle 15°, R/R, 0.7g	Leakage greater than 17 oz./min.
2/27	11	3	1972 Pinto	N/A	21.47 mph, FIXED BARRIER	Filler pipe and tank leakage greater than 12 oz./min. (Stoddard Solvent)
2/28	12	14	1971 Impala	1971 Chev. Impala	34.59 mph, in-line, 0.7g	Could not measure

FIGURE 1
Fuel Tank Integrity Collision Tests Results (continued)

DATE	TEST NO.	MATRIX NO.	STATIONARY VEHICLE	STRICKING VEHICLE	TEST CONDITIONS	RESULTS
3/3	13	6	1972 Vega	N/A	21.38 mph, FIXED BARRIER	Leakage less than 1 ounce, total
3/21	14	13	1974 Pinto	1971 Chev. Impala	35.32 mph, 0.6g	Filler pipe and tank leakage greater than 500 oz./min.
3/21	15	18	1972 Pinto Sta. Wagon	"	35.57 mph, 0.6g	No leakage. Filler pipe partially pulled out
3/22	16	16	1976 Pinto	"	35.30 mph, 0.6g	Filler pipe and tank leakage greater than 450 oz./min.
3/23	17	15	1974 Pinto	"	29.89 mph, normal att.	Filler pipe partially pulled out. Leakage greater than 10 oz./min.
3/27	18	19	1976 Pinto Sta. Wagon	"	35.18 mph, normal att.	Leakage less than 1 oz. total. Filler neck pulled out 2½". No punctures in tank.
3/28	19	17	1976 Pinto	"	30.31 mph, normal att.	Leakage of total tank contents in 1 minute. 4" Dia. puncture.

DENNIS A. GIOIA

7

Pinto Fires and Personal Ethics:
A Script Analysis of Missed Opportunities*

ABSTRACT. This article details the personal involvement of the author in the early stages of the infamous Pinto fire case. The paper first presents an insider account of the context and decision environment within which he failed to initiate an early recall of defective vehicles. A cognitive script analysis of the personal experience is then offered as an explanation of factors that led to a decision that now is commonly seen as a definitive study in unethical corporate behavior. The main analytical thesis is that script schemas that were guiding cognition and action at the time precluded considerations of issues in ethical terms because the scripts did not include ethical dimensions.

In the summer of 1972 I made one of those important transitions in life, the significance of which becomes obvious only in retrospect. I left academe with a BS in Engineering Science and an MBA to enter

---

* Reprinted, with editorial changes, by permission of Kluwer Academic Publishers from the *Journal of Business Ethics* 11 (1992) pp. 379–389.

the world of big business. I joined Ford Motor Company at World Headquarters in Dearborn, Michigan, fulfilling a long-standing dream to work in the heart of the auto industry. I felt confident that I was in the right place at the right time to make a difference. My initial job title was "Problem Analyst"—a catchall label that superficially described what I would be thinking about and doing in the coming years. On some deeper level, however, the title paradoxically came to connote the many critical things that I would *not* be thinking about and acting upon.

By that summer of 1972 I was very full of myself. I had met my life's goals to that point with some notable success. I had virtually everything I wanted, including a strongly-held value system that has led me to question many of the perspectives and practices I observed in the world around me. Not the least of these was a profound distaste for the Vietnam war, a distaste that had found me participating in various demonstrations against its conduct and speaking as a part of a collective voice on the moral and ethical failure of a democratic government that would attempt to justify it. I also found myself in MBA classes railing against the conduct of businesses of the era, whose actions struck me as ranging from inconsiderate to indifferent to simply unethical. To me the typical stance of business seemed to be one of disdain for, rather than responsibility toward, the society of which they were prominent members. I wanted something to change. Accordingly, I cultivated my social awareness; I held my principles high; I espoused my intention to help a troubled world; and I wore my hair long. By any measure I was a prototypical "Child of the '60s."

Therefore, it struck quite a few of my friends in the MBA program as rather strange that I was in the program at all. ("If you are so disappointed in business, why study business?"). Subsequently, they were practically dumbstruck when I accepted the job offer from Ford, apparently one of the great purveyors of the very actions I reviled. I countered that it was an ideal strategy, arguing that I would have a greater chance of influencing social change in business if I worked behind the scenes on the inside, rather than as a strident voice on the outside. It was clear to me that somebody needed to prod these staid companies into socially responsible action. I certainly aimed to do my part. Besides, I liked cars.

INTO THE FRAY: SETTING THE PERSONAL STAGE

Predictably enough, I found myself on the fast track at Ford, participating in a "tournament" type of socialization (Van Maanen,

1978), engaged in a competition for recognition with other MBA's who had recently joined the company. And I quickly became caught up in the game. The company itself was dynamic; the environment of business, especially the auto industry, was intriguing; the job was challenging and the pay was great. The psychic rewards of working and succeeding in a major corporation proved unexpectedly seductive. I really became involved in the job.

Market forces (international competition) and government regulation (vehicle safety and emissions) were affecting the auto industry in disruptive ways that only later would be common to the wider business and social arena. They also produced an industry and a company that felt buffeted, beleaguered, and threatened by the changes. The threats were mostly external, of course, and led to a strong feeling of we-vs-them, where we (Ford members) needed to defend ourselves against them (all the outside parties and voices demanding that we change our ways). Even at this time, an intriguing question for me was whether I was a "we" or a "them." It was becoming apparent to me that my perspective was changing. I had long since cut my hair.

By the summer of 1973 I was pitched into the thick of the battle. I became Ford's Field Recall Coordinator—not a position that was particularly high in the hierarchy, but one that wielded influence far beyond its level. I was in charge of the operational coordination of all of the recall campaigns currently underway and also in charge of tracking incoming information to identify developing problems. Therefore, I was in a position to make initial recommendations about possible future recalls. The most critical type of recalls were labeled "safety campaigns"—those that dealt with the possibility of customer injury or death. These ranged from straight-forward occurrences such as brake failure and wheels falling off vehicles, to more exotic and faintly humorous modes such as detaching axles that announced their presence by spinning forward and slamming into the startled driver's door and speed control units that locked on, and refused to disengage, as the car accelerated wildly while the spooked driver futilely tried to shut it off. Safety recall campaigns, however, also encompassed the more sobering possibility of on-board gasoline fires and explosions.

THE PINTO CASE: SETTING THE CORPORATE STAGE

In 1970 Ford introduced the Pinto, a small car that was intended to compete with the then current challenge from European cars and the ominous presence on the horizon of Japanese manufacturers. The Pinto was brought from inception to production in the record time of approximately 25 months (compared to the industry average of 43 months), a time frame that suggested the necessity for doing things expediently. In addition to the time pressure, the engineering and development teams were required to adhere to the production "limits of 2000" for the diminutive car: it was not to exceed either $2000 in cost or 2000 pounds in weight. Any decisions that threatened these targets or the timing of the car's introduction were discouraged. Under normal conditions design, styling, product planning, engineering, etc., were completed prior to production tooling. Because of the fore-shortened time frame, however, some of these usually sequential processes were executed in parallel.

As a consequence, tooling was already well under way (thus "freezing" the basic design) when routine crash testing revealed that the Pinto's fuel tank often ruptured when struck from the rear at a relatively low speed (31 mph in crash tests). Reports (revealed much later) showed that the fuel tank failures were the result of some rather marginal design features. The tank was positioned between the rear bumper and the rear axle (a standard industry practice for the time). During impact, however, several studs protruding from the rear of the axle housing would puncture holes in the tank; the fuel filler neck also was likely to rip away. Spilled gasoline then could be ignited by sparks. Ford had in fact crash-tested 11 vehicles; 8 of these cars suffered potentially catastrophic gas tank ruptures. The only 3 cars that survived intact had each been modified in some way to protect the tank.

These crash tests, however, were conducted under the guidelines of Federal Motor Vehicle Safety Standard 301 which had been proposed in 1968 and strenuously opposed by the auto industry. FMVSS 301 was not actually adopted until 1976; thus, at the time of the tests, Ford was not in violation of the law. There were several possibilities for fixing the problem, including the option of redesigning the tank integrity in a high-speed crash. That solution, however, was not only time consuming and expensive, but also usurped trunk space, which was seen as a critical competitive sales factor. One of the production modifications to the tank, however, would have cost only $11 to install, but given the tight margins and restrictions of the "limits of 2000," there was reluctance to make even this relatively minor change. There were other reasons for not approving the change, as well, including a widespread industry belief that all small cars were inherently unsafe solely because of their size and weight. Another more prominent reason was a corporate belief that "safety doesn't sell." This observation was attributed to Lee Iacocca and stemmed from Ford's earlier attempt to make safety a sales theme, an attempt that failed rather dismally in the marketplace.

Perhaps the most controversial reason for rejecting the production change to the gas tank, however, was Ford's use of cost-benefit analysis to justify the decision. The National Highway Traffic Safety Association (NHTSA, a federal agency) had approved the use of cost-benefit analysis as a appropriate means for establishing automotive safety design standards. The controversial aspect in making such calculations was that they required the assignment of some specific value for a human life. In 1970, that value was deemed to be approximately $200,000 as a "cost to society" for each fatality. Ford used NHTSA's figures in estimating the costs and benefits of altering the tank production design. An internal memo, later revealed in court, indicates the following tabulations concerning potential fires (Dowie, 1977):

Costs: $137,000,000
(Estimated as the costs of a production fix to all similarly designed cars and trucks with the gas tank aft of the axle (12,500,000 vehicles × $11/vehicle))

Benefits: $49,530,000
(Estimated as the savings from preventing (180 projected deaths × $200,000/death) +(180 projected burn injuries × $67,000/injury) + (2100 burned cars × $700/car))

The cost-benefit decision was then construed as straightforward: No production fix would be undertaken. The philosophical and ethical implications of assigning a financial value for human life or disfigurement do not seem to have been a major consideration in reaching this decision.

PINTOS AND PERSONAL EXPERIENCE

When I took over the Recall Coordinator's job in 1973 I inherited the oversight of about 100 active recall campaigns, more than half of which were safety-related. These ranged from minimal in size (replacing front wheels that were likely to break on 12 heavy trucks) to maximal (repairing the power steering pump on millions of cars). In addition, there were quite a number of safety problems that were under consideration as candidates for addition to the recall list. (Actually, "problem" was a word whose public use was forbidden by the legal office at the time, even in service bulletins, because it suggested corporate admission of culpability. "Condition" was the sanctioned catchword.) In addition to these potential recall candidates, there were many files containing field reports of alleged component failure (another forbidden word) that had led to accidents, and in some cases, passenger injury. Beyond these existing files, I began to construct my own files of incoming safety problems.

One of these new files concerned reports of Pintos "lighting up" (in the words of a field representative) in rear-end accidents. There were actually very few reports, perhaps because component failure was not initially assumed. These cars simply were consumed by fire after apparently very low speed accidents. Was there a problem? Not as far as I was concerned. My cue for labeling a case as a problem either required high frequencies of occurrence or directly traceable causes. I had little time for speculative contemplation on potential problems that did not fit a pattern that suggested known courses of action leading to possible recall. I do, however, remember being disquieted by a field report accompanied by graphic, detailed photos of the remains of a burned-out Pinto in which several people had died. Although that report became part of my file, I did not flag it as any special case.

It is difficult to convey the overwhelming complexity and pace of the job of keeping track of so many active or potential recall campaigns. It remains the busiest, most information-filled job I have ever held or would want to hold. Each case required a myriad of information-gathering and execution stages. I distinctly remember that the information-processing demands led me to confuse the facts of one problem case with another on several occasions because the tell-tale signs of recall candidate cases were so similar. I thought of myself as a fireman—a fireman who perfectly fit the description by one of my colleagues: "In this office everything is a crisis. You only have time to put out the big fires and spit on the little ones." By those standards the Pinto problem was distinctly a little one.

It is also important to convey the muting of emotion involved in the Recall Coordinator's job. I remember contemplating the fact that my job literally involved life-and-death matters. I was sometimes responsible for finding and fixing cars NOW, because somebody's life might depend on it. I took it *very* seriously. Early in the job, I sometimes woke up at night wondering whether I had covered all the bases. Had I left some unknown person at risk because I had not thought of something? That soon faded, however, and of necessity the consideration of people's lives became a fairly removed, dispassionate process. To do the job "well" there was little room for emotion. Allowing it to surface was potentially paralyzing and prevented rational decisions about which cases to recommend for recall. On moral grounds I knew I could recommend most of the vehicles on my safety tracking list for recall (and risk earning the label of a "bleeding heart"). On practical grounds, I recognized that people implicitly accept risks in cars. We could not recall all cars with *potential* problems and stay in business. I learned to be responsive to those cases that suggested an imminent, dangerous problem.

I should also note, that the country was in the midst of its first, and worst, oil crisis at this time. The effects of the crisis had cast a pall over Ford and the rest of the automobile industry. Ford's product line, with the perhaps notable exception of the Pinto and Maverick small cars, was not well-suited to dealing with the crisis. Layoffs were imminent for many people. Recalling the Pinto in this context would have damaged one of the few trump cards the company had (although, quite frankly, I do not remember overtly thinking about that issue).

Pinto reports continued to trickle in, but at such a slow rate that they really did not capture particular attention relative to other, more pressing safety problems. However, I later saw a crumpled, burned car at a Ford depot where alleged problem components and vehicles were delivered for inspection and analysis (a place known as the "Chamber of Horrors" by some of the people who worked there). The revulsion on seeing this incinerated hulk was immediate and pro-found. Soon afterwards, and despite the fact that the file was very sparse, I recommended the Pinto case for preliminary department-level review concerning possible recall. After the usual round of discussion about criteria and justification for recall, everyone voted against recommending recall—including me. It did not fit the pattern of recallable standards; the evidence was not overwhelming that the car was defective in some way, so the case was actually fairly straight-forward. It was a good business decision, even if people might be dying. (We did not then know about the preproduction crash test data that suggested a high rate of tank failures in "normal" accidents (cf., Perrow, 1984) or an abnormal failure mode.)

Later, the existence of the crash test data did become known within Ford, which suggested that the Pinto might actually have a recallable problem. This information led to a reconsideration of the case within our office. The data, however, prompted a comparison of the Pinto's survivability in a rear end accident with that of other competitor's small cars. These comparisons revealed that although many cars in this subcompact class suffered appalling deformation in relatively low speed collisions, the Pinto was merely the worst of a bad lot. Furthermore, the gap between the Pinto and the competition was not dramatic in terms of the speed at which fuel tank rupture was likely to occur. On that basis it would be difficult to justify the recall of cars that were comparable with others on the market. In the face of even more compelling evidence that people were probably going to die in this car, I again included myself in a group of decision makers who voted not to recommend recall to the higher levels of the organization.

CODA TO THE CORPORATE CASE

Subsequent to my departure from Ford in 1975, reports of Pinto fires escalated, attracting increasing media attention, almost all of it critical of Ford. Anderson and Whitten (1976) revealed the internal memos concerning the gas tank problem and questioned how the few dollars saved per car could be justified when human lives were at stake. Shortly thereafter, a scathing article by Dowie (1977) attacked not only the Pinto's design, but also accused Ford of gross negligence, stonewalling, and unethical corporate conduct by alleging that Ford knowingly sold "firetraps" after willfully calculating the cost of lives against profits (see also Gatewood and Carroll, 1983). Dowie's provocative quote speculating on "how long the Ford Motor Company would continue to market lethal cars were Henry Ford II and Lee Iacocca serving 20 year terms in Leavenworth for consumer homicide" (1977, p. 32) was particularly effective in focusing attention on the case. Public sentiment edged toward labeling Ford as socially deviant because management was seen as knowing that the car was defective, choosing profit over lives, resisting demands to fix the car, and apparently showing no public remorse (Swigert and Farrell, 1980–81). Shortly after Dowie's (1977) exposé, NHTSA initiated its own investigation. Then, early in 1978 a jury awarded a Pinto burn victim $125 million in punitive damages (later reduced to $6.6 million, a judgment upheld on an appeal that prompted the judge to assert that "Ford's institutional mentality was shown to be one of callous indifference to public safety" (quoted in Cullen *et. al.*, 1987, p. 164)). A siege atmosphere emerged at Ford. Insiders characterized the mounting media campaign as "hysterical" and "a crusade against us" (personal communications). The crisis deepened. In the summer of 1978 NHTSA issued a formal determination that the Pinto was defective. Ford then launched a reluctant recall of all 1971–1976 cars (those built for the 1977 model year were equipped with a production fix prompted by the adoption of the FMVSS 301 gas tank standard). Ford hoped that the issue would then recede, but worse was yet to come.

The culmination of the case and the demise of the Pinto itself began in Indiana on August 10, 1978, when three teenage girls died in a fire triggered after their 1973 Pinto was hit from behind by a van. A grand jury took the unheard of step of indicting Ford on charges of reckless homicide (Cullen *et al.*, 1987). Because of the precedent-setting possibilities for all manufacturing industries, Ford assembled a formidable legal team headed by Watergate prosecutor James Neal to defend itself at the trial. The trial was a media event; it was the first time that a corporation was tried for alleged *criminal* behavior. After a protracted, acrimonious courtroom battle that included vivid clashes among the opposing attorneys, surprise witnesses, etc., the jury ultimately found in favor of Ford. Ford had dodged a bullet in the form of a consequential legal precedent, but because of the negative publicity of the case and the charges of corporate crime and ethical deviance, the conduct of manufacturing businesses was altered, probably forever. As a relatively minor footnote to the case, Ford ceased production of the Pinto.

CODA TO THE PERSONAL CASE

In the intervening years since my early involvement with the Pinto fire case, I have given repeated consideration to my role in it. Although most of the ethically questionable actions that have been cited in the press are associated with Ford's intentional stonewalling after it was clear that the Pinto was defective (see Cullen *et al.*, 1986; Dowie, 1977; Gatewood and Carroll, 1983)—and thus postdate my involvement with the case and the company—I still nonetheless wonder about my own culpability. Why didn't I see the gravity of the problem and its ethical overtones? What happened to the value system I carried with me into Ford? Should I have acted differently, given what I knew then? The experience with myself has sometimes not been pleasant. Somehow, it seems I should have done *something* different that might have made a difference.

As a consequence of this line of thinking and feeling, some years ago I decided to construct a "living case" out of my experience with the Pinto fire problem for use in my MBA classes. The written case description contains many of the facts detailed above; the analytical task of the class is to ask appropriate questions of me as a figure in the case to reveal the central issues involved. It is somewhat of a trying experience to get through these classes. After getting to know me for most of the semester, and then finding out that I did *not* vote to recommend recall, students are often incredulous, even angry at me for apparently not having lived what I have been teaching. To be fair and even-handed here, many students understand my actions in the context of the times and the attitudes prevalent then. Others, however, are very disappointed that I appear to have failed during a time of trial. Consequently, I am accused of being a charlatan and otherwise vilified by those who maintain that ethical and moral principles should have prevailed in this case no matter what the mitigating circumstances. Those are the ones that hurt.

Those are also the ones, however, that keep the case and its lessons alive in my mind and cause me to have an on-going dialogue with myself about it. It is fascinating to me that for several years after I first conducted the living case with myself as the focus, I remained convinced that I had made the "right" decision in not recommending recall of the cars. In light of the times and the evidence available, I thought I had pursued a reasonable course of action. More recently, however, I have come to think that I really should have done everything I could to get those cars off the road.

In retrospect I know that in the context of the times my actions were *legal* (they were all well within the framework of the law); they probably also were *ethical* according to most prevailing definitions (they were in accord with accepted professional standards and codes of conduct); the major concern for me is whether they were *moral* (in the sense of adhering to some higher standards of inner conscience and conviction about the "right" actions to take). This simple typology implies that I had passed at least two hurdles on a personal continuum that ranged from more rigorous, but arguably less significant criteria, to less rigorous, but more personally, organizationally, and perhaps societally significant standards:

X	X	?
Legal	Ethical	Moral

It is that last criterion that remains troublesome.

Perhaps these reflections are all just personal revisionist history. After all, I am still stuck in my cognitive structures, as everyone is. I do not think these concerns are all retrospective reconstruction, however. Another telling piece of information is this: The entire time I was dealing with the Pinto fire problem, I owned a Pinto (!). I even sold it to my sister. What does that say?

WHAT HAPPENED HERE?

I, of course, have some thoughts about my experience with this damningly visible case. At the risk of breaking some of the accepted rules of scholarly analysis, rather than engaging in the usual comprehensive, dense, arms-length critique, I would instead like to offer a rather selective and subjective focus on certain characteristics of human information processing relevant to this kind of situation, of which I was my own unwitting victim. I make no claim that my analysis necessarily "explains more variance" than other possible explanations. I do not think that this selective view is enlightening in that it offers an alternative explanation for some ethically questionable actions in business.

The subjective stance adopted in the analysis is intentional also. This case obviously stems from a series of personal experiences, accounts, and introspections. The analytical style is intended to be consistent with the self-based case example; therefore, it appears to be less "formal" than the typical objectivist mode of explanation. I suspect that my chosen focus will be fairly non-obvious to the reader familiar with the ethical literature (as it typically is to the ethical actor). Although this analysis might be judged as somewhat self-serving, I nonetheless believe that it provides an informative explanation for some of the ethical foibles we see enacted around us.

To me, there are two major issues to address. First, how could my value system apparently have flip-flopped in the relatively short space of 1–2 years? Secondly, how could I have failed to take action on a retrospectively obvious safety problem when I was in the perfect position to do so? To begin, I would like to consider several possible explanations for my thoughts and actions (or lack thereof) during the early stages of the Pinto fire case.

One explanation is that I was simply revealed as a phony when the chips were down; that my previous values were not strongly inculcated; that I was all bluster, not particularly ethical, and as a result acted expediently when confronted with a reality test of those values. In other words, I turned traitor to my own expressed values. Another explanation is that I was simply intimidated; in the face of strong pressure to heel to company preferences, I folded—put ethical concerns aside, or at least traded them for a monumental guilt trip and did what everybody would do to keep a good job. A third explanation is that I was following a strictly utilitarian set of decision criteria (Valasquez *et al.*, 1983) and, predictably enough, opted for a personal form of Ford's own cost-benefit analysis, with similar disappointing results. Another explanation might suggest that the interaction of my stage or moral development (Kohlberg, 1969) and the culture and decision environment at Ford led me to think about and act upon an ethical dilemma in a fashion that reflected a lower level of actual moral development than I espoused for myself (Trevino, 1986 and this issue). Yet another explanation is that I was co-opted; rather than working from the inside to change a lumbering system as I had intended, the tables were turned and the system beat me at my own game. More charitably, perhaps, it is possible that I simply was a good person making bad ethical choices because of the corporate milieu (Gellerman, 1986).

I doubt that this list is exhaustive. I am quite sure that cynics could match my own MBA students' labels, which in the worst case include phrases like "moral failure" and "doubly reprehensible because you were in a position to make a difference." I believe, however, on the basis of a number of years of work on social cognition in organizations that a viable explanation is one that is not quite so melodramatic. It is an explanation that rests on a recognition that even the best-intentioned organization members organize information into cognitive structures or schemas that serve as (fallible) mental templates for handling incoming information and as guides for acting upon it. Of the many schemas that have been hypothesized to exist, the one that is most relevant to my experience at Ford is the notion of a script (Abelson, 1976, 1981).

My central thesis is this: *My own schematized (scripted) knowledge influenced me to perceive recall issues in terms of the prevailing decision environment and to unconsciously overlook key features of the Pinto case, mainly because they did not fit an existing script. Although the outcomes of the case carry retrospectively obvious ethical overtones, the schemas driving my perceptions and actions precluded consideration of the issues in ethical terms because the scripts did not include ethical dimensions.*

SCRIPT SCHEMAS

A *schema* is a cognitive framework that people use to impose structure upon information, situations, and expectations to facilitate understanding (Gioia and Poole, 1984; Taylor and Crocker, 1981). Schemas derive from consideration of prior experience or vicarious learning that results in the formation of "organized" knowledge—knowledge that, once formed, precludes the necessity for further active cognition. As a consequence, such structured knowledge allows virtually effortless interpretation of information and events (cf., Canter and Mischel, 1979), a *script* is a specialized type of schema that retains knowledge of actions appropriate for specific situations and contexts (abelson, 1976, 1981). One of the most important characteristics of scripts is that they simultaneously provide a cognitive framework for *understanding* information and events as well as a guide to appropriate *behavior* to deal with the situation faced. They thus serve as linkages between cognition and action (Gioia and Manz, 1985).

The structuring of knowledge in scripted form is a fundamental human information processing tendency that in many ways results in a relatively closed cognitive system that influences both perception and action. Scripts, like all schemas, operate on the basis of prototypes, which are abstract representations that contain the main features or characteristics of a given knowledge category (e.g., "safety problems"). Protoscripts (Gioia and Poole, 1984) serve as templates against which incoming information can be assessed. A pattern in current information that generally matches the template associated with a given script signals that active thought and analysis is not required. Under these conditions the entire existing script can be called forth and enacted automatically and unconsciously, usually without adjustment for subtle differences in information patterns that might be important.

Given the complexity of the organizational world, it is obvious that the schematizing or scripting of knowledge implies a great information processing advantage—a decision maker need not actively think about each new presentation of information, situations, or problems; the mode of handling such problems has already been worked out in advance and remanded to a working stock of knowledge held in individual (or organizational) memory. Scripted knowledge saves a significant amount of mental work, a savings that in fact prevents the cognitive paralysis that would inevitably come from trying to treat each specific instance of a class of problems as a unique case that requires contemplation. Scripted decision making is thus efficient decision making but not necessarily good decision making (Gioia and Poole, 1984).

Of course, every advantage comes with its own set of built-in disadvantages. There is a price to pay for scripted knowledge. On the one hand, existing scripts lead people to selectively perceive information that is consistent with a script and thus to ignore anomalous information. Conversely, if there is missing information, the gaps in knowledge are filled with expected features supplied by the script (Bower *et al.*, 1979; Graesser *et al.*, 1980). In some cases, a pattern that matches an existing script, except for some key differences, can be "tagged" as a distinctive case (Graaesser *et al.*, 1979) and thus be made more memorable. In the worst case scenario, however, a situation that does not fit the characteristics of the scripted perspective for handling problem cases often is simply not noticed. Scripts thus offer a viable explanation for why experienced decision makers (perhaps *especially* experienced decision makers) tend to overlook what others would construe as obvious factors in making a decision.

Given the relatively rare occurrence of truly novel information, the nature of script processing implies that it is a default mode of organizational cognition. That is, instead of spending the predominance of their mental energy thinking in some active fashion, decision makers might better be characterized as typically *not* thinking, i.e., dealing with information in a mode that is akin to "cruising on automatic pilot" (cf., Gioia, 1986). The scripted view casts decision makers as needing some sort of prod in the form of novel or unexpected information to kick them into a thinking mode—a prod that often does not come because of the wealth of similar data that they must process. Therefore, instead of focusing what people pay attention to, it might be more enlightening to focus on what they do *not* pay attention to.

PINTO PROBLEM PERCEPTION AND SCRIPTS

It is illustrative to consider my situation in handling the early stages of the Pinto fires case in light of script theory. When I was dealing with the first trickling-in of field reports that might have suggested a significant problem with the Pinto, the reports were essentially similar to many others that I was dealing with (and dismissing) all the time. The sort of information they contained, which did not convey enough prototypical features to capture my attention, never got past my screening script. I had seen this type of information pattern before (hundreds of times!); I was making this kind of decision automatically every day. I had trained myself to respond to proto-typical cues, and these didn't fit the relevant prototype for crisis cases. (Yes, the Pinto reports fit a prototype—but it was a prototype for "normal accidents" that did not deviate significantly from expected problems). The frequency of the reports relative to other, more serious problems (i.e., those that displayed more characteristic features of safety problems) also did not pass my scripted criteria for singling out the Pinto case. Consequently, I looked right past them.

Overlooking uncharacteristic cues also was exacerbated by the nature of the job. The overwhelming information overload that charac-terized the role as well as its hectic pace actually forced a greater reliance on scripted responses. It was impossible to handle the job requirements *without* relying on some sort of automatic way of assessing whether a case deserved active attention. There was so much to do and so much information to attend to that the only way to deal with it was by means of schematic processing. In fact, the one anomaly in the case that might have cued me to gravity of the problem (the field report accompanied by graphic photographs) still did not distinguish the problem as one that was distinctive enough to snap me out of my standard response mode and tag it as a failure that deserved closer monitoring.

Even the presence of an emotional component that might have short-circuited standard script processing instead became part of the script itself. Months of squelching the disturbing emotions associated with serious safety problems soon made muffled emotions a standard (and not very salient) component of the script for handling *any* safety problem. This observation, that emotion was muted by experience, and therefore de-emphasized in the script, differs from Fiske's (1982) widely accepted position that emotion is tied to the top of a schema (i.e., is the most salient and initially-tapped aspect of schematic processing). On the basis of my experience, I would argue that for organization members trained to control emotions to perform the job role (cf., Pitre, 1990), emotion is either not a part of the internalized script, or at best becomes a difficult-to-access part of any script for job performance.

The one instance of emotion penetrating the operating script was the revulsion that swept over me at the sight of the burned vehicle at the return depot. That event was so strong that it prompted me to put the case up for preliminary consideration (in theoretical terms, it prompted me cognitively to "tag" the Pinto case as a potentially distinctive one). I soon "came to my senses," however, when rational consideration of the problem characteristics suggested that they did not meet the scripted criteria that were consensually shared among members of the Field Recall Office. At the preliminary review other members of the decision team, enacting their own scripts in the absence of my emotional experience, wondered why I had even brought the case up. To me this meeting demonstated that even when controlled analytic information processing occurred, it was nonetheless based on prior schematization of information. In other words, even when information processing was not automatically executed, it still depended upon schemas (cf., Gioia, 1986). As a result of the social construction of the situation, I ended up agreeing with my colleagues and voting not to recall.

The remaining major issue to be dealt with, of course, concerns the apparent shift in my values. In a period of less than two years I appeared to change my stripes and adopt the cultural values of the organization. How did that apparent shift occur? Again, scripts are relevant. I would argue that my pre-Ford values for changing corporate America were bona fide. I had internalized values for doing what was right as I then understood "rightness" in grand terms. The key is, however, that I had not internalized a *script* for enacting those values in any specific context outside my limited experience. The insider's view at Ford, of course, provided me with a specific and immediate context for developing such a script. Scripts are formed from salient experience and there was no more salient experience in my relatively young life than joining a major corporation and moving quickly into a position of clear and present responsibility. The strongest possible parameters for script formation were all there, not only because of the job role specifications, but also from the corporate culture. Organizational culture, in one very powerful sense, amounts to a collection of scripts writ large. Did I sell out? No. Were my cognitive structures altered by salient experience? Without question. Scripts for understanding and action were formed and reformed in a relatively short time in a way that not only altered perceptions of issues but also the likely actions associated with those altered perceptions.

I might characterize the differing cognitive structures as "outsider" versus "insider" scripts. I view them also as "idealist" versus "realist" scripts. I might further note that the outsider/idealist script was one that was more individually-based than the insider/realist script, which was more collective and subject to the influence of the corporate milieu and culture. Personal identity as captured in the revised script became much more corporate than individual. Given that scripts are socially constructed and reconstructed cognitive structures, it is understandable that their content and process would be much more responsive to the corporate culture, because of its saliency and immediacy.

The recall coordinator's job was serious business. The scripts associated with it influenced me much more than I influenced it. Before I went to Ford I would have argued strongly that Ford had an ethical obligation to recall. After I left Ford I now argue and teach that Ford had an ethical obligation to recall. But, *while I was there*, I perceived no strong obligation to recall and I remember no strong *ethical* overtones to the case whatsoever. It was a very straightforward decision, driven by dominant scripts for the time, place, and context.

WHITHER ETHICS AND SCRIPTS?

Most models of ethical decision making in organizations implicitly assume that people recognize and think about a moral or ethical dilemma when they are confronted with one (cf., Kohlberg, 1969 and Trevino's review in this issue). I call this seemingly fundamental assumption into question. The unexplored ethical issue for me is the arguably prevalent case where organizational representatives are not aware that they are dealing with a problem that might have ethical overtones. If the case involves a familiar class of problems or issues, it is likely to be handled via existing cognitive structures or scripts—*scripts that typically include no ethical component in their cognitive content.*

Although we might hope that people in charge of important decisions like vehicle safety recalls might engage in active, logical analysis and consider the subtleties in the many different situations they face, the context of the decisions and their necessary reliance on schematic processing tends to preclude such consideration (cf., Gioia, 1989). Accounting for the subtleties of ethical consideration in work situations that are typically handled by schema-based processing is very difficult indeed. Scripts are built out of situations that are normal, not those that are abnormal, ill-structured, or unusual (which often can characterizse ethical domains). The ambiguities associated with most ethical dilemmas imply that such situations demand a "custom" decision, which means that the inclusion of an ethical dimension as a component of an evolving script is not easy to accomplish.

How might ethical considerations be internalized as part of the script for understanding and action? It is easier to say what will *not* be likely to work than what will. Clearly, mere mention of ethics in policy or training manuals will not do the job. Even exhortations to be concerned with ethics in decision making are seldom likely to migrate into the script. Just as clearly, codes of ethics typically will not work. They are too often cast at a level of generality that can not be associated with any specific script. Furthermore, for all practical purposes, codes of ethics often are stated in a way that makes them "context-free," which makes them virtually impossible to associate with active scripts, which always are context-bound.

Tactics for script *development* that have more potential involve learning or training that concentrates on exposure to information or models that explicitly display a focus on ethical considerations. This implies that ethics be included in job descriptions, management development training, mentoring, etc. Tactics for script *revision* involve learning or training that concentrate on "script-breaking" examples. Organization members must be exposed either to vicarious or personal experiences that interrupt tacit knowledge of "appropriate" action so that script revision can be initiated. Training scenarios, and especially role playing, that portray expected sequences that are then interrupted to call explicit attention to ethical issues can be tagged by the perceiver as requiring attention. This tactic amounts to installing a decision node in the revised scripts that tells the action "Now think" (Abelson, 1981). Only by means of similar script-breaking strategies can existing cognitive structures be modified to accommodate the necessary cycles of automatic and controlled processing (cf., Louis and Sutton, 1991).

The upshot of the scripted view of organizational understanding and behavior is both an encouragement and an indictment of people facing situations laced with ethical overtones. It is encouraging because it suggests that organizational decision makers are not necessarily lacking in ethical standards; they are simply fallible information processors who fail to notice the ethical implications of a usual way of handling issues. It is an indictment because ethical dimensions are not usually a central feature of the cognitive structures that drive decision making. Obviously, they should be, but it will take substantial concentration on the ethical dimension of the corporate culture, as well as overt attempts to emphasize ethics in education, training, and decision making before typical organizational scripts are likely to be modified to include the crucial ethical component.

REFERENCES

Abelson, R.P. 1976, "Script Processing in Attitude Formation and Decision-making," in J. S. Carroll and J. W. Payne (eds.), *Cognitive and Social Behavior* (Earlbaum, Hillsdale, NJ), pp. 33–45

Abelson, R. P. 1981, "Psychological Status of the Script Concept," *American Psychologist* 36, pp. 715–729.

Anderson, J. and Whitten, L. 1976, "Auto Maker Shuns Safer Gas Tank," *Washington Post* (December 30), p. B–7.

Bower, G. H., Black, J. B. and Turner, T. J. 1979, "Scripts in Memory for Text," *Cognitive Psychology* 11, pp. 177–220.

Cantor, N. and Mischel, W. 1979, "Prototypes in Person Perception," in L. Berkowitz (ed.), *Advances in Experimental Social Psychology* 12 (Academic Press, New York), pp. 3–51.

Cullen, F. T., Maakestad, W. J. and Cavender, G. 1987, *Corporate Crime Under Attack* (Anderson Publishing Co., Chicago).

Dowie, M. 1977, "How Ford Put Two Million Firetraps on Wheels," *Business and Society Review* 23, pp. 46–55.

Fiske, S. T. 1982, "Schema-Triggered Affect: Applications to Social Perception," in M. S. Clark and S. T. Fiske (eds.), *Affect and Cognition* (Earlbaum, Hillsdale, NJ), pp. 55–78.

Gatewood, E. and Carroll, A. B. 1983, "The Anatomy of Corporate Social Response: The Rely, Firestone 500, and Pinto Cases," *Business Horizons*, pp. 9–16.

Gellerman, S. 1986, "Why 'Good' Managers Make Bad Ethical Choices," *Harvard Business Review* (July–August), pp. 85–90.

Gioia, D. A. 1989, "Self-Serving Bias as a Self-Sensemaking Strategy," in P. Rosenfeld and R. Giacalone (eds.), *Impression Management in the Organization* (LEA, Hillsdale, NJ), pp. 219–234.

Gioia, D. A. 1986, "Symbols, Scripts, and Sensemaking: Creating Meaning in the Organizational Experience," in H. P. Sims, Jr. and D. A. Gioia (eds.), *The Thinking Organization: Dynamics of Organizational Social Cognition* (Jossey-Bass, San Francisco), pp. 49–74.

Gioia, D. A. and Manz, C. C. 1985, "Linking Cognition and Behavior: A Script Processing Interpretatin of Vicarious Learning," *Academy of Management Review* 10, pp. 527–539.

Gioia, D. A. and Poole, P. P. 1984, "Scripts in Organizational Behavior," *Academy of Management Review* 9, pp. 449–459.

Graesser, A. C., Gordon, S. G. and Sawyer, J. D. 1979, "Recognition Memory for Typical and Atypical Actions in Scripted Activities: Test of Script Pointer and Tag Hypothesis," *Journal of Verbal Learning and Verbal Behavior* 18, pp. 319–332.

Graesser, A. C., Woll, S. B., Kowalski, D. J. and Smith, D. A. 1980, "Memory for Typical and Atypical Actions in Scripted Activities," *Journal of Experimental psychology* 6, pp. 503–515.

Kohlberg, L. 1969, "Stage and Sequence: The Cognitive-Development Approach to Socialization," in D. A. Goslin (ed.), *Handbook of Socialization Theory and Research* (Rand-McNally, Chicago), pp. 347–480.

Louis, M. R. and Sutton, R. I. 1991, "Switching Cognitive Gears: From Habits of Mind to Active Thinking," *Human Relations* 44, pp. 55–76.

Perrow, C. 1984, *Normal Accidents* (Basic Books, New York).

Pitre, E. 1990, "Emotional Control," working paper, the Pennsylvania State University.

Swigert, V. L. and Farrell, R. A. 1980–81, "Corporate Homicide: Definitional Processes in the Creation of Deviance," *Law and Society Review* 15, pp. 170–183.

Taylor, S. E. and Crocker, J. 1981, "Schematic Bases of Social Information Processing," in E. T. Higgins, C. P. Herman, and M. P. Zanna (eds.), *Social Cognition*1 (Earlbaum, Hillsdale, NJ), pp. 89–134.

Trevino, L. 1986, "Ethical Decision Making in Organizations: A Person-Situation Interactionist Model," *Academy of Management Review* 11, pp. 601–617.

Trevino, L. 1992, "Moral Reasoning and Business Ethics: Implications for Research, Education and Management," *Journal of Business Ethics* 11, 445–459.

Valasquez, M., Moberg, D. J. and Cavanaugh, G. F. 1983, "Organizational Statesmanship and Dirty Politics: Ethical Guidelines for the Organizational Politician," *Organizational Dynamics* (Autumn), pp. 65–80.

Van Maanen, J. 1978, "People Processing: Strategies of Organizational Socialization," *Organizational Dynamics* (Summer), pp. 19–36.

Part II

COST-BENEFIT ANALYSIS

Introduction: Cost-Benefit Analysis

As we saw in Part I, the Ford engineers who worked on the Pinto were aware of the design problems with the fuel system. The design cost (the price of materials and labor) for the alterations being considered, either the body side rails, the fuel tank "flak vest," the plastic shields, or the fuel tank bladder, and the flexible filler pipe, would have been low, but no changes were made to upgrade the safety of the car. Why did Ford management decide not to upgrade the safety of the car prior to 1978? The charge made by Mark Dowie, and later by the *Chicago Tribune*, was that Ford did not fix the car because they used a management decision-making technique called cost-benefit analysis.

A cost-benefit analysis may be described as an attempt to identify and analyze a set of costs and benefits in order to present decision makers with an economic justification for making a certain choice. "Costs" represent expenditures of money for businesses and organizations, although often these costs are only probable. "Benefits" refers to monetary gains or to the avoidance of expenditures and, once again, are often only probable. The basic idea is that a manager can identify the alternatives, distinguish the costs and benefits associated with each, translate the costs and benefits into monetary units, calculate the sums and differences, and justify the alternative which provides the largest net monetary benefit. In the Pinto case, the alternatives were either upgrading or not upgrading the integrity of the fuel system. All the costs and benefits associated with each alternative need to be identified and translated into monetary units; for example, upgrading the fuel system for a particular model year would have been a cost to Ford of approximately $2,880,000. In a strict cost-benefit analysis, if a factor cannot be translated into money, it is disregarded. The managers would have added up the net loss or gain for each alternative and would have picked the one that provided the largest net gain for the company.

The articles in Part II explore the ethics of cost-benefit analysis in general, and the supposed use of it in the Pinto case. Steven Kelman's article "Cost-Benefit Analysis: An Ethical Critique" is the first essay in this part of the book. Kelman argues that there are serious ethical problems with cost-benefit analysis; for example, that there are cases where a decision might be right even though the monetary benefits do not outweigh the monetary costs. The pieces that follow Kelman's article (by James V. DeLong, Robert M. Solow, Gerard Butters, John Calfee and Pauline Ippolito and, Robert A. Nisbet) are replies to Kelman that defend the use of cost-benefit analysis. Taken together, Kelman's article and the replies to it provide some insight into the debate over the ethics of cost-benefit analysis.

Focusing on the Pinto case, Mark Dowie's claim was that Ford's analysis showed that the monetary costs of upgrading the safety of the fuel system would have outweighed the monetary benefits of doing so, i.e., the money saved by having fewer civil suits brought against the company. Therefore, they chose to allow the tank to remain as it was for economic benefit. This decision seems inhuman to Dowie since it means that Ford management was allowing people to die whose lives might have been saved by an inexpensive improvement.

Whether or not Ford used a cost-benefit analysis in the Pinto case is a controversial matter. The third article in Part II, Douglas Birsch's article "Product Safety, Cost-Benefit Analysis, and the Ford Pinto Case" explores product safety and cost-benefit analysis that places a monetary value on human life in connection with the Pinto case and Ford's use of a fuel system cost-benefit analysis. Birsch discusses product safety and claims that, based on product safety considerations, the Ford Pinto was an inadequate vehicle. Ford never admitted deciding not to upgrade the fuel system because of a cost-benefit analysis, but Birsch reviews the indirect evidence that suggests they did. He concludes that the question is impossible to answer definitively. Birsch's article proceeds by analyzing the ethics of cost-benefit analysis that places a monetary value on human life. He suggests that arguments can be made that the use of cost-benefit analysis that places a monetary value on human life is unethical in general and in the Pinto case. If Ford managers did base the decision on this kind of cost-benefit analysis, there are reasons to believe that they acted unethically.

Dowie's argument that Ford used a cost-benefit analysis was based on the general use of cost-benefit analysis at Ford which he illustrated with a cost-benefit analysis contained in a document Ford submitted to the NHTSA. This document, "Fatalities Associated with Crash-Induced Fuel Leakage and Fires" has come to be identified with the Pinto case and is the final selection in Part II. We received it from NHTSA as a supplement to the Investigation Report. It suggests that the seriousness of the fire problem in motor vehicles, in general, has been overstated and that the costs of implementing fire related safety regulation would exceed the expected benefit. The cost-benefit analysis contained in the document is not specifically about Ford Pintos or about rear-end collisions; it is about fuel leakage from rollovers in cars and trucks. Thus, even though this memorandum is associated in the literature with the Pinto case, it does not provide direct proof that Ford used a cost-benefit analysis as the basis for the decision not to improve the safety of the fuel system in the Pinto.

8

Cost-Benefit Analysis: An Ethical Critique*

At the broadest and vaguest level, cost-benefit analysis may be regarded simply as systematic thinking about decision making. Who can oppose, economists sometimes ask, efforts to think in a systematic way about the consequences of different courses of action? The alternative, it would appear, is unexamined decision making. But defining cost-benefit analysis so simply leaves it with few implications for actual regulatory decision making. Presumably, therefore, those who urge regulators to make greater use of the technique have a more extensive prescription in mind. I assume here that their prescription includes the following views:

1. There exists a strong presumption that an act should not be undertaken unless its benefits outweigh its costs.
2. In order to determine whether benefits outweigh costs, it is desirable to attempt to express all benefits and costs in a common

---

* Reprinted, with editorial changes, with the permission of The American Enterprise Institute for Public Policy Research, Washington, D.C.

scale or denominator, so that they can be compared with each other, even when some benefits and costs are not traded on markets and hence have no established dollar values.

3. Getting decision-makers to make more use of cost-benefit techniques is important enough to warrant both the expense required to gather the data for improved cost-benefit estimation and the political efforts needed to give the activity higher priority compared to other activities, also valuable in and of themselves.

My focus is on cost-benefit analysis as applied to environmental safety, and health regulation. In that context, I examine each of the above propositions from the perspective of formal ethical theory, that is, the study of what actions it is morally right to undertake. My conclusions are:

1. In areas of environmental, safety, and health regulation, there may be many instances where a certain decision might be right even though its benefits do not outweigh its costs.
2. There are good reasons to oppose efforts to put dollar values on non-marketed benefits and costs.
3. Given the relative frequency of occasions in the areas of environmental, safety, and health regulation where one would not wish to use a benefits-outweigh-costs test as a decision rule, and given the reasons to oppose the monetizing of non-marketed benefits or costs that is a prerequisite for cost-benefit analysis, it is not justifiable to devote major resources to the generation of data for cost-benefit calculations or to undertake efforts to "spread the gospel" of cost-benefit analysis further.

I

How do we decide whether a given action is morally right or wrong and hence, assuming the desire to act morally, why it should be undertaken or refrained from? Like the Molière character who spoke prose without knowing it, economists who advocate use of cost-benefit analysis for public decisions are philosophers without knowing it: the answer given by costs benefit analysis, that actions should be undertaken so as to maximize net benefits, represents one of the classic answers given by moral philosophers—that given by utilitarians. To determine whether an action is right or wrong, utilitarians tote up all the positive consequences of the action in terms of human satisfaction. The act that maximizes attainment of satisfaction under the circumstances is the right act. That the economists' answer is also the answer of one school of philosophers should not be surprising. Early on, economics was a branch of moral philosophy, and only later did it become an independent discipline.

Before proceeding further, the subtlety of the utilitarian position should be noted. The positive and negative consequences of an act for satisfaction may go beyond the act's immediate consequences. A facile version of utilitarianism would give moral sanction to a lie, for instance, if the satisfaction of an individual attained by telling the lie was greater than the suffering imposed on the lie's victim. Few utilitarians would agree. Most of them would add to the list of negative consequences the effect of the one lie on the tendency of the person who lies to tell other lies, even in instances when the lying produced less satisfaction for him than dissatisfaction for others. They would also add the negative effects of the lie on the general level of social regard for truth-telling, which has many consequences for future utility. A further consequence may be added as well. It is sometimes said that we should include in a utilitarian calculation the feeling of dissatisfaction produced in the liar (and perhaps in others) because, by telling a lie, one has "done the wrong thing." Correspondingly, in this view, among the positive consequences to be weighed into a utilitarian calculation of truth-telling is satisfaction arising from "doing the right thing." This view rests on an error, however, because it *assumes* what it is the purpose of the calculation to *determine*— that telling the truth in the instance in question is indeed the right thing to do. Economists are likely to object to this point, arguing that no feeling ought "arbitrarily" to be excluded from a complete costs benefit calculation, including a feeling of dissatisfaction at doing the wrong thing. Indeed, the economists' cost-benefit calculations would, at least ideally, include such feelings. Note the difference between the economist's and the philosopher's cost-benefit calculations, however. The economist may choose to include feelings of dissatis-faction in his cost-benefit calculation, but what happens if somebody asks the economist, "Why is it right to evaluate an action on the basis of a cost-benefit test?" If an answer is to be given to that question (which does not normally preoccupy economists but which does concern both philosophers and the rest of us who need to be persuaded that cost-benefit analysis is right), then the circularity problem reemerges. And there is also another difficulty with counting feelings of dissatisfaction at doing the wrong thing in a cost-benefit calculation. It leads to the perverse result that under certain circumstances a lie, for example, might be morally right if the individual contemplating the lie felt no compunction about lying and morally wrong only if the individual felt such a compunction!

This error is revealing, however, because it begins to suggest a critique of utilitarianism. Utilitarianism is an important and powerful moral doctrine. But it is probably a minority position among contemporary moral philosophers. It is amazing that economists can proceed in unanimous endorsement of cost-benefit analysis as if unaware that their conceptual framework is highly controversial in the discipline from which it arose—moral philosophy.

Let us explore the critique of utilitarianism. The logical error discussed before appears to suggest that we have a notion of certain things being right or wrong that *predates* our calculation of costs and benefits. Imagine the case of an old man in Nazi Germany who is hostile to the regime. He is wondering whether he should speak out against Hitler. If he speaks out, he will lose his pension. And his action will have done nothing to increase the chances that the Nazi regime will be overthrown: he is regarded as somewhat eccentric by those around him, and nobody has ever consulted his views on political questions. Recall that one cannot add to the benefits of speaking out any satisfaction from doing "the right thing," because the purpose of the exercise is to determine whether speaking out *is* the right thing. How would the utilitarian calculation go? The benefits of the old man's speaking out would, as the example is presented, be nil, while the costs would be his loss of his pension. So the costs of the action would outweigh the benefits. By the utilitarians' cost-benefit calculation, it would be *morally wrong* for the man to speak out.

Another example: two very close friends are on an Arctic expedition together. One of them falls very sick in the snow and bitter cold, and sinks quickly before anything can be done to help him. As he is dying, he asks his friend one thing, "Please, make me a solemn promise that ten years from today you will come back to this spot and place a lighted candle here to remember me." The friend solemnly promises to do so, but does not tell a soul. Now, ten years later, the friend must decide whether to keep his promise. It would be inconvenient for him to make the long trip. Since he told nobody, his failure to go will not affect the general social faith in promise-keeping. And the incident was unique enough so that it is safe to assume that his failure to go will not encourage him to break other promises. Again, the costs of the act outweigh the benefits. A utilitarian would need to believe that it would be *morally wrong* to travel to the Arctic to light the candle.

A third example: a wave of thefts has hit a city and the police are having trouble finding any of the thieves. But they believe, correctly, that punishing someone for theft will have some deterrent effect and will decrease the number of crimes. Unable to arrest any actual perpetrator, the police chief and the prosecutor arrest a person whom they know to be innocent and, in cahoots with each other, fabricate a convincing case against him. The police chief and the prosecutor are about to retire, so the act has no effect on any future actions of theirs. The fabrication is perfectly executed, so nobody finds out about it. Is the *only* question involved in judging the act of framing the innocent man that of whether his suffering from conviction and imprisonment will be greater than the suffering avoided among potential crime victims when some crimes are deterred? A utilitarian would need to believe that it is *morally right to punish the innocent man* as long as it can be demonstrated that the suffering prevented outweighs his suffering.

And a final example: imagine two worlds, each containing the same sum total of happiness. In the first world, this total of happiness came about from a series of acts that included a number of lies and injustices (that is, the total consisted of the immediate gross sum of happiness created by certain acts, minus any long-term unhappiness occasioned by the lies and injustices). In the second world the same amount of happiness was produced by a different series of acts, none of which involved lies or injustices. Do we have any reason to prefer the one world to the other? A utilitarian would need to believe that the choice between the two worlds is a *matter of indifference.*

To those who believe that it would not be morally wrong for the old man to speak out in Nazi Germany or for the explorer to return to the Arctic to light a candle for his deceased friend, that it would not be morally right to convict the innocent man, or that the choice between the two worlds is not a matter of indifference—to those of us who believe these things, utilitarianism is insufficient as a moral view. We believe that some acts whose costs are greater than their benefits may be morally right and, contrariwise, some acts whose benefits are greater than their costs may be morally wrong.

This does not mean that the questions whether benefits are greater than costs is morally irrelevant. Few would claim such. Indeed, for a broad range of individual and social decisions, whether an act's benefits outweigh its costs is a sufficient question to ask. But not for all such decisions. These may involve situations where certain duties—duties not to lie, break promises, or kill, for example—make an act wrong, even if it would result in an excess of benefits over costs.

Or they may involve instances where people's rights are at stake. We would not permit rape even if it could be demonstrated that the rapist derived enormous happiness from his act, while the victim experienced only minor displeasure. We do not do cost-benefit analyses of freedom of speech or trial by jury. The Bill of Rights was not RARGed. As the United Steelworkers noted in a comment on the Occupational Safety and Health Administration's economic analysis of its proposed rule to reduce worker exposure to carcinogenic coke-oven emissions, the Emancipation Proclamation was not subjected to an inflationary impact statement. The notion of human rights involves the idea that people may make certain claims to be allowed to act in certain ways or to be treated in certain ways, even if the sum of benefits achieved thereby does not outweigh the sum of costs. It is this view that underlies the statement that "workers have a right to a safe and healthy work place" and the expectation that OSHA's decisions will reflect that judgment.

In the most convincing versions of non-utilitarian ethics, various duties or rights are not absolute. But each has a *prima facie* moral validity so that, if duties or rights do not conflict, the morally right act is the act that reflects a duty or respects a right. If duties or rights do conflict, a moral judgment, based on conscious deliberation, must be made. Since one of the duties non-utilitarian philosophers enumerate is the duty of beneficence (the duty to maximize happiness), which in effect incorporates all of utilitarianism by reference, a non-utilitarian who is faced with conflicts between the results of cost-benefit analysis and non-utility-based considerations will need to undertake such deliberation. But in that deliberation additional elements, which cannot be reduced to a question of whether benefits outweigh costs, have been introduced. Indeed, depending on the moral importance we attach to the right or duty involved, cost-benefit questions may, within wide ranges, become irrelevant to the outcome of the moral judgment.

In addition to questions involving duties and rights, there is a final sort of question where, in my view, the issue of whether benefits outweigh costs should not govern moral judgment. I noted earlier that, for the common run of questions facing individuals and societies, it is possible to begin and end our judgment simply by finding out if the benefits of contemplated act outweigh the costs. This very fact means that one way to show the great importance, or value, attached to an area is to say that decisions involving the area should not be determined by cost-benefit calculations. This applies, I think, to the view many environmentalists have of decisions involving our natural environment. When officials are deciding what level of pollution will harm certain vulnerable people—such as asthmatics or the elderly—while not harming others, one issue involved may be the right of those people not to be sacrificed on the altar of somewhat higher living standards for the rest of us. But more broadly than this, many environmentalists fear that subjecting decisions about clean air or water to the cost-benefit tests that determine the general run of decisions removes those matters from the realm of specially valued things.

II

In order for cost-benefit calculations to be performed the way they are supposed to be, all costs and benefits must be expressed in a common measure, typically dollars, including things not normally bought and sold on markets, and to which dollar prices are therefore not attached. The most dramatic example of such things is human life itself; but many of the other benefits achieved or preserved by environmental policy—such as peace and quiet, fresh-smelling air, swimmable rivers, spectacular vistas—are not traded on markets either.

Economists who do cost-benefit analysis regard the quest after dollar values for non-market things as a difficult challenge—but one to be met with relish. They have tried to develop methods for imputing a person's "willingness to pay" for such things, their approach generally involving a search for bundled goods that *are* traded on markets and that vary as to whether they include a feature that is, *by itself*, not marketed. Thus, fresh air is not marketed, but houses in different parts of Los Angeles that are similar except for the degree of smog are. Peace and quiet is not marketed, but similar houses inside and outside airport flight paths are. The risk of death is not marketed, but similar jobs that have different levels of risk are. Economists have produced many often ingenious efforts to impute dollar prices to non-marketed things by observing the premiums accorded homes in clean air areas over similar homes in dirty areas or the premiums paid for risky jobs over similar nonrisky jobs.

These ingenious efforts are subject to criticism on a number of technical grounds. It may be difficult to control for all the dimensions of quality other than the presence or absence of the non-marketed thing. More important, in a world where people have different preferences and are subject to different constraints as they make their choices, the dollar value imputed to the non-market things that most people would wish to avoid will be lower than otherwise, because people with unusually weak aversion to those things or unusually strong constraints on their choices will be willing to take the bundled good in question at less of a discount than the average person. Thus, to use the property value discount of homes near airports as a measure of people's willingness to pay for quiet means to accept as a proxy for the rest of us the behavior of those least sensitive to noise of airport employees (who value the convenience of a near-airport location) or of others who are susceptible to an agent's assurances that "it's not so bad." To use the wage premiums accorded hazardous work as a measure of the value of life means to accept as proxies for the rest of us the choices of people who do not have many choices or who are exceptional risk-seekers.

A second problem is that the attempts of economists to measure people's willingness to pay for non-marketed things assume that there is no difference between the price a person would require for *giving up* something to which he has a preexisting right and the price he would pay to *gain* something to which he enjoys no right. Thus, the analysis assumes no difference between how much a homeowner would need to be paid in order to give up an unobstructed mountain view that he already enjoys and how much he would be willing to pay to get an obstruction moved once it is already in place. Available evidence suggests that most people would insist on being paid far more to assent to a worsening of their situation than they would be willing to pay to improve their situation. The difference arises from such factors as being accustomed to and psychologically attached to that which one believes one enjoys by right. But this creates a circularity problem for any attempt to use cost-benefit analysis to determine *whether* to assign to, say, the homeowner the right to an unobstructed mountain view. For willingness to pay will be different depending on whether the right is assigned initially or not. The value judgment about whether to assign the right must thus be made first. (In order to set an upper bound on the value of the benefit, one might hypothetically assign the right to the person and determine how much he would need to be paid to give it up.)

Third, the efforts of economists to impute willingness to pay invariably involve bundled goods exchanged in *private* transactions. Those who use figures garnered from such analysis to provide guidance for public decisions assume no difference between how people value certain things in private individual transactions and how they would wish those same things to be valued in public collective decisions. In making such assumptions, economists insidiously slip into their analysis an important and controversial value judgment, growing naturally out of the highly individualistic microeconomic tradition—namely, the view that there should be no difference between private behavior and the behavior we display in public social life. An alternative view—one that enjoys, I would suggest, wide resonance among citizens—would be that public, social decisions provide an opportunity to give certain things a higher valuation than we choose, for one reason or another, to give them in our private activities.

Thus, opponents of stricter regulation of health risks often argue that we show by our daily risk-taking behavior that we do not value life infinitely, and therefore our public decisions should not reflect the high value of life that proponents of strict regulation propose. However, an alternative view is equally plausible. Precisely because we fail, for whatever reasons, to give life-saving the value in everyday personal decisions that we in some general terms believe we should give it, we may wish our social decisions to provide us the occasion to display the reverence for life that we espouse but do not always show. By this view, people do not have fixed-unambiguous "preferences" to which they give expression through private activities and which therefore should be given expression in public decisions. Rather, they may have what they themselves regard as "higher" and "lower" preferences. The latter may come to the fore in private decisions, but people may want the former to come to the fore in public decisions. They may sometimes display racial prejudice, but support antidiscrimination laws. They may buy a certain product after seeing a seductive ad, but be skeptical enough of advertising to want the government to keep a close eye on it. In such cases, the use of private behavior to impute the values that should be entered for public decisions, as is done by using willingness to pay in private transactions, commits grievous offense against a view of the behavior of the citizen that is deeply engrained in our democratic tradition. It is a view that denudes politics of any independent role in society, reducing it to a mechanistic, mimicking recalculation based on private behavior.

Finally, one may oppose the effort to place prices on a non-market thing and hence in effect incorporate it into the market system out of a fear that the very act of doing so will reduce the thing's perceived value. To place a price on the benefit may, in other words, reduce the value of that benefit. Cost-benefit analysis thus may be like the thermometer that, when placed in a liquid to be measured, itself changes the liquid's temperature.

Examples of the perceived cheapening of a thing's value by the very act of buying and selling it abound in everyday life and language. The disgust that accompanies the idea of buying and selling human beings is based on the sense that this would dramatically diminish human worth. Epithets such as "he prostituted himself," applied as linguistic analogies to people who have sold something, reflect the view that certain things should not be sold because doing so diminishes their value. Praise that is bought is worth little, even to the person buying it. A true anecdote is told of an economist who retired to another university community and complained that he was having difficulty making friends. The laconic response of a critical colleague—"If you want a friend why don't you buy yourself one"—illustrates in a pithy way the intuition that, for some things, the very act of placing a price on them reduces their perceived value.

The first reason that pricing something decreases its perceived value is that, in many circumstances, non-market exchange is associated with the production of certain values not associated with market exchange. These may include spontaneity and various other feelings that come from personal relationships. If a good becomes less associated with the production of positively valued feelings because of market exchange, the perceived value of the good declines to the extent that those feelings are valued. This can be seen clearly in instances where a thing may be transferred both by market and by non-market mechanisms. The willingness to pay for sex bought from a prostitute is less than the perceived value of the sex consummating love. (Imagine the reaction if a practitioner of cost-benefit analysis computed the benefits of sex based on the price of prostitute services.)

Furthermore, if one values in a general sense the existence of a non-market sector because of its connection with the production of certain valued feelings, then one ascribes added value to any non-marketed good simply as a repository of values represented by the non-market sector one wishes to preserve. This seems certainly to be the case for things in nature, such as pristine streams or undisturbed forests: for many people who value them, part of their value comes from their position as repositories of values the non-market sector represents.

The second way in which placing a market price on a thing decreases its perceived value is by removing the possibility of proclaiming that the thing is "not for sale," since things on the market by definition are for sale. The very statement that something is not for sale affirms, enhances, and protects a thing's value in a number of ways. To begin with, the statement is a way of showing that a thing is valued for its own sake, whereas selling a thing for money demonstrates that it was valued only instrumentally. Furthermore, to say that something cannot be transferred in that way places it in the exceptional category—which requires the person interested in obtaining that thing to be able to offer something else that is exceptional, rather than allowing him the easier alternative of obtaining the thing for money that could have been obtained in an infinity of ways. This enhances its value. If I am willing to say "You're a really kind person" to whoever pays me to do so, my praise loses the value that attaches to it from being exchangeable only for an act of kindness.

In addition, if we have already decided we value something highly, one way of stamping it with a cachet affirming its high value is to announce that it is "not for sale." Such an announcement does more, however, than just reflect a preexisting high valuation. It signals a thing's distinctive value to others and helps us persuade them to value the thing more highly than they otherwise might. It also expresses our resolution to safeguard that distinctive value. To state that something is not for sale is thus also a source of value for that thing, since if a thing's value is easy to affirm or protect, it will be worth more than an otherwise similar thing without such attributes.

If we proclaim that something is not for sale, we make a once-and-for-all judgment of its special value. When something is priced, the issue of its perceived value is constantly coming up, as a standing invitation to reconsider that original judgment. Were people constantly faced with questions such as "how much money could get you to give up your freedom of speech?" or "how much would you sell your vote for if you could?", the perceived value of the freedom to speak or the right to vote would soon become devastated as, in moments of weakness, people started saying "maybe it's not worth *so much* after all." Better not to be faced with the constant questioning in the first place. Something similar did in fact occur when the slogan "better red than dead" was launched by some pacifists during the Cold War. Critics pointed out that the very posing of this stark choice—in effect, "would you *really* be willing to give up your life in exchange for not living under communism?"—reduced the value people attached to freedom and thus diminished resistance to attacks on freedom.

Finally, of some things valued very highly it is stated that they are "priceless" or that they have "infinite value." Such expressions are reserved for a subset of things not for sale, such as life or health. Economists tend to scoff at talk of pricelessness. For them, saying that something is priceless is to state a willingness to trade off an infinite quantity of all other goods for one unit of the priceless good, a situation that empirically appears highly unlikely. For most people, however, the word priceless is pregnant with meaning. Its value-affirming and value-protecting functions cannot be bestowed on expressions that merely denote a determinate, albeit high, valuation. John Kennedy in his inaugural address proclaimed that the nation was ready to "pay any price [and] bear any burden...to assure the survival and the success of liberty." Had he said instead that we were willing to "pay a high price" or "bear a large burden" for liberty, the statement would have rung hollow.

III

An objection that advocates of cost-benefit analysis might well make to the preceding argument should be considered. I noted earlier that, in cases where various non-utility-based duties or rights conflict with the maximization of utility, it is necessary to make a deliberative judgment about what act is finally right. I also argued earlier that the search for commensurability might not always be a desirable one, that the attempt to go beyond expressing benefits in terms of (say) lives saved and costs in terms of dollars is not something devoutly to be wished.

In situations involving things that are not expressed in a common measure, advocates of cost-benefit analysis argue that people making judgments "in effect" perform cost-benefit calculations anyway. If government regulators promulgate a regulation that saves 100 lives at a cost of $1 billion, they are "in effect" valuing a life at (a minimum of) $10 million, whether or not they say that them are willing to place a dollar value on a human life. Since, in this view, cost-benefit analysis "in effect" is inevitable, it might as well be made specific.

This argument misconstrues the real difference in the reasoning processes involved. In cost-benefit analysis, equivalencies are established *in advance* as one of the raw materials for the calculation. One determines costs and benefits, one determines equivalencies (to be able to put various costs and benefits into a common measure), and then one sets to toting things up—waiting, as it were, with bated breath for the results of the calculation to come out. The outcome is determined by the arithmetic; if the outcome is a close call or if one is not good at long division, one does not know how it will turn out until the calculation is finished. In the kind of deliberative judgment that is performed without a common measure, no establishment of equivalencies occurs in advance. Equivalencies are not aids to the decision process. In fact, the decision-maker might not even be aware of what the "in effect" equivalencies were, at least before they are revealed to him afterwards by someone pointing out what he had "in effect" done. The decision-maker would see himself as simply having made a deliberative judgment; the "in effect" equivalency number did-not play a causal role in the decision but at most merely reflects it. Given this, the argument against making the process explicit is the one discussed earlier in the discussion of problems with putting specific quantified values on things that are not normally quantified—that the very act of doing so may serve to reduce the value of those things.

My own judgment is that modest efforts to assess levels of benefits and costs are justified, although I do not believe that government agencies ought to sponsor efforts to put dollar prices on non-market things. I also do not believe that the cry for more cost-benefit analysis in regulation is, on the whole, justified. If regulatory officials were so insensitive about regulatory costs that they did not provide acceptable raw material for deliberative judgments (even if not of a strictly cost-benefit nature), my conclusion might be different. But a good deal of research into costs and benefits already occurs—actually, far more in the U.S. regulatory process than in that of any other industrial society. The danger now would seem to come more from the other side.

9

Defending Cost-Benefit Analysis:
Replies to Steven Kelman*

JAMES V. DELONG

Steven Kelman's "Cost-Benefit Analysis—An Ethical Critique" presents so many targets that it is difficult to concentrate one's fire. However, four points seem worth particular emphasis:

(1) The decision to use cost-benefit analysis by no means implies adoption of the reductionist utilitarianism described by Kelman. It is based instead on the pragmatic conclusion that any value system one adopts is more likely to be promoted if one knows something about the consequences of the choices to be made. The effort to put dollar values on noneconomic benefits is nothing more than an effort to find some common measure for things that are not easily comparable when, in the real world, choice must be made. Its object is not to write a computer program but to improve the quality of difficult social

* Reprinted, with editorial changes, with the permission of The American Enterprise Institute for Public Policy Research, Washington, D.C.

choices under conditions of uncertainty, and no sensible analyst lets himself become the prisoner of the numbers.

(2) Kelman repeatedly lapses into "entitlement" rhetoric, as if an assertion of a moral claim closes an argument. Even leaving aside the fundamental question of the philosophical basis of those entitlements, there are two major problems with this style of argument. First, it tends naturally toward all-encompassing claims.

Kelman quotes a common statement that "workers have a right to a safe and healthy workplace," a statement that contains no recognition that safety and health are not either/or conditions, that the most difficult questions involve gradations of risk, and that the very use of entitlement language tends to assume that a zero-risk level is the only acceptable one. Second, entitlement rhetoric is usually phrased in the passive voice, as if the speaker were arguing with some omnipotent god or government that is maliciously withholding the entitlement out of spite. In the real world, one person's right is another's duty, and it often clarifies the discussion to focus more precisely on who owes this duty and what it is going to cost him or her. For example, the article posits that an issue in government decisions about acceptable pollution levels is "the right" of such vulnerable groups as asthmatics or the elderly "not to be sacrificed on the altar of somewhat higher living standards for the rest of us." This defends the entitlement by assuming the costs involved are both trivial and diffused. Suppose, though, that the price to be paid is not "somewhat higher living standards," but the jobs of a number of workers?

Kelman's counter to this seems to be that entitlements are not firm rights, but only presumptive ones that prevail in any clash with nonentitlements, and that when two entitlements collide the decision depends upon the "moral importance we attach to the right or duty involved." So the above collision would be resolved by deciding whether a job is an entitlement and, if it is, by then deciding whether jobs or air have greater "moral importance."

I agree that conflicts between such interests present difficult choices, but the quantitative questions, the cost-benefit questions, are hardly irrelevant to making them. Suppose taking X quantity of pollution from the air of a city will keep one asthmatic from being forced to leave town and cost 1,000 workers their jobs? Suppose it will keep 1,000 asthmatics from being forced out and cost one job? These are not equivalent choices, economically or morally, and the effort to decide them according to some abstract idea of moral importance only obscures the true nature of the moral problems involved.

(3) Kelman also develops the concept of things that are "specially valued," and that are somehow contaminated if thought about in monetary terms. As an approach to personal decision making, this is silly. There are many things one specially values—in the sense that one would find the effort to assign a market price to them ridiculous—which are nonetheless affected by economic factors. I may specially value a family relationship, but how often I phone is influenced by long-distance rates. I may specially value music, but be affected by the price of records or the cost of tickets at the Kennedy Center.

When translated to the realm of government decisions, however, the concept goes beyond silliness. It creates a political grotesquerie. People specially value many different things. Under Kelman's assumptions, people must, in creating a political coalition, recognize and accept as legitimate everyone's special value; without concern for cost. Therefore, everyone becomes entitled to as much of the thing he specially values as he says he specially values, and it is immoral to discuss vulgar questions of resource limitations. Any coalition built on such premises can go in either of two directions: It can try to incorporate so many different groups and interests that the absurdity of its internal contradictions becomes manifest. Or it can limit its membership at some point and decide that the special values of those left outside are not legitimate and should be sacrificed to the special values of those in the coalition. In the latter case, of course, those outside must be made scapegoats for any frustration of any group member's entitlement, a requirement that eventually leads to political polarization and a holy war between competing coalitions of special values.

(4) The decisions that must be made by contemporary government indeed involve painful choices. They affect both the absolute quantity and the distribution not only of goods and benefits, but also of physical and mental suffering. It is easy to understand why people would want to avoid making such choices and would rather act in ignorance than with knowledge and responsibility for the consequences of their choices. While this may be understandable, I do not regard it as an acceptable moral position. To govern is to choose, and government officials—whether elected or appointed—betray their obligations to the welfare of the people who hired them if they adopt a policy of happy ignorance and nonresponsibility for consequences.

The article concludes with the judgment that the present danger is too much cost-benefit analysis, not too little. But I find it hard to believe, looking around the modern world, that its major problem is that it suffers from an excess of rationality. The world's stock of ignorance is and will remain quite large enough without adding to it as a matter of deliberate policy.

ROBERT M. SOLOW

I am an economist who has no personal involvement in the practice of cost-benefit analysis, who happens to think that modern economics underplays the significance of ethical judgments both in its approach to policy and its account of individual and organizational behavior, and who once wrote in print:

> It may well be socially destructive to admit the routine exchange-ability of certain things. We would prefer to maintain that they are beyond price (although this sometimes means only that we would prefer not to know what the price really is).

You might expect, therefore, that I would be in sympathy with Steven Kelman's ethical critique of cost-benefit analysis. But I found the article profoundly, and not entirely innocently, misleading. I would like to say why.

First of all, it is not the case that cost-benefit analysis works, or must work, by "monetizing" everything from mother love to patriotism. Cost-benefit analysis is needed only when society must give up some of one good thing in order to get more of another good thing. In other cases the decision is not problematical. The underlying rationale of cost-benefit analysis is that the cost of the good thing to be obtained is precisely the good thing that must or will be given up to obtain it. Wherever he reads "willingness to pay" and balks, Kelman should read "willingness to sacrifice" and feel better. In a choice between hospital beds and preventive treatment, lives are traded against lives. I suppose it is only natural that my brethren should get into the habit of measuring the sacrifice in terms of dollars forgone. In the typical instance in which someone actually does a cost-benefit analysis, the question to be decided is, say, whether the public should be taxed to pay for a water project—a context in which it does not seem far-fetched to ask whether the project will provide services for which the public would willingly pay what it would have to give up in taxes. But some less familiar unit of measurement could be used.

Let me add here, parenthetically, that I do agree with Kelman that there are situations in which the body politic's willingness to sacrifice may be badly measured by the sum of individuals' willingnesses to sacrifice in a completely "private" context. But that is at worst an error of technique, not a mistaken principle.

Second, Kelman hints broadly that "economists" are so morally numb as to believe that a routine cost-benefit analysis could justify killing widows and orphans, or abridging freedom of speech, or outlawing simple evidences of piety or friendship. But there is nothing in the theory or the practice of cost-benefit analysis to justify that judgment. Treatises on the subject make clear that certain ethical or political principles may irreversibly dominate the advantages and disadvantages capturable by cost-benefit analysis. Those treatises make a further point that Kelman barely touches on: since the benefits and the costs of a policy decision are usually enjoyed and incurred by different people, a distributional judgment has to be made which can override any simple-minded netting out. In addition, Kelman's point that people may put different values on the acquisition of a good for the first time and on the loss of a preexisting entitlement to the same good is not exactly a discovery. He should look up "compensating variation" 'and "equivalent variation" in a good economics textbook.

Third, Kelman ends by allowing that it is not a bad thing to have a modest amount of cost-benefit analysis going on. I would have supposed that was a fair description of the state of affairs. Do I detect a tendency to eat one's cost-benefit analysis and have it too? If not, what is the point of all the overkill? As a practical matter, the vacuum created by diminished reliance on cost-benefit analysis is likely to be filled by a poor substitute for ethically informed deliberation. Is the capering of Mr. Stockman more to Mr. Kelman's taste?

GERARD BUTTERS, JOHN CALFEE, AND PAULINE IPPOLITO

In his article, Steve Kelman argues against the increased use of cost-benefit analysis for regulatory decisions involving health, safety, and the environment. His basic contention is that these decisions are moral ones, and that cost-benefit analysis is therefore inappropriate because it requires the adoption of an unsatisfactory moral system. He supports his argument with a series of examples, most of which involve private decisions. In these situations, he asserts, cost-benefit advocates must renounce any moral qualms about lies, broken promises, and violations of human rights.

We disagree (and in doing so, we speak for ourselves, not for the Federal Trade Commission or its staff). Cost-benefit analysis is not a means for judging private decisions. It is a guide for decision making involving others, especially when the welfare of many individuals must be balanced. It is designed not to dictate individual values, but to take them into account when decisions must be made collectively. Its use is grounded on the principle that, in a democracy, government must act as an agent of the citizens.

We see no reason to abandon this principle when health and safety are involved. Consider, for example, a proposal to raise the existing federal standards on automobile safety. Higher standards will raise the costs, and hence the price, of cars. From our point of view, the appropriate policy judgment rests on whether customers will value the increased safety sufficiently to warrant the costs. Any violation of a cost-benefit criterion would require that consumers purchase something they would not voluntarily purchase or prevent them from purchasing something they want. One might argue, in the spirit of Kelman's analysis, that many consumers would want the government to impose a more stringent standard than they would choose for themselves. If so, how is the cost safety trade-off that consumers really want to be determined? Any objective way of doing this would be a natural part of cost-benefit analysis.

Kelman also argues that the process of assigning a dollar value to things not traded in the marketplace is rife with indignities, flaws, and biases. Up to a point, we agree. It *is* difficult to place objective dollar values on certain intangible costs and benefits. Even with regard to intangibles which have been systematically studied, such as the "value of life," we know of no cost-benefit advocate who believes that regulatory staff economists should reduce every consideration to dollar terms and simply supply the decision maker with the bottom line. Our main concerns are twofold: (1) to make the major costs and benefits explicit so that the decision maker makes the trade-offs consciously and with the prospect of being held accountable, and (2) to encourage the move toward a more consistent set of standards.

The gains from adopting consistent regulatory standards can be dramatic. If costs and benefits are not balanced in making decisions, it is likely that the returns per dollar in terms of health and safety will be small for some programs and large for others. Such programs present opportunities for saving lives, and cost-benefit analysis will reveal them. Perhaps, as Kelman argues, there is something repugnant about assigning dollar values to lives. But the alternative can be to sacrifice lives needlessly by failing to carry out the calculations that would have revealed the means for saving them. It should be kept in mind that the avoidance of cost-benefit analysis has its own cost, which can be gauged in lives as well as in dollars.

Nonetheless, we do not dispute that cost-benefit analysis is highly imperfect. We would welcome a better guide to public policy, a guide that would be efficient, morally attractive, and certain to ensure that governments follow the dictates of the governed. Kelman's proposal is to adopt an ethical system that balances conflicts between certain unspecified "duties" and "rights" according to "deliberate reflection." But who is to do the reflecting, and on whose behalf? His guide places no clear limits on the actions of regulatory agencies. Rather than enhancing the connections between individual values and state decisions, such a vague guideline threatens to sever them. Is there a common moral standard that every regulator will magically and independently arrive at through "deliberate reflection"? We doubt it. Far more likely is a system in which bureaucratic decisions reflect the preferences, not of the citizens, but of those in a peculiar position to influence decisions. What concessions to special interests cannot be disguised by claiming that it is degrading to make explicit the trade-offs reflected in the decision? What individual crusade cannot be rationalized by an appeal to "public values" that "rise above" values revealed by individual choices?

ROBERT A. NISBET

A considerable distance separates Steven Kelman's views and mine on, first, the appositeness of cost-benefit analysis and, second, the historical context in which we live. No matter: his thoughtful and gracefully written article empresses a point of view that is widespread and must not be disregarded by those of us who see the matter somewhat differently.

(1) I question Kelman's use of "utilitarianism." It seems to me that he has in mind, rather, Bentham's notable (or notorious) hedonic calculus—which does indeed posit that the morally right act is always the one that maximizes satisfaction. Granted that utilitarian theory was originated by Bentham, with the assistance of James Mill. But there is much warrant and precedent for taking it as we find it in John Stuart Mill's *Utilitarianism.*

Mill, like Bentham and the great English utilitarians of the late nineteenth century, believes the end of government should be to accomplish the greatest possible good for the greatest possible number. But Mill will have none of the hedonic calculus. "He who saves a fellow creature from drowning does what is morally right, whether his motive be duty, or the hope of being paid for his trouble; he who betrays a friend that trusts him is guilty of a crime, even if his object be to serve another friend to whom he is under greater obligation." And there is more: "It is confessedly unjust," says Mill, "to break faith with anyone, to violate an engagement, either express or implied, or disappoint expectations raised by our own conduct...." So much for Kelman's illustrations with respect to the irrelevance or impiety of cost-benefit assessment.

In addition, the conviction that utility ought to be the ultimate standard of value is, for Mill, quite compatible with the belief that "certain social utilities...are vastly more important and therefore more absolute and imperative than any others are as a class"—and, further, that these utiiities should be and are "guarded bv a sentiment not only different in degree but in kind." Mill lists a number of such "utilities," chief among them liberty. Were he living today, he might very well—in fact, probably would—add conservation of resources to his list of overriding utilities.

(2) That leads me to Kelman's worthy insistence that there are certain values in life for which cost-benefit assessment is inappropriate, even immoral or illogical. I dare say there are, most of them being highly subjective and egocentric. But consider so subjective a state of mind as, say, one's love of another human being. We stipulate the crassness and venality of claiming to love another if the loved one's exclusive attraction is an abundance of worldly goods. There have been other ages, however, not without honor, and there are even now peoples whose morality must be presumed at least as elevated as ours who take a less subjective (and romantic) view of this matter than we contemporary Americans do. In many a newspaper in India we find advertisements for spouses, with everything from a Ph.D. to a given number of cows put on the negotiation counter. Marriages are not to be allowed, in such a culture, to run the risk of foundering on mere human passion—call it love—and on subjective assessment free of cost-benefit analysis. Marriage is too serious in the Hindu's mind, too sacred, too vital. I do not recommend the Hindu dogma of marriage to this generation of Americans, but from all I have been able to discover from Indian records, as many happy marriages proceed from naked cost-benefit analysis there as from whatever most marriages proceed from in the United States. In fact, I know of virtually nothing, really, in mankind's history, however sacred—birth, marriage, and death foremost—that has not been and is not today in many places subjected to cost-benefit consideration.

To take a less universal crisis of the human condition, the care of the handicapped is, I believe, an obligation of any civilized society.

But are we being callous to see economic disaster ahead if we dismiss altogether cost-benefit criteria in our search for ways of increasing their mobility? Is it inhumane to look for other ways of helping wheelchair users than by spending tens of millions on ramps and lifts?

Or take the environment. As far as I am concerned, laws against pollution and resource depletion are always called for, within reasonable limits. And doubtless some parts of the wilderness should be maintained as nearly as possible in their pristine state. But not, I would argue, with such zeal that even prospecting for vital fuels and minerals is outlawed. There is no evidence in this area—or elsewhere, for that matter—of the surfeit of cost-benefit balancing Kelman seems to have observed. With memory fresh of the Alaskan wilderness bill that President Carter signed, I am obliged to conclude that proper balance lies a long way ahead of us—meaning a balance under which private industry has a great deal more leeway than it now has to explore, mine, or otherwise develop these areas. We should remember that serious environmentalism (conservation, as it was called then) began under such prescient minds as Theodore Roosevelt and Gifford Pinchot, who repeatedly declared that the purpose of conservation was *not* idle preservation but rather to prevent wanton desolation and to guarantee a future in which people could continue to rise in the scale of economy and civilization.

Unoccupied land is exactly a place where cost-benefit analysis is vital—in the sheer interest of the large numbers of underprivileged among us, including the young not yet established in a career and most emphatically blacks, Hispanics, and other minorities whose rise to middle-class status is among the highest items on our national social agenda. What they, and all others who are currently disadvantaged and in need of channels of upward mobility, require most is economic growth and increased productivity. For without the certain prospect of a vast number of new jobs in the private sector, much of the foundation for what we call the American way of life is destroyed. It is truly unfortunate that the once noble conservation movement in this country has fallen, for the most part, into the hands of those less interested in the welfare of posterity than in the preservation of a wilderness that has become an end in itself, a source of happiness for a tiny few who, I fear, love the wilderness above man. Environmentalism is rapidly becoming the socialism, not of fools, but of the middle and upper classes.

In sum, I agree with Kelman that there assuredly are considerations of the quality of life which should be free of cost-benefit analysis. But I am too avid a student of the great civilizations of past and present to believe that there are very many of these considerations. Protagoras' seminal aphorism is worth calling to mind: "Man is the measure of all things." And also the words of that author of Genesis who wrote: "Be fruitful and multiply; and fill the earth and subdue it; and have dominion over the fish of the sea and the birds of the air and over every living thing that moves upon the earth." St. Francis was a great and good man, and we can applaud his devotion to beasts, birds, and fishes. But the Church, rooted as it was in the Jewish-Greek philosophy I have just cited, came to see this extraordinary man in different light. It was when in some degree St. Francis and in much larger degree certain of his disciples argued as though *nature* must be allowed *to subdue man*, as though the *beasts, birds,* and *fishes* must have *dominion over man*, that the Franciscan message was properly checked.

Alas, the Franciscan heresy is spreading today in America, and it is precisely in the enclaves of the affluent and privileged that we find it most at work—to the lasting disadvantage of those who did not happen to get there first.

10

Product Safety, Cost-Benefit Analysis, and the Ford Pinto Case

During the 1970s, Ford Motor Company produced a subcompact automobile called the Pinto. Critics charged that the car had a design deficiency involving the fuel system and that Ford failed to respond adequately to this problem. In a 1977 article entitled "Pinto Madness," Mark Dowie claimed that Ford engineers and executives knew, prior to production, that low-speed, rear-end collisions would rupture the Pinto's fuel tank and that they waited for years to fix the car. He charged that management delayed upgrading the integrity of the fuel system because they used a cost-benefit analysis to determine that it was not profitable to do so.[1] In a series of articles in October of 1979, the *Chicago Tribune* also charged that Ford knew the car's gas-tank design was more susceptible to fire and explosion in low-speed crashes than other available designs, that the car could have been made significantly safer for less than $10 a car, and that Ford executives on two occasions recommended delaying changes to the fuel system in order to save money.[2] These are serious charges, and by investigating them we can draw some conclusions about Ford's actions, as well as about ethical management practices, product safety, and the use of cost-benefit analysis that places a monetary value on human life. The discussion of these issues and the Pinto case will be framed by a set of questions about product safety and one question about cost-benefit analysis: (1) Is it wrong for manufacturers to market any product that could be made safer using current technology? If a safer product can be made, should companies be required to give the public the option of purchasing the safer product? Is it wrong for businesses to market products that are not as safe as competing products on the market? Should manufacturers be forbidden to market products that do not meet the reasonable safety expectations of consumers? (2) Is it unethical for a company to use a cost-benefit analysis that places a monetary value on human life? My conclusion is that, with respect to product safety, manufacturers should be required to obey the law, follow industry standards, and meet the reasonable safety-related expectations of consumers. In the Pinto case, Ford failed to do the latter and hence produced an unsafe vehicle. In regard to the ethical evaluation of cost-benefit analysis that places a monetary value on human life, both human rights advocates and utilitarians might make a case that Ford acted unethically by performing such an analysis and using it as the justification for not making the car safer. Of course, in the Pinto case, there is uncertainty about whether or not Ford actually used a cost-benefit analysis as the basis for the decision not to upgrade the integrity of the fuel system. Even if the company did not, I believe that their money-saving decision was foolish and unethical.

THE PINTO CRASH TESTS

Was the Pinto an unsafe automobile and should Ford have known that it was? This question can best be answered by reviewing the crash testing done to Pintos and other cars modified to have the Pinto fuel system. Do the results of the crash testing reveal an unsafe vehicle? A breakdown of the crash tests reported by the *Chicago Tribune* is as follows:

June 1969: Engineers crash tested a foreign-made compact with a fuel system modified to resemble the proposed Pinto fuel system. The gas tank ruptured in a 21-mph crash.

May–November 1969: Three subcompacts, altered to have Pinto type fuel systems, were crash tested. In two 21-mph tests and one

18-mph test the fuel tanks were punctured or split apart and the filler pipe was pulled loose.

October 10, 1970: A production model Pinto was crashed backward into a fixed barrier at 21 mph. A bolt on the differential housing punctured the tank and the filler pipe was pulled loose. Similar results were achieved in several other tests.

December 2, 1970: Pintos with rubber and nylon "bladders" were crash tested. The arrangement proved successful in withstanding rear-end crashes of 20 and 26 mph.[3]

The key test in the series was on October 10, 1970, and showed that a production model Pinto was susceptible to bursting into flames when crashed into a fixed barrier at 21.5 mph (equivalent to about a 28.3-mph moving barrier test). This result should have raised serious questions about the safety of the Pinto since it demonstrated that a vehicle-to-vehicle crash below 30 mph could cause fatalities.

The problem with the Pinto fuel system was further confirmed by a series of fixed-barrier crash tests performed, in April 1972, on 1971 and 1972 Pintos. The first test of a station wagon at 16.8 mph (equivalent to a 21.8-mph moving-barrier test) showed slight leakage from the tank and the filler pipe was pulled out. The second test of a three-door or hatchback model at 15.5 mph (equivalent to a 20-mph moving-barrier test) showed only slight leakage from the filler pipe at the tank inlet. The third test of a two-door model was done at 26.3 mph (equivalent to a 34.7-mph moving-barrier test). The tank leaked from the filler pipe and was severely deformed, but did not leak further because a rubber bladder had been installed in the steel tank. The fourth test vehicle was also a two-door model and was crashed at 20.8 mph (equivalent to a 27-4-mph moving-barrier test). It showed no leakage, but the car had been modified by the addition of two longitudinal side rails in the rear of the car. The fifth car was a two-door crashed at 21 mph (equivalent to a 27.9-mph moving-barrier test). The car leaked less than one ounce per minute because a rubber bladder had been installed in the tank. The last test car, another two-door, was crashed at 21.5 mph (equivalent to a 28.3-mph moving-barrier test). The filler pipe was pulled out of the fuel tank, and the tank was punctured by the axle housing bolt. These tests should have reinforced the conclusion that the car was not as safe as it should have been and also revealed that it was possible to obtain significantly better results without changing the placement of the gas tank or making major modifications to the car.[4] Besides the rubber bladder and the longitudinal side rails, Ford engineers also considered a "flak vest" or rubber cushion surrounding the tank as a means of upgrading the integrity of the fuel tank. The "flak vest" proved effective in laboratory tests, but, like the rubber bladder, it was never implemented.[5]

The crash tests demonstrated that there was a safety problem with the early Ford Pintos because the fuel tanks and filler pipes were vulnerable to damage in low-speed, rear-end collisions. Ford engineers developed low-cost methods to improve the integrity of the fuel system, and Ford management must have considered whether or not to implement these changes. In the next section of the paper, I will explore the question of whether considerations of product safety ought to have led management to order the changes to be made.

THE PINTO AND SAFETY

Given this crash test information concerning the Pinto, we can proceed with the set of questions concerning product safety. Is it wrong for manufacturers to market any product that could be made safer using current technology? An affirmative answer to this question would produce an unreasonable standard. Many products can be made safer than they are, but consumers would not necessarily want them to be safer if the safety improvement forced other desirable qualities to be sacrificed. Companies could build automobiles that looked tank-like, with massive amounts of steel and devices that limited their speeds. Drivers, however, would not want improved safety at the cost of exorbitant car prices, extremely poor gas mileage, and low speed or handling capabilities. The Pinto was a low-cost, subcompact car; it would be unreasonable to expect it to be made as safe as possible since the nature of the automobile would be radically changed.

Another question that could be asked in relation to the Pinto is: if a safer product can be produced, should companies be required to give the public the option of purchasing the safer product? Should Ford have been required to market an alternative version of the Pinto equipped with the rubber bladder or the plastic shield that eventually made the car safer? While this option at first may seem reasonable, it would have serious implications. Automobiles have a large number of parts and many of them might be able to be modified to improve safety. In order for consumers to make informed decisions, they would need information about the effect on price, fuel-economy, comfort, handling, and durability caused by each change. To compile this information on hundreds of parts would be extremely expensive and would produce a huge buyers' guide, which would probably go unread by most consumers. An even more serious consequence is that it would be a financial disaster to require an automaker to offer a car that could be bought with one or more of several hundred different modifications. The company might end up having to build a special order car for each customer, which would be economically unreasonable.

Is it wrong for businesses to market products which are not as safe as competing products on the market, and was it wrong of Ford to have marketed the Pinto if it were not as safe as the Japanese subcompacts or the Chevrolet Vega? This question is more difficult to answer than the earlier ones. There are industry standards that guide engineering practices. If an engineer designed something that was not up to the industry standard, he or she would be a poor engineer. Thus, in the sense that all products should meet the relevant engineering standards, all products ought to be made as well as the competing products, and they should all be similar with respect to safety. This solution leaves room, however, for a certain amount of leeway. It would be almost impossible to make all products equally safe without making them identical in construction. If consumers are going to have different options available, there are going to be differences in safety. Different subcompact cars, the Pinto and the Vega for example, will have different safety records. As long as the safety records are all considered acceptable by consumers and government regulators, there ought to be no problems. It is unreasonable to expect competing products to have identical safety records, and we should not forbid companies from marketing products that are not as safe as competing products. The key question seems to be: are all the safety records acceptable? We should not ask whether the Pinto was as safe as the Vega, but was the Pinto's safety record acceptable? This question, however, introduces the idea that there is some standard of safety that is "acceptable." I believe that an "acceptable" standard of safety is related to the reasonable safety expectations of consumers, and I will investigate this next.

The final question with regard to product safety is: should manufacturers be forbidden to market products that do not meet the reasonable safety expectations of consumers, and did the Pinto meet the reasonable safety expectations of customers? One difficulty connected to answering these questions is defining the phrase "reasonable safety expectations of consumers." I cannot offer a definition for this phrase in terms of necessary and sufficient conditions, but I will suggest a preliminary account involving three elements: technology, product character, and consumer knowledge. First, the "reasonable safety expectations of consumers" would be those safety-related expectations that are technologically feasible. It is not a reasonable expectation if the business cannot make the product safer. Second, a "reasonable safety expectation" should fit the character of the product. A consumer does not have a reasonable expectation if meeting it would require the company to change the basic character of the product, for instance, to turn an economy or subcompact car into a regularly priced or a compact car. The dividing lines between what is and what is not technologically feasible, and between a product of one character or another, cannot be stated precisely in a general way. Therefore, I believe that our practical evaluations of products will have to be made on a case by case basis. Third, there may be "reasonable safety expectations" even if consumers do not actually have them. If a business conceals the potential for a safer product from consumers, those consumers will not be able to make an informed judgment about what to expect from the product. They may not have any actual safety expectations, but this condition does not mean that safety expectations are not appropriate. A business should be held accountable for the reasonable safety expectations consumers would have if they knew all of the relevant information about the product.

It is impossible to make a completely safe automobile. The use of automobiles always involves some risk, and for many people, a safe car is one that allows the person to drive with an acceptable degree of risk. In the Pinto case, it seems that both the supporters and critics of Ford agreed that, in general, automobile fuel systems were hazardous in 50-mph crashes. People should have expected serious injury or death if they were involved in rear-end collisions at that speed. While this situation presented a risk of death or serious injury, it was an acceptable risk. The National Highway Traffic Safety Administration (NHTSA) and most people involved in the case also seem to have agreed that drivers and passengers should sustain only minor injuries in crashes at or below 30 mph. Driving a car that might burst into flames in a 25-mph crash would have been an unacceptable risk. I am unclear about what people believed about the range from 31- to 49-mph crashes. Therefore, I will simply consider whether the belief that they would sustain only minor injuries in 30-mph or slower crash was a reasonable safety expectation with respect to the Ford Pinto.

Consumers would have expected to survive low-speed, rear-end collisions, and in connection with the Pinto, it would have been a reasonable safety expectation since it was technologically feasible without changing the basic characteristics of the product. The installation of either the "flak vest," the rubber bladder, or the plastic shield would have been an easy and low-cost improvement that would not have changed the basic character of the car. The October 1970 crash test showed the car was unsafe in a vehicle to vehicle crash at 28.3 mph. These results violate the reasonable consumer expectation because the car was unsafe in a low-speed crash. Assuming that consumers did expect to survive low-speed crashes, the Pinto did not meet the reasonable safety expectations of consumers, and therefore with respect to product safety, Ford engineers and executives produced an inadequate vehicle.

There is, of course, a practical problem which has been avoided in the previous paragraphs: how do we discover the safety expectations of consumers, and would they be willing to pay the cost it would take to have those expectations realized? As an economic matter, companies constantly do market research. If a business can research other aspects of consumer preferences, they also can discover consumers' expectations with regard to safety. It is also possible, although perhaps more difficult, to survey the willingness of consumers to pay a proposed amount for an improvement. Fortunately or unfortunately, these market research influenced decisions tend to be cases where the majority wins. If their research had showed them that most people were not willing to pay $8 to improve the integrity of their fuel systems and survive 30-mph crashes, the company would have had a reason not to improve the car. In the Pinto case, however, my judgment is that consumers would have expected to survive low-speed crashes and would have been willing to pay the additional $8 in order to do so.

Should business people attempt to satisfy the reasonable safety expectations of consumers? I believe there are practical and ethical reasons why they should. One practical reason is that meeting customers' expectations produces satisfied customers and hopefully repeat business. Thus, meeting the reasonable safety expectations of consumers ought to increase sales and profits. Ethical reasons could also be advanced for satisfying consumers' safety expectations. A case could be made that doing this would be consistent with an act utilitarian approach to ethics since it usually maximizes net benefits to the greatest number of people. In the Pinto case, upgrading the integrity of the fuel system would have allowed the car to meet the reasonable safety expectation of the consumers: that they survive low-speed crashes. This outcome would have produced satisfied customers and repeat business for Ford, while promoting safety and therefore minimizing danger to consumers. It also would have allowed Ford to avoid many of the liability suits and much of the bad publicity. It seems that all those involved would benefit. These benefits would appear to outweigh the harm of slightly higher car prices and lost money for either Ford, the consumers, or both. Thus, it might be suggested that meeting the reasonable safety expectations of consumers is the ethical thing to do from a utilitarian viewpoint, although utilitarians would want a much more extensive analysis than I have provided.

An argument could be also advanced supporting the view that meeting the reasonable safety expectations of consumers would be in accord with a human rights approach to ethics. Doing so would respects the rights to life and well-being of the consumers by helping to protect them from death or injury. It also respects the right to liberty of customers by not deceiving them about the product they are buying since they are getting a product that meets their expectations. Unless there are human rights being violated by meeting these reasonable safety expectations, it also would be ethical to meet them on human rights grounds. While this human rights analysis is only a first approximation, it reaches the same conclusion as the utilitarian view: that if companies want to act ethically, they should attempt to satisfy the reasonable safety expectations of consumers. Proponents of the human rights approach to ethics would also want a more substantial analysis of the issue than the short discussion offered here.

COST-BENEFIT ANALYSIS AND THE PINTO CASE

For many economists and business people, a cost-benefit analysis is an attempt to identify and analyze a set of costs and benefits in order to present decision-makers with an economic justification for making a certain choice. "Costs" represent expenditures of money for the business or organization, although often these costs are only probable. "Benefits" refer to monetary gains or to the avoidance of expenditures, and once again are often only probable. The basic idea is that the analyst can identify the alternatives, distinguish the costs and benefits associated with each, translate the costs and benefits into monetary units, calculate the sums and differences, and justify the alternative that provides the largest net monetary benefit. In the Pinto case, the alternatives were either upgrading or not upgrading the integrity of the fuel system. All the costs and benefits associated with each alternative needed to be identified and translated into monetary units; for example, upgrading the fuel system for a particular model year would be a cost to Ford of approximately $2,880,000. In a strict cost-benefit analysis, if a factor cannot be translated into money, it is disregarded. The managers would have calculated the net loss or gain for each alternative, and would have picked the one that provided the largest net gain for the company. Cost-benefit analysis is a common procedure in business and government, but it has some inherent problems. First, there are difficulties connected to predicting the consequences of the action and the costs and benefits that will accrue. In analyzing the consequences of not upgrading the integrity of the Pinto fuel system, it would have been difficult for Ford to predict the number of low-speed, rear-end collisions, and the number of lawsuits that would follow. Thus, it would be difficult to predict the cost of having to settle the lawsuits. Second, there may be difficult and controversial assumptions that must be made about what will count as a cost and a benefit; for example, is it legitimate to disregard things that cannot be translated into monetary units? Third, there are problems with translating all the costs and benefits into a common monetary unit of measurement, such as, how should the person doing the analysis translate the loss of a life into an amount of money? These problems make cost-benefit analysis controversial, but no decision-making technique is flawless, and cost-benefit analysis is considered to be vital by many businesses.

In this article, I will not discuss cost-benefit analysis in general, but will focus on cost-benefit analysis that places a monetary value on human life. (For a general ethical discussion of cost-benefit analysis see the articles "Cost-Benefit Analysis: An Ethical Critique" and "Defending Cost-Benefit Analysis: Replies to Steven Kelman," which are contained in this part of the book.) As stated earlier, it has been charged that Ford's decision not to upgrade the integrity of the fuel system was based on a cost-benefit analysis that placed a monetary value on human life. There is some controversy connected to whether or not this charge was accurate. There are four main pieces of evidence that suggest Ford managers did use a cost-benefit analysis. First, there is Mark Dowie's claim that federal regulators and automobile industry experts agreed in the 1960s that cost-benefit analysis would be the basis for making auto safety decisions.[6] If this claim was accurate, then it is logical to assume that a cost-benefit analysis was the basis for Ford's decision not to upgrade the safety of the Pinto since the procedure would have been the foundation for all safety decisions. The second piece of evidence is a cost-benefit analysis submitted to the NHTSA by Ford executives in connection with an effort to lobby against legislation concerning fuel leakage during rollovers. (This document, written by E.S. Grush and C.S. Saunby is reprinted in this part of the book.) Mark Dowie and the *Chicago Tribune* believed that since Ford executives or safety engineers were willing to use cost-benefit analysis in connection with fuel leakage from rollover, they also must have used it with rear-impact fuel leakage. The point is that cost-benefit analysis was being used at Ford, and therefore it must have been employed in the Pinto case. Third, there are parts of two Ford documents that discuss delaying improvements to the fuel systems of Ford cars, including Pintos, in order to achieve cost savings. One document, reprinted in *Reckless Homicide ?: Ford's Pinto Trial* by Lee Strobel, contains the recommendation: "Defer adoption of the "flak" unit or bladder on all affected cars until 1976 to realize a design cost savings of $20.9 million compared to incorporation in 1974."[7] Another document, the "Fuel System Integrity Program Financial Review," discusses delaying the "flak suit" or rubber tank bladder and concludes: "A design cost savings $10.9 million (1974–1975) can be realized by this delay."[8] (The different numbers apparently reflect a two-year delay in the first document as opposed to a one-year delay in the second. Note also that these numbers are for all affected cars, not just Pintos.) These documents suggest that Ford executives used a cost-benefit analysis and concluded that the costs of upgrading the integrity of the fuel systems of Ford cars, including the Pinto, outweighed the benefits of doing so. Whether or not the recommendations of these documents were compelling to those at Ford responsible for the final decision is unknown. The final piece of evidence is the testimony of Harley Copp, a former Ford engineer and executive in charge of the Pinto crash-testing program. He testified that the management decision not to upgrade the integrity of the fuel system was based on the cost savings that would result from delaying the improvements.[9] Thus, while there is no direct evidence to show that Ford's decision not to upgrade the fuel system of the Pinto was based on a cost-benefit analysis, there is a good deal of indirect evidence to support the claim. My personal conclusion is that while there is no way to determine conclusively whether the Pinto decision was based on a cost-benefit analysis, cost-benefit calculations played some role in the reasoning of Ford managers.

The evidence, discussed in the previous paragraph, does not establish conclusively that Ford used cost-benefit analysis in the Pinto case. They may have done so, but they also may have used one of a couple of other reasons to justify not fixing the car. It is even more likely that there were multiple reasons behind the decision. One complete or partial explanation is that they decided not to fix the car because they were worried about bad publicity connected to a recall. They could have neglected an actual cost-benefit analysis and just decided that the bad publicity had to be avoided at any cost. Another complete or partial reason might have been that they concluded that if the law did not require them to fix the car, they were not going to do so. Ford might have based its decision on a cost-benefit analysis and/or either or both of the previous reasons. My personal view is that both of these considerations, in addition to cost-benefit calculations, played some role in making and justifying the decision. While it is not possible for me to determine what actually happened, I wish to explore what a cost-benefit analysis for the Pinto might have looked like if they had done one.

If a fuel system cost-benefit analysis had been done for the Pinto, what might it have looked like? It is possible to approximate such an analysis by using the basic form of the Grush and Saunby cost-benefit analysis and inserting values more appropriate for the Pinto. I will provide the analysis only for the alternative of upgrading the integrity of the fuel system for a particular model year, 1973. It will represent the approximate situation Ford managers would have faced. The analysis of the other alternative, not improving the fuel system, would contain all the same considerations, but on the opposite sides; i.e., benefits would be costs and vice versa. The Grush and Saunby document uses government estimates of $200,000 for a death and $67,000 for a serious burn injury. These figures presumably represent the estimated cost to society of the loss of life or a serious injury, and thus might be expected to approximate the expected settlements in civil suits where the company was held liable. The NHTSA and Ford figures mentioned in the Investigation Report disagree on the number of fatalities. We might compromise between these numbers and use five deaths and five serious injuries a year. As discussed in that introduction, these numbers are too low, but probably are reasonable approximations of the numbers Ford executives might have used at that time. The Grush and Saunby document includes burned vehicles at a ratio of about 11 for each burn death. This would suggest about 55 burned vehicles. The confidential Ford document, that recommends delaying an upgrade to the integrity of the fuel system, mentions a figure of $8 as the cost of the "flak" suit or rubber bladder required to improve the safety of the car. Finally, based on production numbers from the NHTSA Investigation Report, it might be estimated that Ford managers would anticipate selling about 360,000 Pintos in 1973 since Ford sold about 358,273 Pinto sedans in 1972. (Ford managers would not have included Pinto station wagons since these vehicles did not have the rear-end impact, fuel system problem.) Using these rough values and assuming that Ford executives or engineers were trying to decide whether it would have been cost effective to upgrade the fuel system of the Pinto for a particular model year, their results might have looked like this:

Benefits and Costs Related to Upgrading the Integrity of the Fuel System of the Pinto in Connection with Fuel Leakage Associated with Rear-Impact

---

Benefits:

Savings: 5 burn deaths, 5 burn injuries, 55 burned vehicles
Unit Cost: $200,000 per death, $67,000 per injury, $700 per vehicle
Total Benefit: $1,373,500

Costs:

Sales: 360,000
Unit Cost: $8 per car
Total Cost: $2,880,000

Results:

Net Costs: $1,506,500

Therefore, Ford could have saved about a million and a half dollars by not upgrading the integrity of the fuel system for a particular model year. If the decision was based on this purely economic criteria, it would be clear that the car should not be made safer.[10] I must emphasize that this is only an approximation of a Pinto fuel system cost-benefit analysis. It assumes that Ford does not intend to pass the cost along to the customer. Ford could have simply charged the customer an additional $8 for the car and realized an initial net benefit of $1,373,500 by saving the money spent to settle the civil suits. Of course, if the additional $8 led some people to buy another car instead of a Pinto, the company would have incurred costs through lost profits. Exactly how many sales Ford would have lost and whether these lost profits would outweigh the money saved on civil suits seems difficult to calculate, but if Ford management wanted to find the most cost-effective solution, they also should have attempted to do this cost-benefit analysis. Another solution would be for the company to split the cost of the improvement with the customer by raising the price of the car $4. This would presumably mean fewer lost sales and a cost of only about $1,440,000 to fix the car. Thus, the cost to fix the car would be only slightly higher than the cost of settling the civil suits. In order to find the most cost-effective answer, Ford management also should have done this third cost-benefit analysis.

Given this information about the Pinto case, we may proceed to ask the general question about whether it is unethical for companies to use cost-benefit analysis that places a monetary value on human life, and the more specific question about the ethical evaluation of Ford's use of such a cost-benefit analysis in the Pinto case assuming that they did do this.

THE ETHICS OF COST-BENEFIT ANALYSIS

Is it unethical for a company to use a cost-benefit analysis that places a dollar value on human life? Also, was it ethical for Ford to use this kind of analysis in the Pinto case? This kind of cost-benefit analysis raises serious ethical questions from the perspectives of both the human rights and the utilitarian ethical theories. A proponent of human rights might argue that a cost-benefit analysis that places a monetary value on human life is prima facie unethical. Human rights advocates assert that actions that violate human rights are unethical, and that the intention to act in a way that would violate human rights also would be unethical. The cost-benefit analysis seems to demonstrate a disregard for, at least, the rights to life and well-being. If Ford managers were truly willing to allow some people to die or be injured whose lives would have been saved or who would not have been injured, they were not respecting the rights to life and well-being, and prima facie were acting unethically. Unless they argued that other fundamental rights were involved, perhaps the rights to liberty or private property, and that these considerations outweighed the lack of consideration for the rights to life and well-being, it would seem impossible to justify a cost-benefit analysis that placed a monetary value on a human life from a human rights perspective. The key point would seem to be that analysts cannot simply place a monetary value on peoples' lives without considering their basic human rights, and if they do so, they have acted unethically. This would be relevant in all cases of cost-benefit analysis that placed a monetary value on human life. If Ford did the cost-benefit analysis discussed in Part III and disregarded the human rights of those involved, the company executives acted unethically according to the human rights ethical theory, although proponents of that theory would want to offer a much more detailed ethical analysis than I have presented here.

From an act utilitarian point of view, we would not be able to get a general answer to the question about cost-benefit analysis that places a monetary value on a human life. An act utilitarian evaluates each action and would want to evaluate each cost-benefit analysis separately on the consequences that would arise from doing it. If the analysis leads directly to the performing or not performing of some action, then the consequences of the action or inaction are relevant to the evaluation of the analysis. Assume that Ford performed the cost-benefit analysis included in Part III and that this analysis led directly to not upgrading the safety of the car. We would then have to compare the benefits from the action to the harms caused by it. These "harms" and "benefits" would be any harmful or beneficial consequences to any people involved in the case. They would not have to be translated into monetary units, as is done in a cost-benefit analysis, and would include harms and benefits to all people, not just costs and benefits to the company.[11] A simplified version of the ethical analysis would look like this:

Utilitarian Ethical Analysis Related to Performing
the Pinto Cost-Benefit Analysis and to Not Upgrading the Integrity
of the Fuel System of the Pinto in Connection with
Fuel Leakage Associated with Rear-Impact

Benefits:

Ford avoided recalling the car until 1978 and thus postponed the bad publicity associated with a recall until then.

Ford saved about $2,880,000 dollars in upgrade costs each year from 1971–1976 (a total of about $17,280,000).

Harms:

At least 27 people were killed in low-speed rear-end collisions involving Pintos. (I used the numbers documented by the NHTSA Investigation Report. See page 82.)

At least 24 people were seriously burned in low-speed rear-end collisions involving Pintos.

At least 38 vehicles were destroyed.

Ford spent millions of dollars to settle the civil suits. (It is impossible to say how many millions, but the average settlement was a lot higher than the numbers used in the Grush and Saunby cost-benefit analysis.)

Ford spent at least 20 million dollars to recall the 1971–1976 Pintos.

Ford's reputation was harmed temporarily by the bad publicity associated with the accidents, deaths and burn injuries, as well as by the bad publicity associated with not improving the safety of the car.

Results:

The harms associated with doing the cost-benefit analysis and not upgrading the safety of the car would outweigh the benefits. At least 27 people were killed and 24 were injured, 38 vehicles were destroyed, Ford lost millions of dollars, and its reputation was temporarily harmed. Nothing on the benefit side balances out these harms. Therefore, if a utilitarian agreed with the enumeration of the harms and benefits, he or she would conclude that it was unethical to do the cost-benefit analysis and not to upgrade the integrity of the fuel system.

The previous analysis presents only an approximation of a utilitarian ethical analysis, but does suggest how a more comprehensive one might begin. While that comprehensive utilitarian ethical analysis is beyond the scope of this paper, I believe it would ultimately reach the same conclusion: it was unethical to do the analysis and not upgrade the integrity of the fuel system since the harmful consequences of that sequence outweighed the beneficial consequences. Therefore, I conclude that arguments can be made that both the human rights and the utilitarian approaches to ethics would agree that if Ford used a cost-benefit analysis in the Pinto case, it was unethical.

Even if Ford did not use a cost-benefit analysis that placed a monetary value on human life as the basis of their decision not to upgrade the integrity of the fuel system, arguments can be made that their actions in the Pinto case were foolish and unethical. The act utilitarian analysis showed that whatever the source of the decision, it cost the company millions of dollars, a great deal of bad publicity, and caused many unnecessary deaths and injuries. The decision was a poor financial decision, as well as being unethical. The human rights analysis also demonstrated that whatever the reason for their decision, Ford managers acted unethically if they failed to consider the human rights of the drivers and passengers. For whatever reason, Ford managers seem to have decided to allow people to die or to be injured who could have been saved from harm at a small cost, and this decision was unethical and financially unwise.

I argued that the use of a cost-benefit analysis that placed a monetary value on human life was unethical if it was the source of the decision not to make the Pinto safer. If such an analysis is unethical, how should the Ford managers have made the decision about whether or not to upgrade the integrity of the fuel system? One answer is the conclusion reached in Part II: they could have tried to meet the reasonable safety expectations of their customers. This tactic would have led them to try to make the car safe in low-speed collisions and resulted in their saving lives, avoiding injuries, and saving Ford millions of dollars.

The Ford Pinto case was a significant event for the automobile industry, the National Highway Traffic Safety Administration, and for consumers. Partly because the number of deaths and injuries was exaggerated and the information about Ford's use of cost-benefit analysis was distorted, the Pinto case raised the national and the industry consciousness about safety. It may have helped bring about the passage of Standard 301 and even may have changed the attitudes of some industry executives about whether safety could be used as a selling point for automobiles. Ford managers made a foolish and unethical decision in the Pinto case, but perhaps the automobile industry and the driving public have derived some benefit from it. This benefit, however, also could have been derived from a more progressive attitude towards safety by government and the automobile industry, and without the sacrifice of the people who died or were injured in Ford Pintos.

NOTES

1. Mark Dowie, "Pinto Madness," *Mother Jones*, September–October 1977, pp. 18–32.

2. *Chicago Tribune*, October 14, 1979.

3. Ibid.

4. Lee Patrick Strobel, *Reckless Homicide?: Ford's Pinto Trial* (South Bend, Indiana: And Books, 1980) p. 278.

5. *Chicago Tribune*, October 13, 1979.

6. Mark Dowie, "Pinto Madness," p. 24.

7. Lee Strobel, p. 284.

8. *West's California Reporter*, Volume 176, p. 361.

9. Ibid.

10. While a million dollars is a large amount of money, the loss of that sum would not have damaged Ford too seriously. Ford's net income varied during the years the Pinto fuel system remained unimproved, from a high in 1974 of about $906 million to a low in 1976 of about $322 million. (Source: *Fortune Magazine*)

11. There are of course other differences between the simplified utilitarian analysis offered here and the cost-benefit analysis presented earlier. The cost-benefit analysis was a projection, this ethical analysis looks back on the decision based on the actual consequences. Also the cost-benefit analysis was for one model year, while this ethical analysis covers the period from 1971–1976. Finally, the cost-benefit analysis was for upgrading the integrity of the fuel system, while this ethical analysis is for doing a cost-benefit analysis and deciding not to upgrade the safety of the fuel system.

E. S. GRUSH AND C. S. SAUNBY

11

Fatalities Associated with Crash-Induced Fuel Leakage and Fires*

PURPOSE AND BACKGROUND

The NHTSA has issued Notice 2 of Docket 70–20 and Notice 1 of Docket 73–20, both regarding fuel system integrity. In this study, information has been developed concerning two of the issues raised in the Notices: the frequency of fire-related fatalities and the distribution and likelihood of fuel spillage by impact direction and type.

CONCLUSION

The NHTSA estimate of 2000 to 3500 fatalities yearly in fire-involved motor vehicle crashes appears to overstate the seriousness of the fire problem. Examination of in-depth accident data sources indicates that most fatalities in fire-accompanied crashes die from

* Received as a supplement to the NHTSA Investigation Report.

injuries not associated with the fire itself. Thus the National Safety Council estimate of 600 to 700 fire deaths each year is probably more appropriate than the higher NHTSA figure.

The actual number of fuel leakage incidents is relatively evenly distributed into four basic crash types: frontal, side, rear, and rollover. However, the likelihood of a given crash resulting in fuel spillage is much higher for rear impacts (26 percent with spillage in the sample studied) than for other crash types, such as frontals (3.5 percent spillage).

The cost of implementing the rollover portion of the amended Standard has been calculated to be almost three times the expected benefit, even using very favorable benefit assumptions. The yearly benefits of compliance were estimated at just under $50 million, with an associated customer cost of $137 miilion. Analysis of other portions of the proposed regulation would also be ejected to yield poor benefit-to-cost ratios.

METHOD AND RESULTS

Number of Fire Fatalities

The NHTSA states that "motor vehicle collisions accompanied by fire account for between 2000 and 3500 fatalities annually." This range is about the same as that proposed by Sliepcevich and others from the University of Oklahoma Research Institute in an NHTSA-sponsored report. The National Safety Council (NSC), on the other hand, has suggested a somewhat lesser number (600–700) of persons dying annually in motor-vehicle fires resulting from accidents.

One explanation for the large difference in these estimates may relate to what is actually being counted: *total* deaths in fire-involved motor vehicle crashes or deaths *from fire* in fire-involved crashes. It has been reported that, as crash severity increases, the chance of a resultant fire increases in turn. Thus the set of crashes which do involve fire tends to include severe accidents which are believed to be more likely to result in fatality regardless of the occurrence of fire. It may be, therefore, that many fatalities in fire-involved crashes result from the crash forces themselves, with fire being simply a concomitant and not causal variable.

The data source available to cheek this proposition was the CPIR III File of in-depth accident investigations maintained by the University of Michigan Highway Safety Research Institute. This file of 3500 crash-involved vehicles. Each crash was included in the data file due to some "special-interest" feature, typically an injury in a recent-model car; thus the file essentially consists of late-model cars and light trucks (up to 10,000 lbs. GVW) in injury-producing accidents.

From this data source were selected those occupants who were fatally injured in vehicles which sustained crash-induced fires. The 24 such occupants who were found comprise about seven percent of the total of 358 fatalities in the data sample. Extending this percentage to the nationwide total of some 40,000 occupant fatalities yields an estimate of 2800 deaths in motor vehicle accidents in which a fire took place, a number in agreement with the NHTSA and Oklahoma estimate.

The complete crash history on file for each of the 24 supposed fire fatalities was examined in detail to ascertain the actual circumstances surrounding the death, and the findings are out lined in Table 1. In over half of the instances the deceased was not burned at all, and death can be attributed only to the impact injuries. In these instances the occupant was typically ejected or extracted prior to spread of the fire. In one-fourth of the fatalities, fatal injuries were attributed to both impact and burns. These occupants most likely would have died even had there been no fire—in fact, the fire may well have burned an already-dead body. For only five of the 24 fatalities examined was fire reasonably classifiable as the clear cause of the death. Brief synopses of the crashes from which each of the 24 deaths resulted are attached in the Appendix.

TABLE 1

Fatally-Injured Occupants of Burned Vehicles

24

Death Due to Impact Injuries with No Accompanying Burns	Fatal Level Impact Injuries with Accompanying Body Burns	Death Due to Burns Only
13	6	5

The efficacy of the proposed fuel integrity regulation was examined for the five incidents in which occupants were burned to death. In three of the cases (AA-00143, ML-70003, SU-00041) a gross separation or rupture of the fuel system was reported. One of the cases (TR-01212), involving an improperly replaced gas tank was really not crash-related. The fifth fatality (AA-00155) was not fuel related at all, but involved a major post-crash passenger compartment fire. Thus, in the total data file concerning more than 5700 occupants, no burn deaths were reasonably attributable to fuel-fed fires except when accompanied by massive fuel tab or filler neck failure. Results from this rather small sample of fatalities taken from a specialized data source perhaps cannot be considered definitive, in terms of predicting exact numbers. The analysis does indicate, however, that the NSC estimate of 600 to 700 yearly motor vehicle fire fatalities is certainly within reason. In addition, the detailed evaluation shows that, while the higher NHTSA estimate of deaths in cars with fire may be correct, most of these occupants in fact sustain fatal injuries not at all related to the associated fire.

The results discussed here refer to the types of vehicles in service at the present time. In future cars, with improved ejection-prevention and injury-mitigation properties, fewer occupants may sustain impact-induced fatal injuries. This would brighten the overall fatality and injury picture, of course, but might increase occupant exposure to situations in which fire would be the only hazard. On the other hand, occupants sustaining lesser injuries might be better able to cope with and escape from fire impacts which do occur, thereby reducing the risk of serious burns. Thus the influence vehicle improvements will have on the relative risk associated with fire is not clear, and cannot be practicably quantified with the limited data available.

Fuel Spillage

An NHTSA-sponsored study conducted by Brayman at Calspan, Inc. contains data concerning fuel leakage for different impact directions. The source for these data was the Automotive Crash Injury Research (ACIR) accident file maintained by Calspan. The ACIR data concern rural, injury-producing accidents. Accident cases analyzed by Calspan between June 1968 and May 1969 were used by Brayman as the data sample for his study.

Table 2 shows some information developed from the Brayman study. It indicates that fuel leaks themselves are relatively evenly split among four basic crash types: frontal, side (mostly to rear half of car), rear and rollover. Thus no particular crash type is especially outstanding with regard to its contribution to any fuel spillage problem.

Certain crash types have a much greater likelihood of producing fuel spillage, however. Among 933 frontal impacts in the sample, 33, or 3.5 percent, resulted in fuel spillage. In contrast, over one-fourth of all rear impacts produced fuel leakage. Other crash types had

TABLE 2
Distribution and Likelihood by Impact Type of Impact-Induced
Spillage for Passenger Cars in Rural Injury-Producing Accidents

Impact Direction	Number of Fuel Leaks	Percent of Fuel Leaks	Likelihood of Fuel Leak
Front	33	25.8	33/933 = 3.5%
Side, Front Half of Car	8	6.2	8/169 = 4.7%
Side, Rear Half of Car	23	18.0	23/160 = 14.8%
Rear	37	28.9	37/140 = 26.8%
Rollover	27	21.1	27/333 = 8.1%
Total	128	100.0	128/1735 = 7.3%

SOURCE: Calspan Report No. VJ-2839-K, Dated April 1970.
Note: Accident cases in this file are significantly biased toward high severity collisions; they are all rural, and to qualify for filing, an injury had to occur. But injuries are not nearly so frequent in rear-end crashes, in general. As a result, the proportion of fuel leaks in rear-end crashes reported here, 29%, cannot be the nationwide average. Rather, in 29% of rural rear-end collisions sufficiently severity to cause an injury, fuel leaks occur.

intermediate likelihoods of leaking fuel. Thus it is clear that different crash types have widely varying propensities for resulting in fuel leaks.

It is noteworthy that, while seven percent of the cars in the Brayman sample developed fuel leaks, fires (both fuel-fed and otherwise) were reported for .5 percent of the cars in this ACIR data file. Thus it appears as though less than seven percent of cars which develop fuel leaks subsequently burn.

COST/BENEFIT ANALYSIS OF STATIC ROLLOVER REQUIREMENT

The analysis discussed below concerns the static rollover requirement proposed for FMVSS 301. This discussion represents an attempt to outline an approach which can be used to address this and similar problems. While the benefit analysis is not meant to be definitive and beyond criticism, it is based on assumptions and derivations believed to be quite representative of an *upper bound* on the possible benefits accruing from compliance with the requirement.

Table 3 outlines the pertinent benefit and cost. The relevant benefits are those associated with the consequences of reduction in the frequency of fires in rollovers, while the presented costs relate to the incremental cost associated with meeting the specific static rollover aspects of the Standard.

Benefits

The appropriateness of the estimate of 700 burn deaths each year resulting from motor vehicle crashes has been discussed in the main text of this study. Data from both the Calspan fire study and the Oklahoma analysis of a New York State fire study suggest that when occupants are burned, the injuries tend to be quite serious, and about half of the casualties sustain fatal injuries. Thus the 700 fatalities should be complemented by another 700 non-fatally (though seriously) injured occupants. Given the NSC estimate of 10,000 yearly crash induced vehicle fires, about 8,500 of these fire crashes occur with no resultant occupant burns each year. Benefits from FMVSS 301 compliance based on these numbers represent an overestimate, since some undetermined number of these instances relate to large trucks not covered by the proposed Standard.

The proportion of fuel leaks which occur in rollovers is indicated in Table 2 to be slightly less than one-fourth.* If this proportion is applied to the fire numbers themselves, the consequences of fire rollovers can be estimated as 180 deaths, 180 non-fatal injuries, and 2100 other fire crashes. These values are predicated upon two postulations: rollover fuel leaks result in fire just as often as other fuel leaks, and rollover fires are just as likely to result in burns as other fires.

This analysis assumes that *all* these fires and the resultant casualties can be eliminated entirely through compliance with the rollover requirement. In addition, it is assumed that vehicle modifications designed to ensure compliance with non-rollover portions of the Standard will not reduce at all the number of rollover fires. The extent to which either of these assumptions is not completely accurate represents a measure of the extent to which benefits derived here are overestimates of the true values.

---

* That is, the 21.1% associated with rollovers from Table 2. In this and subsequent calculations, figures have been rounded upward. In that way, not only are the statistical assumptions in a conservative direction, but also the arithmetic.

TABLE 3
Benefits and Costs Relating to Fuel Leakage Associated with the
Static Rollover Test Portion of FMVSS 208

Benefits:

Savings — 180 burn deaths, 180 serious burn injuries, 2100 burned vehicles.
Unit Cost: — $200,000 per death, $67,000 per injury, $700 per vehicle.
Total — 180×($200,000) + 180×($67,000) + 2100×($700) = *$49.5 million.*
Benefit

Costs:

Sales — 11 million cars, 1.5 million light trucks.
Unit Cost — $11 per car, $11 per truck.
Total Cost — 11,000,000×($11) + 1,500,000×($11) = *$137 million.*

To compare the benefits of eliminating the consequences of these rollover fires with the requisite costs, the benefits and costs must be expressed in terms of some common measure. The measure typically chosen is dollars; this requires, then, converting the casualty losses to this metric. The casualty to dollars conversion factors used in this study were the societal cost values prepared by the NHTSA. These values are generally higher than similarly-defined costs from other sources, and their use does not signify that Ford accepts or concurs in the values. Rather, the NHTSA figures are used only to be consistent with the attempt not to understate the relevant benefits.

The NHTSA has calculated a value of $200,000 for each fatality. While the major portion of this amount relates to lost future wages, the total also includes some consideration for property damage. The NHTSA average loss for all injuries was about $7,000. Burn injuries which do occur tend to be quite serious, however, as discussed above. Thus a higher value of $67,000, which is the NHTSA estimate of partial disability injuries, was used for each of the 180 non-fatal burn injuries. The $700 property damage per vehicle is the NHTSA estimate of vehicle property damage costs in non-disabling injury crashes.

Costs

The Retail Price Equivalent (the customer sticker price with no provision for Ford profit) of vehicle modifications necessary to assure compliance with the static rollover portion of the proposed Standard has been determined by Ford to be an average of $11 per passenger car and $11 per light truck. While these are Ford costs, they have been applied across the industry in this analysis. Total yearly sales estimates of 11 million passenger cars and 1.5 million light trucks (under 6,000 lbs GVW) were used in conjunction with the rollover requirement cost effective.

Benefit and Cost Comparison

The total benefit is shown in Table 3 to be just under $50 million, while the associated cost is $137 million. Thus the cost is almost three times the benefits, even using a number of highly favorable benefit assumptions. As better estimates of the parameters used in the benefit analysis become available, they would be inserted into the general analysis framework. It does not appear likely, however, that such alternate estimates could lead to the substantial benefit estimate increase which would be required to make compliance with the roll over requirement cost effective.

Benefits and Costs For Other Impact Modes

The analysis discussed above concerns only rollover consequences and costs. Similar analysis for other impact modes would be expected to yield comparable results, with the implementation costs far outweighing the expected benefits.

E. S. Grush
Impact Factors

C. S. Saunby
Impact Factors

Concurred By:

J. D. Hromi
Principal Staff Engineer

R. B. MacLean

REFERENCES

Sliepcevich, C. M., et al, *Escape Worthiness of Vehicles and Occupant Survival*, University of Oklahoma Research Institute, NHTSA Contract No. FH-11-7303, PB 198 772, December 1970.

National Safety Council, *Accident Facts*, 1968 Edition.

Robinson, S. J., *Observation On Fire In Automobile Accidents*, CAL Report No. VJ-1823-R14, February 1965.

Brayman, A. F., *Impact Intrusion Characteristics of Fuel Systems*, CAL Report No. VJ-2839-K, NHTSA Contract No. FH-11-7309, April 1970.

Moore, J. O., and Negri, D. B., *Fire In Automobile Accidents*, New York State Department of Motor Vehicles, Research Report 1969–2, October 1969.

National Highway Traffic Safety Administration, *Societal Costs of Motor Vehicle Accidents*, Preliminary Report, April 1972.

Part III

WHISTLE BLOWING

Introduction: Whistle Blowing

While Part II focused on management decision making and cost-benefit analysis, this section is centered on the engineers who worked on the Ford Pinto. At least some of the engineers at Ford were concerned about the safety of the Pinto. In 1971, a report was written by a Ford engineer listing several options for upgrading the integrity of the fuel system: an over-the-axle tank, a repositioned spare tire, installation of body rails, a redesigned filler pipe, or an inner-tank rubber bladder. The rubber fuel tank bladder was seriously considered, at least by the engineers. Ford engineers also tested a gas tank "flak suit" and a plastic shield as ways to improve the integrity of the fuel system. If there were engineers who were convinced that the Pinto was an unsafe car and if they could not get Ford management to pay attention to their concerns about the fuel system, they might have considered blowing the whistle on Ford Motor Company.

Whistle blowers attempt to disclose wrongdoing within or by an organization to the public, government, media or members of their organization other than their immediate, superiors. The purpose of their disclosure is to prevent the wrongdoing from continuing. Whistle blowing may be internal, with the information being provided to an ombudsman or some corporate official other than one's superior, or external, with the facts being supplied to the media, a government official, or another outside party. It may also be open, where the whistle blower makes no attempt to conceal his or her identity, or anonymous, where he or she tries to keep anyone from knowing who provided the material.[1] Whistle blowing is a serious endeavor since whistle blowers often experience some kind of retaliation by their employers. Whistle blowers have been fired, demoted, involuntarily transferred to less desirable positions, ostracized, or have suffered job discrimination. The stakes in whistle blowing are high; when deciding whether or not to take action, the safety of consumers or other employees must often be weighed against the harm that will be done to the potential whistle blow   er.

Part III begins with Richard De George's important article "Ethical Responsibilities of Engineers in Large Organizations: The Pinto Case," which discusses when it is ethically permissible and ethically obligatory for engineers to blow the whistle. De George uses the Pinto case to illustrate his views. His article represents arguably the best example of an analysis of whistle blowing in terms of specific criteria to establish an ethical framework for this action. Hart T. Mankin's commentary on De George's article criticizes this view of whistle blowing. He claims that De George creates a situation which is too easy on engineers. Douglas Birsch's article "Whistle Blowing, Ethical Obligation, and the Pinto Case" argues that De George's position overprotects companies and does not make adequate moral demands on employees. Birsch presents an alternative view which, contrary to De George's stance, holds that the Pinto engineers were obligated to blow the whistle.

NOTES

1. These distinctions are made by Gene James in his article "Whistle Blowing: Its Moral Justification." See Gene James, "Whistle Blowing: Its Moral Justification," W. Michael Hoffman & Jennifer Moore, *Business Ethics*, (New York: McGraw Hill, 1984) pp. 332–33.

RICHARD T. DE GEORGE

12

Ethical Responsibilities of Engineers in Large Organizations: The Pinto Case*

The myth that ethics has no place in engineering has been attacked, and at least in some corners of the engineering profession has been put to rest.[1] Another myth, however, is emerging to take its place—the myth of the engineer as moral hero. A litany of engineering saints is slowly taking form. The saints of the field are whistle blowers, especially those who have sacrificed all for their moral convictions. The zeal of some preachers, however, has gone too far, piling moral responsibility upon moral responsibility on the shoulders of the engineer. This emphasis, I believe, is misplaced. Though engineers are members of a profession that holds public safety paramount,[2] we cannot reasonably expect engineers to be willing to sacrifice their jobs each day for principle and to have a whistle ever by their sides ready to blow if their firm strays from what they perceive to be the morally

---

right course of action. If this is too much to ask, however, what then is the actual ethical responsibility of engineers in a large organization?

I shall approach this question through a discussion of what has become known as the Pinto case, i.e., the trial that took place in Winamac, Indiana, and that was decided by a jury on March 16, 1980.

In August 1978 near Goshen, Indiana, three girls died of burns in a 1973 Pinto that was rammed in traffic by a van. The rear-end collapsed "like an accordian,"[3] and the gas tank erupted in flames. It was not the first such accident with the Pinto. The Pinto was introduced in 1971 and its gas tank housing was not changed until the 1977 model. Between 1971 and 1978 about fifty suits were brought against Ford in connection with rear-end accidents in the Pinto.

What made the Winamac case different from the fifty others was the fact that the State prosecutor charged Ford with three (originally four, but one was dropped) counts of reckless homicide, a *criminal* offense, under a 1977 Indiana law that made it possible to bring such criminal charges against a corporation. The penalty if found guilty, was a maximum fine of $10,000 for each count, for a total of $30,000. The case was closely watched, since it was the first time in recent history that a corporation was charged with this criminal offense. Ford spent almost a million dollars in its defense.

With the advantage of hindsight I believe the case raised the right issue at the wrong time.

The prosecution had to show that Ford was reckless in placing the gas tank where and how it did. In order to show this the prosecution had to prove that Ford consciously disregarded harm it might cause and the disregard, according to the statutory definition of "reckless," had to involve "substantial deviation from acceptable standards of conduct."[4]

The prosecution produced seven witnesses who testified that the Pinto was moving at speeds judged to be between 15 and 35 mph when it was hit. Harly Copp, once a high ranking Ford engineer, claimed that the Pinto did not have a balanced design and that for cost reasons the gas tank could withstand only a 20 mph impact without leaking and exploding. The prosecutor, Michael Cosentino, tried to introduce evidence that Ford knew the defects of the gas tank, that its executives knew that a $6.65 part would have made the car considerably safer, and that they decided against the change in order to increase their profits.

Federal safety standards for gas tanks were not introduced until 1977. Once introduced, the National Highway Traffic Safety

Administration (NHTSA) claimed a safety defect existed in the gas tanks of Pintos produced from 1971 to 1976. It ordered that Ford recall 1.9 million Pintos. Ford contested the order. Then, without ever admitting that the fuel tank was unsafe, it "voluntarily" ordered a recall. It claimed the recall was not for safety but for "reputational" reasons.[5] Agreeing to a recall in June, its first proposed modifications failed the safety standards tests, and it added a second protective shield to meet safety standards. It did not send out recall notices until August 22. The accident in question took place on August 10. The prosecutor claimed that Ford knew its fuel tank was dangerous as early as 1971 and that it did not make any changes until the 1977 model. It also knew in June of 1978 that its fuel tank did not meet federal safety standards; yet it did nothing to warn owners of this fact. Hence, the prosecution contended, Ford was guilty of reckless homicide.

The defense was led by James F. Neal who had achieved national prominence in the Watergate hearings. He produced testimony from two witnesses who were crucial to the case. They were hospital attendants who had spoken with the driver of the Pinto at the hospital before she died. They claimed she had stated that she had just had her car filled with gas. She had been in a hurry and had left the gas station without replacing the cap on her gas tank. It fell off the top of her car as she drove down the highway. She noticed this and stopped to turn around to pick it up. While stopped, her car was hit by the van. The testimony indicated that the car was stopped. If the car was hit by a van going 50 mph, then the rupture of the gas tank was to be expected. If the cap was off the fuel tank, leakage would be more than otherwise. No small vehicle was made to withstand such impact. Hence, Ford claimed, there was no recklessness involved. Neal went on to produce films of tests that indicated that the amount of damage the Pinto suffered meant that the impact must have been caused by the van's going at least 50 mph. He further argued that the Pinto gas tank was at least as safe as the gas tanks on the 1973 American Motors Gremlin, the Chevrolet Vega, the Dodge Colt, and the Toyota Corolla, all of which suffered comparable damage when hit from the rear at 50 mph. Since no federal safety standards were in effect in 1973, Ford was not reckless if its safety standards were comparable to those of similar cars made by competitors; that standard represented the state of the art at that time, and it would be inappropriate to apply 1977 standards to a 1973 car.[6]

The jury deliberated for four days and finally came up with a verdict of not guilty. When the verdict was announced at a meeting of the Ford Board of Directors then taking place, the members broke out in a cheer.[7]

These are the facts of the case. I do not wish to second-guess the jury. Based on my reading of the case, I think they arrived at a proper decision, given the evidence. Nor do I wish to comment adversely on the judge's ruling that prevented the prosecution from introducing about 40% of his case because the evidence referred to 1971 and 1972 models of the Pinto and not the 1973 model.[8]

The issue of Ford's being guilty of acting recklessly can, I think, be made plausible, as I shall indicate shortly. But the successful strategy argued by the defense in this case hinged on the Pinto in question being hit by a van at 50 mph. At that speed, the defense successfully argued, the gas tank of any subcompact would rupture. Hence that accident did not show that the Pinto was less safe than other subcompacts or that Ford acted recklessly. To show that would require an accident that took place at no more than 20 mph.

The contents of the Ford documents that Prosecutor Cosentino was not allowed to present in court were published in the *Chicago Tribune* on October 13, 1979. If they are accurate, they tend to show grounds for the charge of recklessness.

Ford had produced a safe gas tank mounted over the rear axle in its 1969 Capri in Europe. It tested that tank in the Capri. In its over-the-axle position, it withstood impacts of up to 30 mph. Mounted behind the axle, it was punctured by projecting bolts when hit from the rear at 20 mph. A $6.65 part would help make the tank safer. In its 1971 Pinto, Ford chose to place the gas tank behind the rear axle without the extra part. A Ford memo indicates that in this position the Pinto has more trunk space, and that production costs would be less than in the over-the-axle position. These considerations won out.[9]

The Pinto was first tested it seems in 1971, after the 1971 model was produced, for rear-end crash tolerance. It was found that the tank ruptured when hit from the rear at 20 mph. This should have been no surprise, since the Capri tank in that position had ruptured at 20 mph. A memo recommends that rather than making any changes Ford should wait until 1976 when the government was expected to introduce fuel tank standards. By delaying making any change, Ford could save $20.9 million, since the change would average about $10 per car.[10]

In the Winamac case Ford claimed correctly that there were no federal safety standards in 1973. But it defended itself against recklessness by claiming its car was comparable to other subcompacts at that time. All the defense showed, however, was that all the subcompacts were unsafe when hit at 50 mph. Since the other subcompacts were not forced to recall their cars in 1978, there is *prima facie* evidence that Ford's Pinto gas tank mounting was substandard. The Ford documents tend to show Ford knew the danger it was inflicting on Ford owners; yet it did nothing, for profit reasons. How short-sighted those reasons were is demonstrated by the fact that the Pinto thus far in litigation and recalls alone has cost Ford $50 million. Some forty suits are still to be settled. And these figures do not take into account the loss of sales due to bad publicity.

Given these facts, what are we to say about the Ford engineers? Where were they when all this was going on, and what is their responsibility for the Pinto? The answer, I suggest, is that they were where they were supposed to be, doing what they were supposed to be doing. They were performing tests, designing the Pinto, making reports. But do they have no moral responsibility for the products they design? What after all is the moral responsibility of engineers in a large corporation? By way of reply, let me emphasize that no engineer can morally do what is immoral. If commanded to do what he should not morally do, he must resist and refuse. But in the Ford Pinto situation no engineer was told to produce a gas tank that would explode and kill people. The engineers were not instructed to make an unsafe car. They were morally responsible for knowing the state of the art, including that connected with placing and mounting gas tanks. We can assume that the Ford engineers were cognizant of the state of the art in producing the model they did. When tests were made in 1970 and 1971, and a memo was written stating that a $6.65 modification could make the gas tank safer,[11] that was an engineering assessment. Whichever engineer proposed the modifcation and initiated the memo acted ethically in doing so. The next step, the administrative decision not to make the modification was, with hindsight, a poor one in almost every way. It ended up costing Ford a great deal more not to put in the part than it would have cost to put it in. Ford still claims today that its gas tank was as safe as the accepted standards of the industry at that time.[12] It must say so, otherwise the suits pending against it will skyrocket. That it was not as safe seems borne out by the fact that only the Pinto of all the subcompacts failed to pass the 30 mph rear impact NHTSA test.

But the question of wrongdoing or of malicious intent or of recklessness is not so easily solved. Suppose the ordinary person were told when buying a Pinto that if he paid an extra $6.65 he could increase the safety of the vehicle so that it could withstand a 30 mph rear-end impact rather than a 20 mph impact, and that the odds of suffering a rear-end impact of between 20 and 30 mph was 1 in 250,000. Would we call him or her reckless if he or she declined to pay the extra $6.65? I am not sure how to answer that question. Was it reckless of Ford to wish to save the $6.65 per car and increase the risk for the consumer? Here I am inclined to be clearer in my own mind. If I choose to take a risk to save $6.65, it is my risk and my $6.65. But if Ford saves the $6.65 and I take the risk, then I clearly lose. Does Ford have the right to do that without informing me, if the going standard of safety of subcompacts is safety in a rear-end collision up to 30 mph? I think not. I admit, however, that the case is not clear-cut, even if we add that during 1976 and 1977 Pintos suffered 13 firey fatal rear-end collisions, more than double that of other U.S. comparable cars. The VW Rabbit and Toyota Corolla suffered none.[13]

Yet, if we are to morally fault anyone for the decision not to add the part, we would censure not the Ford engineers but the Ford executives, because it was not an engineering but an executive decision.

My reason for taking this view is that an engineer cannot be expected and cannot have the responsibility to second-guess managerial decisions. He is responsible for bringing the facts to the attention of those who need them to make decisions. But the input of engineers is only one of many factors that go to make up managerial decisions. During the trial, the defense called as a witness Francis Olsen, the assistant chief engineer in charge of design at Ford, who testified that he bought a 1973 Pinto for his eighteen-year-old daughter, kept it a year, and then traded it in for a 1974 Pinto which he kept two years.[14] His testimony and his actions were presented as an indication that the Ford engineers had confidence in the Pinto's safety. At least this one had enough confidence in it to give it to his daughter. Some engineers at Ford may have felt that the car could have been safer. But this is true of almost every automobile. Engineers in large firms have an ethical responsibility to do their jobs as best they can, to report their observations about safety and improvement of safety to management. But they do not have the obligation to insist that their perceptions or their standards be accepted. They are not paid to do that, they are not expected to do that, and they have no moral or ethical obligation to do that.

In addition to doing their jobs, engineers can plausibly be said to have an obligation of loyalty to their employers, and firms have a right to a certain amount of confidentiality concerning their internal operations. At the same time engineers are required by their professional ethical codes to hold the safety of the public paramount.

Where these obligations conflict, the need for and justification of whistle blowing arises.[15] If we admit the obligations on both sides, I would suggest as a rule of thumb that engineers and other workers in a large corporation are morally *permitted* to go public with information about the safety of a product if the following conditions are met:

1. if the harm that will be done by the product to the public is serious and considerable;
2. if they make their concerns known to their superiors; and
3. if, getting no satisfaction from their immediate superiors, they exhaust the channels available within the corporation, including going to the board of directors.

If they still get no action, I believe they are morally *permitted* to make public their views; but they are not morally *obliged* to do so. Harly Copp, a former Ford executive and engineer, in fact did criticize the Pinto from the start and testified for the prosecution against Ford at the Winamac trial.[16] He left the company and voiced his criticism. The criticism was taken up by Ralph Nader and others. In the long run it led to the Winamac trial and probably helped in a number of other suits filed against Ford. Though I admire Mr. Copp for his actions, assuming they were done from moral motives, I do not think such action was morally required, nor do I think the other engineers at Ford were morally deficient in not doing likewise.

For an engineer to have a moral *obligation* to bring his case for safety to the public, I think two other conditions have to be fulfilled, in addition to the three mentioned above.[17]

4. He must have documented evidence that would convince a reasonable, impartial observer that his view of the situation is correct and the company policy wrong.

Such evidence is obviously very difficult to obtain and produce. Such evidence, however, takes an engineer's concern out of the realm of the subjective and precludes that concern from being simply one person's opinion based on a limited point of view. Unless such evidence is available, there is little likelihood that the concerned engineer's view will win the day simply by public exposure. If the testimony of Francis Olsen is accurate, then even among the engineers at Ford there was disagreement about the safety of the Pinto.

5. There must be strong evidence that making the information public will in fact prevent the threatened serious harm.

This means both that before going public the engineer should know what source (government, newspaper, columnist, TV reporter) will make use of his evidence and how it will be handled. He should also have good reason to believe that it will result in the kind of change or result that he believes is morally appropriate. None of this was the case in the Pinto situation. After much public discussion, five model years, and failure to pass national safety standards tests, Ford plausibly defends its original claim that the gas tank was acceptably safe. If there is little likelihood of his success, there is no moral obligation for the engineer to go public. For the harm he or she personally incurs is not offset by the good such action achieves.[18]

My first substantive conclusion is that Ford engineers had no moral *obligation* to do more than they did in this case.

My second claim is that though engineers in large organizations should have a say in setting safety standards and producing cost-benefit analyses, they need not have the last word. My reasons are two. First, while the degree of risk, e.g., in a car, is an engineering problem, the acceptability of risk is not. Second, an engineering cost-benefit analysis does not include all the factors appropriate in making a policy decision, either on the corporate or the social level. Safety is one factor in an engineering design. Yet clearly it is only one factor. A Mercedes-Benz 280 is presumably safer than a Ford Pinto. But the difference in price is considerable. To make a Pinto as safe as a Mercedes it would probably have to cost a comparable amount. In making cars as in making many other objects some balance has to be reached between safety and cost. The final decision on where to draw the balance is not only an engineering decision. It is also a managerial decision, and probably even more appropriately a social decision.

The difficulty of setting standards raises two pertinent issues. The first concerns federal safety standards. The second concerns cost-benefit analyses. The state of engineering technology determines a floor below which no manufacturer should ethically go. Whether the Pinto fell below that floor, we have already seen, is a controverted question. If the cost of achieving greater safety is considerable—and I do not think $6.65 is considerable—there is a built-in temptation for a producer to skimp more than he should and more than he might like. The best way to remove that temptation is for there to be a national set of standards. Engineers can determine what the state of the art is, what is possible, and what the cost of producing safety is. A panel of informed people, not necessarily engineers, should decide what is acceptable risk and hence what acceptable minimum standards are. Both the minimum standards and the standards attained by a given car should be a matter of record that goes with each car. A safer car may well cost more. But unless a customer knows how much safety he is buying for his money, he may not know which car he wants to buy. This information, I believe, is information a car buyer is entitled to have.

In 1978, after the publicity that Ford received with the Pinto and the controversy surrounding it, the sales of Pintos fell dramatically. This was an indication that consumers preferred a safer car for comparable money, and they went to the competition. The state of Oregon took all its Pintos out of its fleet and sold them off. To the surprise of one dealer involved in selling turned-in Pintos, they went for between $1000 and $1800.[19] The conclusion we correctly draw is that there was a market for a car with a dubious safety record even though the price was much lower than for safer cars and lower than Ford's manufacturing price.

The second issue is the way cost-benefit analyses are produced and used. I have already mentioned one cost-benefit analysis used by Ford, namely the projection that by not adding a part and by placing the gas tank in the rear the company could save $20.9 million. The projection, I noted, was grossly mistaken for it did not consider litigation, recalls, and bad publicity which have already cost Ford over $50 million. A second type of cost-benefit analysis sometimes estimates the number and costs of suits that will have to be paid, adds to it fines, and deducts that total amount from the total saved by a particular practice. If the figure is positive, it is more profitable not to make a safety change than to make it.

A third type of cost-benefit analysis, which Ford and other auto companies produce, estimates the cost and benefits of specific changes in their automobiles. One study, for instance, deals with the cost-benefit analysis relating to fuel leakage associated with static rollover. The unit cost of the part is $11. If that is included in 12.5 million cars, the total cost is $137 million. That part will prevent 180 burn deaths, 180 serious burn injuries and 2100 burned vehicles. Assigning a cost of $200,000 per death, $67,000 per major injury, and $700 per vehicle, the benefit is $49.5 million. The cost-benefit ratio is slightly over 3-1.[20]

If this analysis is compared with a similar cost-benefit analysis for a rear-end collision, it is possible to see how much safety is achieved per dollar spent. This use is legitimate and helpful. But the procedure is open to very serious criticism if used not in a comparative but in an absolute manner.

The analysis ignores many factors, such as the human suffering of the victim and of his or her family. It equates human life to $200,000, which is based on average lost future wages. Any figure here is questionable, except for comparative purposes, in which case as long as the same figure is used it does not change the information as to relative benefit per dollar. The ratio, however, has no *absolute* meaning, and no decision can properly be based on the fact that the resulting ratio of cost to benefit in the above example is 3 to 1. Even more important, how can this figure or ratio be compared with the cost of styling? Should the $11 per unit to reduce death and injury from roll-over be weighed against a comparable $11 in rear-end collision or $11 in changed styling? Who decides how much more to put into safety and how much more to put into styling? What is the rationale for the decision?

In the past consumers have not been given an opportunity to vote on the matter. The automobile industry has decided what will sell and what will not, and has decided how much to put on safety. American car dealers have not typically put much emphasis on safety features in selling their cars. The assumption that American drivers are more interested in styling than safety is a decision that has been made for them, not by them. Engineers can and do play an important role in making cost-benefit analyses. They are better equipped than anyone else to figure risks and cost. But they are not better equipped to figure the acceptability of risk, or the amount that people should be willing to pay to eliminate such risk. Neither, however, are the managers of automobile corporations. The amount of acceptable risk is a public decision that can and should be made by representatives of the public or by the public itself.

Since cost-benefit analyses of the types I have mentioned are typical of those used in the auto industry, and since they are inadequate ways of judging the safety a car should have, given the state of the art, it is clear that the automobile companies should not have the last word or the exclusive word in how much safety to provide. There must be national standards set and enforced. The National Highway Traffic Administration was established in 1966 to set standards. Thus far only two major standards have been established and implemented: the 1972 side impact standard and the 1977 gasoline tank safety standard. Rather than dictate standards, however in which process it is subject to lobbying, it can mandate minimum standards and also require auto manufacturers to inform the public about the safety quotient of each car, just as it now requires each car to specify the miles per gallon it is capable of achieving. Such an approach would put the onus for basic safety on the manufacturers, but it would also make additional safety a feature of consumer interest and competition.

Engineers in large corporations have an important role to play. That role, however, is not usually to set policy or to decide on the acceptability of risk. Their knowledge and expertise are important both to the companies for which they work and to the public. But they are not morally responsible for policies and decisions beyond their competence and control. Does this view, however, let engineers off the moral hook too easily?

To return briefly to the Pinto story once more, Ford wanted a subcompact to fend off the competition of Japanese imports. The order came down to produce a car of 2,000 pounds or less that would cost $2,000 or less in time for the 1971 model. This allowed only 25 months instead of the usual 43 months for design and production of a new car.[21] The engineers were squeezed from the start. Perhaps this is why they did not test the gas tank for rear-end collision impact until the car was produced.

Should the engineers have refused the order to produce the car in 25 months? Should they have resigned, or leaked the story to the newspapers? Should they have refused to speed up their usual routine? Should they have complained to their professional society that they were being asked to do the impossible—if it were to be done right? I am not in a position to say what they should have done. But with the advantage of hindsight, I suggest we should ask not only what they should have done. We should especially ask what changes can be made to prevent engineers from being squeezed in this way in the future.

Engineering ethics should not take as its goal the producing of moral heroes. Rather it should consider what forces operate to encourage engineers to act as they feel they should not; what structural or other features of a large corporation squeeze them until their consciences hurt? Those features should then be examined, evaluated, and changes proposed and made. Lobbying by engineering organizations would be appropriate, and legislation should be passed if necessary. In general I tend to favor voluntary means where possible. But where that is utopian, then legislation is a necessary alternative.

The need for whistle blowing in a firm indicates that a change is necessary. How can we preclude the necessity for blowing the whistle?

The Winamac Pinto case suggests some external and internal modifications. It was the first case to be tried under a 1977 Indiana law making it possible to try corporations as well as individuals for the criminal offenses of reckless homicide. In bringing the charges against Ford, Prosecutor Michael Cosentino acted courageously, even if it turned out to have been a poor case for such a precedent-setting trial. But the law concerning reckless homicide, for instance, which was the charge in question, had not been rewritten with the corporation in mind. The penalty, since corporations cannot go to jail, was the maximum fine of $10,000 per count—hardly a significant amount when contrasted with the 1977 income of Ford International which was $11.1 billion in revenues and $750 million in profits. What Mr. Cosentino did *not* do was file charges against individuals in the Ford Company who were responsible for the decisions he claimed were reckless. Had highly placed officials been charged, the message would have gotten through to management across the country that individuals cannot hide behind corporate shields in their decisions if they are indeed reckless, put too low a price on life and human suffering, and sacrifice it too cheaply for profits.

A bill was recently proposed in Congress requiring managers to disclose the existence of life-threatening defects to the appropriate Federal agency.[22] Failure to do so and attempts to conceal defects could result in fines of $50,000 or imprisonment for a minimum of two years, or both. The fine in corporate terms is negligible. But imprisonment for members of management is not.

Some argue that increased litigation for product liability is the way to get results in safety. Heavy damages yield quicker changes than criminal proceedings. Ford agreed to the Pinto recall shortly after a California jury awarded damages of $127.8 million after a youth was burned over 95% of his body. Later the sum was reduced, on appeal, to $6.3 million.[23] But criminal proceedings make the litigation easier, which is why Ford spent $1,000,000 in its defense to avoid paying $30,000 in fines.[24] The possibility of going to jail for one's actions, however, should have a salutary effect. If someone, the president of a company in default of anyone else, were to be charged in criminal suit, presidents would soon know whom they can and should hold responsible below them. One of the difficulties in a large corporation is knowing who is responsible for particular decisions. If the president were held responsible, outside pressure would build to reorganize the corporation so that responsibility was assigned and assumed.

If a corporation wishes to be moral or if society or engineers wish to apply pressure for organizational changes such that the corporation acts morally and responds to the moral conscience of engineers and others within the organization, then changes must be made. Unless those at the top set a moral tone, unless they insist on moral conduct, unless they punish immoral conduct and reward moral conduct, the corporation will function without considering the morality of questions and of corporate actions. It may by accident rather than by intent avoid immoral actions, though in the long run this is unlikely.

Ford's management was interested only in meeting federal standards and having these as low as possible. Individual federal standards should be both developed and enforced. Federal fines for violations should not be token but comparable to damages paid in civil suits and should be paid to all those suffering from violations.[25]

Independent engineers or engineering societies—if the latter are not co-opted by auto manufacturers—can play a significant role in supplying information on the state of the art and the level of technical feasibility available. They can also develop the safety index I suggested earlier, which would represent the relative and comparative safety of an automobile. Competition has worked successfully in many areas. Why not in the area of safety? Engineers who work for auto manufacturers will then have to make and report the results of standard tests such as the ability to withstand rear-end impact. If such information is required data for a safety index to be affixed to the windshield of each new car, engineers will not be squeezed by management in the area of safety.

The means by which engineers with ethical concerns can get a fair hearing without endangering their jobs or blowing the whistle must be made part of a corporation's organizational structure. An outside board member with primary responsibility for investigating and responding to such ethical concerns might be legally required. When this is joined with the legislation pending in Congress which I mentioned, the dynamics for ethics in the organization will be significantly improved. Another way of achieving a similar end is by providing an inspector general for all corporations with an annual net income of over $1 billion. An independent committee of an engineering association might be formed to investigate charges made by engineers concerning the safety of a product on which they are working;[26] a company that did not allow an appropriate investigation of employee charges would become subject to cover-up proceedings. Those in the engineering industry can suggest and work to implement other ideas. I have elsewhere outlined a set of ten such changes for the ethical corporation.[27]

In addition to asking how an engineer should respond to moral quandaries and dilemmas, and rather than asking how to educate or train engineers to be moral heroes, those in engineering ethics should ask how large organizations can be changed so that they do not squeeze engineers in moral dilemmas, place them in the position of facing moral quandaries, and make them feel that they must blow the whistle.

The time has come to go beyond sensitizing students to moral issues and solving and resolving the old, standard cases. The next and very important questions to be asked as we discuss each case is how organizational structures can be changed so that no engineer will ever again have to face *that* case.

Many of the issues of engineering ethics within a corporate setting concern the ethics of organizational structure, questions of public policy, and so questions that frequently are amenable to solution only on a scale larger than the individual—on the scale of organization and law. The ethical responsibilities of the engineer in a large organization have as much to do with the organization as with the engineer. They can be most fruitfully approached by considering from a moral point of view not only the individual engineer but the framework within which he or she works. We not only need moral people. Even more importantly we need moral structures and organizations. Only by paying more attention to these can we adequately resolve the questions of the ethical responsibility of engineers in large organizations.

NOTES

1. The body of literature on engineering ethics is now substantive and impressive. See, *A Selected Annotated Bibliography of Professional Ethics and Social Responsibility in Engineering*, compiled by Robert F. Ladenson, James Choromokos, Ernest d'Anjou, Martin Pimsler, and Howard Rosen (Chicago: Center for the Study of Ethics in the Professions, Illinois Institute of Technology, 1980). A useful two-volume collection of readings and cases is also available: Robert J. Baum and Albert Flores, *Ethical Problems in Engineering*, 2nd edition (Troy, N.Y.: Rensselaer Polytechnic Institute Center for the Study of the Human Dimensions of Science and Technology, 1980. See also Robert J. Baum's *Ethics and Engineering Curricula* (Hastings-on-Hudson, N.Y.: Hastings Center, 1980).

2. See, for example, the first canon of the 1974 Engineers Council for Professional Development Code, and the draft (by A. Oldenquist and E. Slowter) of a "Code of Ethics for the Engineering Profession" (all reprinted in Baum and Flores, *Ethical Problems in Engineering.*

3. Details of the incident presented in this paper are based on testimony at the trial. Accounts of the trial as well as background reports were carried by both the *New York Times* and the *Chicago Tribune.*

4. *New York Times*, February 17, 1980, IV, p. 9.

5. *New York Times*, February 21, 1980, p. A6. *Fortune*. September 11, 1978, p. 42.

6. *New York Times*, March 14, 1980, p. 1.

7. *Time*, March 24, 1980, p. 24.

8. *New York Times*, January 16, 1980, p. 16; February 7, 1980, p. 16.

9. *Chicago Tribune*, October 13, 1979, p. 1, and Section 2, p. 12.

10. *Chicago Tribune*, October 13, 1979, p. 1; *New York Times*, October 14, 1979, p. 26.

11. *New York Times*, February 4, 1980, p. 12.

12. *New York Times*, June 10, 1978, p. 1; *Chicago Tribune*, October 13, 1979, p. 1, and Section 2, p. 12. The continuous claim has been that the Pinto poses "No serious hazards."

13. *New York Times*, October 26, 1978, p. 103.

14. *New York Times*, February 20, 1980, p. A16.

15. For a discussion of the conflict, see, Sissela Bok, "Whistleblowing and Professional Responsibility," *New York University Educational Quarterly*, pp. 2–10. For detailed case studies see, Ralph Nader, Peter J. Petkas, and Kate Blackwell, *Whistle Blowing* (New York: Grossman Publishers, 1972); Charles Peters and Taylor Branch, *Blowing the Whistle: Dissent in the Public Interest* (New York: Praeger Publishers, 1972); and Robert M. Anderson, Robert Perrucci, Dan E. Schendel and Leon E. Trachtman, *Divided Loyalties: Whistle-Blowing at BART* (West Lafayette, Indiana: Purdue University, 1980).

16. *New York Times*, February 4, 1980, p. 12.

17. The position I present here is developed more fully in my book *Business Ethics* (New York: Macmillan, forthcoming in fall 1981). It differs somewhat from the dominant view expressed in the existing literature in that I consider whistle blowing an extreme measure that is morally obligatory only if the stringent conditions set forth are satisfied. Cf. Kenneth D. Walters, "Your Employees' Right to Blow the Whistle," *Harvard Business Review*, July–August, 1975.

18. On the dangers incurred by whistle blowers, see Gene James, "Whistle-Blowing: Its Nature and Justification," *Philosophy in Context*, 10 (1980), pp. 99–117, which examines the legal context of whistle blowing; Peter Raven-Hansen, "Dos and Don'ts for Whistleblowers: Planning for Trouble," *Technology Review*, May 1980, pp. 34–44, which suggests how to blow the whistle; Helen Dudar, "The Price of Blowing the Whistle," *The New York Times Magazine*, 30 October, 1977, which examines the results for whistleblowers; David W. Ewing, "Canning Directions," *Harpers*, August, 1979, pp. 17–22, which indicates "how the government rids itself of troublemakers" and how legislation protecting whistleblowers can be circumvented; and Report by the U.S. General Accounting Office, "The Office of the Special Counsel Can Improve Its Management of Whistleblower Cases," December 30, 1980 (FPCD-81-10).

19. *New York Times*, April 21, 1978, IV, p. 1, 18.

20. See Mark Dowie, "Pinto Madness," *Mother Jones*, September/October, 1977, pp. 24–28.

21. *Chicago Tribune*, October 13, 1979, Section 2, p. 12.

22. *New York Times*, March 16, 1980, IV, p. 20.

23. *New York Times*, February 8, 1978, p. 8.

24. *New York Times*, February 17, 1980, IV, p. 9; January 6, 1980, p. 24; *Time*, March 24, 1980, p. 24.

25. *The Wall Street Journal*, August 7, 1980, p. 7, reported that the Ford Motor Company "agreed to pay a total of $22,500 to the families of three Indiana teen-age girls killed in the crash of a Ford Pinto nearly two years ago.... A Ford spokesman said the settlement was made without any admission of liability. He speculated that the relatively small settlement may have been influenced by certain Indiana laws which severely restrict the amount of damages victims or their families can recover in civil cases alleging wrongful death."

26. A number of engineers have been arguing for a more active role by engineering societies in backing up individual engineers in their attempts to act responsibly. See, Edwin Layton, *Revolt of the Engineers* (Cleveland: Case Western Reserve, 1971); Stephen H. Unger, "Engineering Societies and the Responsible Engineer," *Annals of the New York Academy of Sciences*, 196 (1973), pp. 433–37 (reprinted in Baum and Flores, *Ethical Problems in Engineering*, pp. 56–59; and Robert Perrucci and Joel Gerstl, *Profession Without Community: Engineers in American Society* (New York: Random House, 1969).

27. Richard T. De George, "Responding to the Mandate for Social Responsibility," *Guidelines for Business When Societal Demands Conflict* (Washington, D.C.: Council for Better Business Bureaus, 1978), pp. 60–80.

13

Commentary on "Ethical Responsibilities of
Engineers in Large Organizations:
The Pinto Case"*

Dr. De George is entirely too easy on engineers or, for that matter,
anyone else who faces a moral dilemma. He would seem to say that
there is no further obligation to do something about a moral problem
on the part of the individual if his personal risks are greater than
the chance of success in affecting a change. I was stunned to read
"...we cannot reasonably expect engineers to be willing to sacrifice
their jobs each day for principle...". I thought that was what principles
were about. If we talk about moral principles, we are removed from
the lesser ethical requirements of the engineers' code. Surely if an
engineer perceives his dilemma to be one of moral principle, can he
do any less than sacrifice his job? (So that obeisance is paid to
pragmatism. I hasten to acknowledge that engineering jobs today are
fairly easy to obtain.) I must inquire, however, why anyone would want
to continue working at a job where his moral principles are violated.

---

* Reprinted, with editorial changes, by permission of the author. Copyright
© 1981 by Hart T. Mankin.

Surely one may disagree with one's supervisor's ignoring his suggestions without it necessarily calling moral issues into play. It could be said that the moral question was answered when the engineer took a job with a weapons manufacturer, an automobile manufacturer, or a bathtub manufacturer (after all, think of the number of deaths and injuries which involve bathtubs).

Dr. De George uses the Pinto case as a vehicle, but he either knowingly or unknowingly involves two other ethical areas—the ethics of journalism and the ethics involved in the Rules of Evidence in the law. Because his use of the Pinto case is not determinative of his conclusions, it shall not be necessary to comment on the quality of the information upon which he relied.

Legal writers are also using the Pinto case in the area of business ethics and the ethics of the corporation—how far can personification of the corporation go?

The corporation's personality and its ethical role in the community is probably determined in large measure by its historical reputation and the quality of its press. It is undoubtedly correct, as Dr. De George stated, that "unless those at the top set a moral tone, unless they insist on moral conduct, unless they punish immoral conduct and reward moral conduct, the corporation will function without considering morality of questions and of corporate actions."

In fact, there is a corporate morality and it is generally set by the Chief Executive Officer and/or the Board of Directors either consciously or subconsciously and is usually considered to be very important. Generally speaking, that attitude does tend to filter down except in those isolated instances where the lower-ranking, result oriented employee thinks that it would be in the corporation's best interest to cut corners. The corner cutting can be deliberate to save costs, or from ignorance, or be presumed to be consistent with the ethics of the marketplace. All three of these considerations are obviously grossly in error and certainly will result in harm done to the corporation. Of course, there are examples of senior management countenancing such conduct, but those are unusual.

Getting back to the Pinto case which Dr. De George uses as a dramatic example, let's examine it a little more closely.

Our exploration must necessarily be based on Dr. De George's description which, in turn, is based on newspaper and magazine accounts which may or may not be accurate. Assuming accuracy, would it not be fair to say that no product can be made 100% safe? Safety standards set by the National Transportation Safety Board with the assistance of other professional and trade organizations, together with standards set by such nongovernmental groups, reflect the state of the engineering art at the time the standards are set and provide for standards that will reflect the intended usage of the product with a small additional margin of safety. The additional margin of safety must necessarily be a subjectively established figure which takes into consideration the design of a product when considering its marketability; that is to say, its desirability by the public for whose intended use it was manufactured. One considers its engineering together with its styling, its price and its probable market. In the case of the Pinto, a subcompact automobile. I suspect that any number of $6.65 and $11 improvements could be made to it to have made it substantially safer than it was. That additional margin of safety would probably have provided for occurrences far beyond its intended use. It is obvious that it could have been made virtually as safe as an armored car with its higher margin of safety, but it probably would not have sold. It sold because the market was there.

It seems to me that the Pinto case best makes the case for a consideration of the study of corporate or organizational ethics rather than to be used as a vehicle for examining the moral or ethical obligations of an engineer. The problem is indeed of a different dimension when the debate is about professional rules generated to reflect society's expectations of engineers and the standards the profession sets for itself. Exploring the ethics of the engineer requires an examination of those engineering standards and codes which are established and which the engineer presumably follows as the standards of his profession. The ethical responsibility of an engineer who believes that the state of the art has surpassed the standards set in a particular engineering discipline does indeed have a significant ethical engineering problem to face. Whether or not it achieves the level of a moral dilemma depends in large measure on the individual engineer's perception. A nice question to be addressed could be simply posed as what service does an engineer provide? Is it one coupled with an ethical overlay beyond simply designing or manufacturing a product to the then current state of the art? In my judgment, even an affirmative answer to a majority of the situations that could arise under such a circumstance would not require or even suggest whistle-blowing. Clearly the engineer should provide his highest degree of expertise to client-employer. His contribution is one of many made to his employer. Beyond his field, he may be entering areas in which he has no particular qualifications. He is a contributor to an ultimate product and short of extraordinary circumstances would be expected to provide his best engineering knowledge. When a manufacturer is designing a subcompact automobile to compete in the subcompact automobile market, he does not do those things that he would do if he were competing in the luxury sedan market. Engineering ethics would presumably view "over-engineering" or "overdesign" with almost as much disdain as cutting corners.

Dr. De George concludes his well reasoned paper with the argument that the questions that we should be facing concern how to change organizational structures so that engineers will not have to be placed in moral dilemmas. It seems to me that the sensitizing of professionals to ethical considerations should be increased so that organizational or institutional structures will reflect enhanced ethical sensitivities as trained professionals move up the organizational ladder to positions of leadership. Organizations may reflect ethics by consensus. The consensus is from individuals, their education, their training, their perceptions and their reactions to external forces. In conclusion, I would suggest that the engineer faces no different moral dilemmas than any other human being. His difficulty comes in determining his response to ethical considerations if those considerations are based on transitory standards of his profession. As an example, if an electrical engineer is ethically bound to design to the standards of the National Electrical Code and does not, he faces a rather simple problem. If, on the other hand, as is suggested in the paper by Dr. De George, he may believe that the Code standards are not strict enough and he insists upon designing to higher standards than the Code provides, he is faced with an entirely different dimension of problem, both philosophical and legal.

Weep not for the engineer who may, on rare occasion, be squeezed because of his ethics. Contemplate instead the responsibilities that we have to assure that all institutions, including business, be operated on an ethical, and perhaps moral level.

14

Whistle Blowing, Ethical Obligation, and the Ford Pinto Case[1]

Whistle blowing is an important and instructive ethical issue since it often highlights a conflict between acting to prevent harm to others or acting in the individual's self-interest. Whistle blowers attempt to disclose wrongdoing within or by an organization to the public, government, media, or members of their organization other than their immediate superiors. The purpose of the disclosure is to prevent the wrongdoing from continuing.[2] Whistle blowers risk their personal well-being because organizations often retaliate against them. Since whistle blowing has the potential to prevent harm to others but often involves personal sacrifice, a crucial question is: when, if ever, are business people or engineers ethically obligated to blow the whistle on their employers?

This article divides the treatment of the question into four parts. First, I present Richard De George's set of conditions, which establish when whistle blowing is ethically permissible and ethically obligatory. These conditions have a major fault: they do not provide a clear, preliminary model for whistle blowing since in almost all complex cases, an employee would not be ethically obligated to blow the whistle. This flaw keeps the conditions from making adequate moral demands on employees and overprotects companies. The second, part applies De George's conditions to the managers and engineers who worked on the Ford Pinto of the early 1970s. This application of the conditions to a case illustrates the problem with them. Part III presents an alternative approach to ethical obligation and whistle blowing which provides more protection for the users of products and services. It leads to the conclusion that engineers and business people have an ethical obligation to blow the whistle more frequently than De George's conditions indicate. The final section of the paper applies this second view to the Pinto case.

PART I

How are we to determine whether business people and engineers are ethically obligated to blow the whistle on their employers? One response to this question has been to try to set out conditions or criteria for whistle blowing. Richard De George claims there are five conditions that determine the moral status of whistle blowing. If the first three are satisfied, whistle blowing is permissible; if all five are satisfied, whistle blowing is morally obligatory. De George's first condition states, "The firm, through its product or policy, will do serious and considerable harm to the public, whether in the person of the user of its product, an innocent bystander, or the general public."[3] By "serious and considerable harm," De George means serious bodily harm or danger to life or health. He wants to limit whistle blowing to situations that threaten death in order to create a set of clear-cut cases. He also thinks that such a limitation would avoid unnecessary harm to companies and keep whistle blowing a rare occurrence, which would make it more effective.

Gene James has criticized De George for limiting the first criterion to cases that threaten serious bodily harm or death.[4] James worries that restricting the discussion to such clear-cut cases will provide a position which ". . . leaves us with no guidance when we are confronted with more usual situations involving other types of harm."[5] James has failed to appreciate De George's strategy, which is to construct a clear, preliminary model for the moral status of whistle blowing and to limit the number of legitimate cases of it. Once De George has created this model, he thinks it will ". . . provide a basis for working out guidelines for more complex cases."[6] Thus, the original model is not supposed to provide guidance in all potential whistle blowing cases, but instead to provide some preliminary common ground where we can agree when whistle blowing is permissible and obligatory. James' criticism that the first condition is too restrictive is not forceful because it would be possible for De George to stipulate additions to the idea of "serious and considerable harm" in order to make the first condition broader. A beginning to this task might be to suggest that "serious and considerable harm" plausibly includes not only death but, at least, disfigurement, sterilization, and injuries that require medical treatment to prevent loss of life. This expansion retains De George's goal of keeping the conditions clear-cut so that we have the best chance of reaching agreement, but extends the realm of legitimate whistle blowing.

The second condition states, "Once employees identify a serious threat to the user of a product or to the general public, they should report it to their immediate superior and make their moral concern known."[7] De George thinks that people have a moral obligation to prevent harm to others if they can do so at relatively little cost to themselves. Presumably, reporting a threat to an immediate supervisor will not harm the employee since reporting problems to supervisors is an ordinary part of the job. Therefore, employees are morally obligated to inform their immediate superiors about serious threats to others. The employee must also report the problem to his or her superior so that the firm has an opportunity to correct the situation. This preserves the employee's loyalty to the employer. De George adds that if the superior already knows of the danger, then reporting it to him or her would be redundant, and the second condition would already be satisfied.

The key to the second condition is the assertion that people have a moral obligation to prevent harm to others if they can do so at relatively little cost to themselves. Thus, even if employees do not have a moral obligation to blow the whistle in a case, De George asserts that they always have a moral obligation to report to their immediate superiors products and practices that threaten to do serious and considerable harm. De George's second condition shows his concern with protecting the public, but as the discussion of the last two conditions will indicate, I question whether his conditions, as a whole, provide sufficient protection.

The third condition reads: "If one's immediate superior does nothing effective about the concern or complaint, the employee should exhaust the internal procedures and possibilities within the firm."[8] This condition also makes sure that employees do not violate their loyalty to their employers. Once the first three conditions are satisfied and the problem has still not been resolved, the employee has gained the right to override the demand of loyalty and blow the whistle on the organization. De George anticipates the most serious problem connected to this condition when he declares that if the harm is imminent, there may not be time to exhaust the internal procedures. He suggests that prudence and judgment should be used, but that at least some effort should be made to make use of available internal procedures. As in condition two, the obligation to make the effort to explore other options within the organization is derived from the general obligation to prevent harm to others if it can be done at relatively little cost.

In general, De George thinks whistle blowing is permissible when there is a threat of serious harm to the public and when the potential whistle blowers have done everything possible to inform their employers of their concerns. Whistle blowing would not be permissible without informing the employer since this would violate the employee's duty of loyalty. Thus, the permissibility of whistle blowing depends upon an action by the employees, making their concerns known within the organization, and a lack of effective action by the employer, failing to resolve the problem.

The fourth condition is the first of the two additional conditions that make whistle blowing ethically obligatory. De George states, "The whistle blower must have, or have accessible, documented evidence that would convince a reasonable, impartial observer that one's view of the situation is correct, and that the company's product or practice poses a serious and likely danger to the public or to the user of the product."[9] This condition raises doubts about whether anyone in a complex case would be ethically obligated to blow the whistle. First, it would be difficult for some potential whistle blowers to get access to such documentation since it might be closely guarded to protect it from competitors. It also might be of questionable legality for them to take the documentation if it is something to which they are not entitled to have access, or if it is proprietary information. Second, an even more serious difficulty is that it is unclear what it takes to convince a "reasonable, impartial observer." Reasonable people can view the same documentary evidence and not come to the same conclusion since "convincing documentation" depends upon the observer's expectations for the product as well as his or her technical evaluation of the documentation. The idea of "convincing documentation" is not value-neutral because the person's evaluative judgments about what the product ought to be like are an essential part of determining what will count as documentation. Product expectations are so diverse and specific that they would prevent any general condition from being successful no matter how it was amended. A potential whistle blower could only determine whether the documentation convinced him or her, not whether it convinced a "reasonable, impartial observer." The subsequent discussion of the Ford Pinto case illustrates this criticism. Potential whistle blowers would always be uncertain to some degree whether the documentation would convince a reasonable, impartial observer, and thus it would be rare for someone to be obligated to blow the whistle in a complex case. These criticisms cannot be avoided by restating De George's claim that these are merely preliminary conditions designed to provide a basis for future refinement. While "serious and considerable harm" could be expanded to avoid James' criticism of the first condition, we cannot salvage condition four. No addition could create a successful general category of "convincing documentation."

The fifth condition and the second of the two necessary to make whistle blowing ethically obligatory reads, "The employee must have good reasons to believe that by going public the necessary changes will be brought about. The chance of being successful must be worth the risk one takes, and the danger to which one is exposed."[10] This last condition is also accompanied by difficulties for those who would like whistle blowing to be a fairly regular occurrence. First, what counts as "good reasons" for believing that the changes will be brought about? Reasonable people might disagree about what constitutes "good reasons." It seems likely that "good reasons" would vary with the circumstances, so there is no independent or general standard for this criterion. Furthermore, one such circumstance is that having "good reasons" is connected to knowing who will use the information and how it will be used, but it is often impossible to predict this with accuracy. A significant degree of uncertainty seems inevitable in any complex case, and hence this condition would often prevent ethical obligation.

A second problem with the fifth condition is connected to the question of how the employee is supposed to know whether the chance for success makes the risk acceptable. The condition forces the employee once again to predict future events and to risk retaliation based on a prediction. De George does claim that the greater the risk to the employee, the greater the chance for success ought to be, but this is not enough help. There are no guidelines for comparing the degree of risk to the chance of success. As with the fourth condition, the fifth condition makes it unlikely that anyone would be obligated to blow the whistle. Potential whistle blowers might always be uncertain about whether the chances for success were worth the risk.

The problems with condition five would not be eliminated by further modifications of it. Since having "good reasons" depends upon the specific circumstances, there is no way to create a general definition in terms of necessary and sufficient conditions for the phrase. Anticipating and evaluating the degree of risk depends on predicting the future, and no further modifications would eliminate that uncertainty. Therefore, any modifications would not make it more likely that people would often be obligated to blow the whistle in complex cases.

Conditions four and five are so demanding that they inject an unavoidable element of uncertainty into the evaluation of any complex case that could not be removed by future modifications of the conditions. Employees will almost never be obligated to blow the whistle on their employers in complicated cases. The fourth condition generates uncertainty about knowing what it would take to convince a reasonable, impartial observer that the employee's view of the situation is correct. In the fifth condition, the uncertainty arises from employees not knowing whether the changes will be brought about and how they should compare the degree of risk to the chances for success. Instead of being conditions designed to determine whether the employee is ethically obligated or not, conditions four and five look more like requirements that prevent ethical obligation in almost all complex cases.

The fact that it would be rare for an employee to be morally obligated to blow the whistle in complicated cases might not be a problem from De George's point of view. As mentioned earlier, he wants to keep whistle blowing a rare phenomenon so that it will be effective and will prevent unnecessary harm to companies. I believe that the first of these concerns is not as serious as De George thinks. Whistle blowing is only of instrumental value; it is the prevention of serious harm that is important. If whistle blowing were to become a relatively regular occurrence, companies might police themselves more effectively to prevent the bad publicity that accompanies a whistle blowing incident. Whistle blowing might be less effective as De George believes, but the added concern of the companies themselves might actually improve the situation with respect to preventing harm. In regard to De George's other concern, we can develop a criterion for whistle blowing that will make it more frequent, but still prevent unnecessary harm to companies. Before turning to this other view, however, let us examine De George's application of his conditions to the Ford Pinto case.

PART II

De George's whistle blowing conditions originally appeared in his article, "Ethical Responsibilities of Engineers in Large Organizations: The Pinto Case."[11] In this essay, he concludes that it would have been permissible for the Pinto engineers to blow the whistle on Ford, but that they were not ethically obligated to do so. This part of my article will review and elaborate on De George's support for this conclusion.

The Ford Pinto, a subcompact car built by Ford Motor Company during the seventies, was introduced into the Ford Line to compete with foreign subcompacts. Controversy surrounded the Pinto for most of its existence with the major problem being connected to the fuel system. The fuel tank was susceptible to rupturing when the car was struck from behind by another vehicle traveling at a relatively low speed, causing the tank to leak gasoline that sometimes produced fires which seriously burned or killed passengers. Engineers and managers at Ford knew of the fire danger but delayed altering the fuel system in a way that would eliminate the problem. In general, critics have charged that the fuel tank was susceptible to this damage because of poor design and that Ford did not respond effectively to this design deficiency.

De George believes that the position of the fuel tank and the nature of the automobile were such that there was a threat of "serious and considerable harm" to passengers when the car was struck from behind at relatively low speeds. There is sufficient evidence from crash tests to support this claim.[12] The Ford engineers knew of this condition at least by 1970 and probably earlier because crash tests were performed in 1969 on subcompacts modified to have fuel tank placement similar to the Pinto design. Thus, we can assume that De George's first condition was satisfied in this case.

By reporting the results of the crash tests, the Ford engineers informed their immediate superiors, and everyone else at Ford who had access to their reports, that at relatively low speeds a rear-end collision involving a Pinto would produce a dangerous fire hazard. Therefore, the engineers had fulfilled condition two.

Condition three may also have been satisfied by the reports on the crash tests results, but this is debatable. The reports do not really show that the engineers had exhausted the internal resources of the corporation. Condition three could have been met, however, by the engineers writing additional memos and sending them to various officials at Ford. They were morally obligated to do this if they thought it might prevent serious harm to others and would have had relatively little cost to themselves. Once they did this, if Ford still took no action to correct the problem, it would have been ethically permissible for them to blow the whistle on the company. It was mentioned earlier that De George states that if the harm is imminent, there may not be time to exhaust the internal procedures. Potential whistle blowers must be prudent and use their judgment, but at least some effort should be made to exhaust the internal procedures of the company. Considering this factor, we might conclude that it would have been permissible for the Pinto engineers to blow the whistle since they had done something and harm was imminent.

De George believes that the Ford engineers were not ethically obligated to blow the whistle because conditions four and five were not fulfilled. Condition four is tied to the issue of whether the engineers could have acquired ". . .documented evidence that would convince a reasonable, impartial observer" that their view of the situation is correct.[13] De George believes that they could not have done this since, according to Ford engineer Francis Olsen, there was disagreement among the engineers about the safety of the Pinto.[14] Thus, even with access to the available documentation, the Ford engineers who believed that the Pinto was a dangerous vehicle were unable to convince their colleagues, like Francis Olsen, that the car was unsafe. It appears that condition four would not be satisfied, but De George would be better off not using the above reasoning to support this claim. The condition states that the documentation must convince impartial observers. The Ford engineers were certainly not impartial about these matters. Francis Olsen might have had his professional reputation and his ego invested in the design of the Pinto's fuel system. Therefore, his assessment of the crash test results may have been biased.

Another difficulty is that De George assumes that there will be no serious problems about what counts as documentation and evidence. The dispute among the engineers, however, shows that different people have different criteria for evidence based on their expectations for the car. The matter of evidence is not value-neutral because the observers' evaluative judgments about what the car ought to be like enter into the matter of what counts as convincing documentation. The resolution to whether condition four was satisfied depends upon agreement about the interpretation of the crash tests results relative to the expectations for the car. The crash tests showed that the car would be unsafe in vehicle to vehicle, rear-end crashes at speeds in the upper twenties. One individual might conclude that this documents that the car was unsafe, that it represented a threat of serious and considerable harm to passengers; but this depends on the assumption that subcompacts should be safe in 25 through 30 mile per hour crashes. Apparently engineers like Francis Olsen believed that this assumption was unrealistic, that subcompacts were not supposed to be safe at these speeds. Their conclusion from the crash tests must have been that the car was safe enough for a subcompact. They would have concluded that the documentation would be inadequate to convince an impartial observer that the car was unsafe, that condition four was not satisfied, and that they were not ethically obligated to blow the whistle. Thus, the question of whether condition four is satisfied does not really depend on the "reasonable, impartial observer," in any objective way, but instead depends on the potential whistle blower's subjective interpretation of the data and his or her safety expectations for the product. This discussion supports the earlier claim that De George's conditions are so strict that even where documentation exists, potential whistle blowers would often be uncertain whether the documentation would convince an impartial observer that their view of the situation was correct. Therefore, whistle blowing would rarely be ethically obligatory.

De George thinks that the fifth condition would not be satisfied either. The condition states, "The employee must have good reasons to believe that by going public the necessary changes will be brought about. The chance of being successful must be worth the risk one takes, and the danger to which one is exposed."[15] According to De George, the Pinto engineers would not have had good reason to believe that the changes would take place since, after much public discussion and failing to pass national safety standards tests, Ford plausibly defended its claim in a criminal trial that the car was adequately safe.[16] (The company was found innocent of producing and keeping a dangerous vehicle on the market.) The results of the trial, however, are inadequate to substantiate his claim since the trial did not prove that making information about the car public would not lead to the fuel system being upgraded. By the time of the trial, the 1971–1976 Pintos had already been recalled and upgraded. Also, the car involved in the crash that led to the trial was a 1973 Pinto. The trial judge refused to allow evidence into court except that which concerned 1973 Pintos. Thus, the prosecutors could not introduce into evidence any of the crash tests or much of the other information about Pintos. Finally, a major issue in the trial was the speed at which the accident occurred. Ford argued that the crash took place at about 50 mph and that no subcompact car's fuel system could have withstood the impact.

The results of the trial were too specialized to support the general claim that public disclosure would not have led to the car's safety being upgraded.

There is, in fact, a line of argument that suggests that the Ford engineers might have gotten safety improvements on the car by blowing the whistle to the media. Mark Dowie's controversial article "Pinto Madness," published in 1977, led to a public debate over the car, which prodded the National Highway Traffic Safety Administration (NHTSA) into an investigation.[17] In 1978, Ford recalled all the 1971–1976 Pintos to upgrade their fuel systems in an effort to avoid NHTSA hearings on the Pinto and to end the controversy. Dowie's article contained anonymous comments from Ford engineers. Instead of waiting for Dowie to discover the Pinto's problem, the engineers could have approached him or another journalist earlier, and perhaps the car would have been recalled sooner. Therefore, by blowing the whistle to the media, the Pinto engineers might have gotten the car's fuel system upgraded earlier. It would, however, have been impossible for the Pinto engineers to be certain of this. Whether they had "good reasons" or not, and whether the chances were worth the risk of losing their jobs cannot be definitively answered. The stringency of De George's condition injects an unavoidable degree of uncertainty into our evaluation of this matter and prevents us from being able to determine conclusively whether condition five was satisfied.

According to De George, it will sometimes be ethically permissible to blow the whistle, but rarely ethically obligatory. Whistle blowing becomes a matter in which the employee must earn the right to blow the whistle by discovering a case of serious harm and giving the company the chance to correct the problem. In almost all complex cases, employees will be uncertain about a crucial element and therefore will not be obligated to blow the whistle. This view of whistle blowing protects individual employees and corporate interests but in many cases risks the lives of people in society at large.

PART III

Are business people and engineers ever ethically obligated to blow the whistle on their employers? While De George's conditions are an interesting approach to whistle blowing, I believe they overprotect employees and companies. I will propose a second approach to the issue that eliminates several features of De George's view and would make legitimate whistle blowing more frequent. Whereas De George's view is better for potential whistle blowers and companies, this second view is more beneficial to the public and to other employees who might be harmed by a product or practice. This second strategy is similar to De George's view in that it is designed to provide a clear, preliminary model on which to base future discussion. A crucial difference, however, is that while additions to conditions four and five cannot resolve the difficulties with them, further discussion of the second model would help to eliminate the problems left by this preliminary treatment.

The second approach to this question will center around a moral principle appropriate to the whistle blowing dilemma instead of appealing to a set of conditions. In his book *Practical Ethics*, Peter Singer proposes a principle that he thinks should be acceptable to most philosophers.[18] A slightly altered version of the principle is: if it is in our power to prevent something bad from happening without thereby sacrificing anything of comparable moral significance, then we ought to do it. If this principle is accepted, it generates ethical obligations and can be used to create ethical obligations connected to whistle blowing. Legitimate whistle blowers attempt to prevent bad things from happening by informing someone of a problem with a product or practice. Questions arise about the action because other people disagree about the badness of the things in question, because they sometimes think that the whistle blowers are sacrificing something of comparable moral significance, and because potential whistle blowers are sometimes unclear about whether it is in their power to prevent the bad thing from happening.

The potential whistle blower's first step is to determine whether there is wrongdoing; i.e., is something bad occurring or about to occur? Second, the question about whether something of comparable moral significance is being sacrificed must be answered. Finally, is it in his or her power to prevent the wrongdoing? The principle states that if one can prevent something bad from happening without sacrificing anything of comparable moral significance, then one ought to do it. In a potential whistle blowing case, if one can prevent a wrongdoing and if this prevention is of more ethical significance than the other factors, then one is obligated to blow the whistle.

How does a whistle blower know if something "bad" has or is about to happen? An interesting approach to this question would be to elaborate on a suggestion by Gene James. James says that whistle blowers should be concerned with situations that involve not just serious harm, but with all violations of fundamental human rights.[19]

Following James, I will suggest that something bad occurs when one or more fundamental human rights are violated, e.g., the rights to life, liberty, well-being, private property, privacy, and so on. Potential whistle blowers would know whether the right was being violated by focusing on the basic good or interest that the right protects. If a product or service kills someone, the right to life has been violated. If it seriously injures someone, the right to well-being has been violated. If the firm is stealing from customers, suppliers, or employees, the right to private property has been violated. There may also be cases where the determination cannot be made; i.e., where we are not sure whether a right has been violated. This approach, however, would allow the potential whistle blower to make a determination in a large number of cases. It also leaves open the possibility of further discussion that would refine the means of detecting when a human right had been violated, and which would elaborate all of the relevant rights.

The second aspect of the principle about "comparable moral significance" produces even greater problems than providing guidelines for what is "bad." How do potential whistle blowers know whether they are sacrificing something of comparable moral significance when they try to prevent something bad from happening? If a fundamental human right has been violated, we really ought to say that something *prima facie* unethical has taken place. There are cases where an individual must violate a right in order to uphold another right. A contemporary example of such a situation is the abortion controversy. Those who believe that the embryo is a human being with the right to life would like to prohibit abortions even though this violates a woman's right to privacy or liberty, in the sense that it violates her right to control her own reproductive life. In cases like abortion, where there is a conflict between different rights, it is difficult to know what is the ethical thing to do. Libertarians and feminists would not defend limiting a woman's freedom to control her reproductive life, while those who rank the right to life above everything are obligated to do so. There are similar conflicts in whistle blowing cases. If we demand that employees blow the whistle on their companies to protect the rights of the public or other employees, we risk violating the rights of the whistle blowers. If whistle blowers are fired, their rights to well-being seem violated, as well as those of their families. Would we be sacrificing something of comparable moral importance, the rights of the whistle blowers and their families, to protect the rights of the public and other employees?

This problem with resolving conflicts between human rights is a major difficulty for a rights-based ethical approach.[20] There are two different kinds of cases that must be considered to resolve this whistle blowing dilemma. First, there are cases where the employees who are potential whistle blowers are involved in producing products or performing services that endanger others. I believe that their rights to life, liberty, and well-being do not justify their harming innocent people or depriving those innocent people of their rights to life or well-being. This is in line with my general view that people's rights never justify their harming or killing innocent people.[21] If a person is employed to produce a harmful product or to provide a harmful service, there is no relevant violation of his or her rights if that employment is lost. There is also no relevant violation of the rights to well-being of family members who are being supported by the harm done to innocent people. Dependent childrens' rights to well-being do not justify their parents killing or harming innocent people in order to support them. If employees are involved in producing harmful products or providing harmful services, we would not be sacrificing anything of comparable moral value by holding them to be obligated to blow the whistle, even if they do lose their jobs. Their rights are not violated since they cannot use those rights to justify harming innocent people, and the obligation to blow the whistle protects the rights of the people who might be harmed or killed by the product or service.

The second kind of case involves employees who are not participating in producing the harmful product or providing the harmful service, but who are in a position to blow the whistle anyway. Their rights to well-being and the rights of their family members would be violated if they lost their jobs. I do not believe that in this kind of case we can justify the protection of one group's rights by violating another group's rights. Therefore, we cannot hold these people to be obligated to blow the whistle if they believe that doing so would cost them their jobs. They would, however, be obligated to do so if there was no serious threat to their jobs. This implies that these employees will not be obligated to blow the whistle very often.

The second view of whistle blowing achieves its goal with the first group of employees, those who are involved in producing harmful products or providing harmful service; it sets up a position where these people would often be obligated to blow the whistle. The treatment of the second group, however, is not an improvement over De George's position. In condition five, De George made the evaluation of risk necessary, and this view does the same thing. Future alterations would not be able to create a general and independent standard for evaluating this risk, and thus ethical obligation will depend upon the individual's assessment of the risk of losing his or her job.

The third aspect of the principle suggests that we should prevent the bad thing from happening if it is in our power to do so. This determination must be made on a case by case basis, and there will be cases where the individual is unsure whether it is in his or her power to prevent the harm. What are we to say about these cases? Our usual reaction in straightforward events is to attempt to prevent a serious harm or a death if there is a chance to do so without incurring a greater or equal harm to ourselves. Even if I am not sure I can reach the drowning boy in time, I will attempt to save him. I send money to the most reputable famine relief organizations I can find, even though I am not certain that the money will reach those who are starving. The uncertainty does not prevent us from trying to prevent great harms. Therefore, in cases of uncertainty where one would not be sacrificing something of equal moral significance, it is the individual's obligation to try to prevent the harm if there is a possibility to do so. This constructs a paradigm where effort, not actual success, is what matters, and sets up a very demanding standard; but without it, it will usually be unclear whether someone is obligated to blow the whistle. There is uncertainty connected to most of the events in life, and if a degree of uncertainty releases us from ethical obligation, there will be very few cases where we are ethically obligated to do anything. Without these stipulations, I would end up in the same position as De George, where uncertainty leads to people not being obligated to blow the whistle and where obligatory whistle blowing is rare in complex cases.

It might be suggested that the whistle blowing literature could be used to provide paradigms which would offer some guidance about the application of this principle to whistle blowing cases. The careful discussion of cases like A.H. Robin's Dalkon Shield, Ford's Pinto of the 1970s, Johns-Manville's treatment of its asbestos workers, McDonnell-Douglas's DC-10, and others might show how people were ethically obligated to blow the whistle in these cases because they had a reasonable chance of preventing something bad from happening and they would not have been sacrificing anything of comparable moral significance.

PART IV

The Ford Pinto case is a good example to use to try out this approach to whistle blowing. The principle which informs this position is: if it is in our power to prevent something bad from happening without thereby sacrificing anything of comparable moral significance, then we ought to do it. Did the Ford engineers know that something "bad" was likely to happen? As we saw earlier, crash tests indicated that in rear-end crashes of between 25 and 30 miles per hour the fuel tank was likely to be ruptured, leading to a fire that could kill the passengers. These deaths were preventable since the integrity of the fuel system could have been upgraded for about eight dollars a car. In the case of a crash and a death, the victim's right to life was violated since the death was preventable. In the case of a crash and a serious burn injury, the victim's right to well-being was violated by the unnecessary injury. Thus, the construction of the Pinto with the flawed fuel system violated the rights of the crash victims and was a potential violation of the rights of anyone who drove or rode in the cars. If the engineers believed that the unmodified Pinto was safe enough, they were underestimating the capabilities of subcompact cars. A car that can be made significantly safer for about eight dollars is not a car that is "safe enough." The fuel system of the Pinto was such that low speed crashes were killing and injuring people unnecessarily, and therefore producing the car and leaving it on the market without alterations violated human rights.

I have argued that something bad was occurring in the Pinto case, but would the engineers have been sacrificing something of comparable harm by blowing the whistle and preventing the violation of the right to life? The Pinto engineers would fit the first situation discussed in the corresponding section of Part III. They were involved in producing a harmful product; i.e., they were involved in allowing others to be harmed. As I stated, my position is that our rights do not justify our harming innocent people or allowing them to be harmed when we could prevent the harm. The drivers and passengers of the Pintos were innocent in the relevant sense that they were not involved in harming or attempting to harm the Pinto engineers. Therefore, the engineers cannot appeal to their rights or their families rights to avoid being obligated to blow the whistle. We would not be sacrificing anything of comparable moral worth by obligating the Pinto engineers to blow the whistle because the engineers' and their families' rights are not relevant in this case, and we are protecting the rights of all the people who drive or ride in Ford Pintos.

This brings us to the final point: Was it in the Ford engineer's power to get the fuel system of the car upgraded? I have already suggested that they did have a chance for success by blowing the whistle to the media. Mark Dowie's article "Pinto Madness" led to a public debate over the car and prompted the NHTSA's investigation. Ford wanted to avoid public hearings on the Pinto and recalled all the 1971–1976 Pintos to upgrade their fuel systems in an effort to avoid NHTSA hearings. If Dowie could initiate events that ultimately led to a recall, why could the Pinto engineers have not done so by blowing the whistle to the media? I believe that there is a good chance that by approaching the media, the Pinto engineers could have gotten the car's fuel system upgraded earlier.

Singer's principle, slightly modified, states that if there is a reasonable chance that we have the power to prevent something bad from happening without thereby sacrificing anything of comparable moral significance, then we ought to do it. The Pinto engineers had reason to believe that something bad would inevitably happen, and their blowing the whistle would not have sacrificed anything of comparable moral importance. They also had a reasonable chance to prevent some of the deaths from happening. Therefore, based on the second position, the engineers were ethically obligated to blow the whistle on Ford.

When, if ever, are business people or engineers ethically obligated to blow the whistle on their employers? The application of De George's conditions is one way to answer this question. Another answer is to say that if there is a reasonable possibility that it is in someone's power to prevent something bad from occurring by blowing the whistle and that by doing so he or she would not sacrifice anything of equal moral significance, then the individual is obligated to do it. De George's conditions overprotect companies and do not make adequate moral demands on employees. The second approach to whistle blowing offers more protection for users of goods and services. Business people and engineers occupy positions where they can contribute to great human harm and benefit. We need to hold them to high standards, like those set up by the second view of whistle blowing and ethical obligation, so that there will be fewer tragedies like the deaths of people in burning Ford Pintos.

NOTES

1. This essay is an altered version of an article of mine entitled, "Whistleblowing, Ethical Obligation and the DC-10 Case." The earlier version appeared in John Fielder and Douglas Birsch, *The DC-10 Case: A Study in Ethics, Technology, and Society* (Albany, New York: SUNY Press, 1992).

2. Slightly different definitions of whistle blowing can be found in the following sources: Norman Bowie, *Business Ethics* (Englewood Cliffs, NJ: Prentice Hall, 1982) and Richard De George, *Business Ethics*, 3rd ed. (New York: Macmillan Publishing Co., 1990).

3. Richard De George, *Business Ethics*, 3rd ed. (New York: Macmillan Publishing Co., 1990) p. 208.

4. Gene James, "Whistle Blowing: Its Moral Justification," in W. Michael Hoffman & Jennifer Mills Moore, *Business Ethics*, 2nd ed., (New York: McGraw-Hill, 1990).

5. Ibid., p. 336.

6. De George, *Business Ethics*, p. 203.

7. Ibid., p. 210.

8. Ibid., p. 211.

9. Ibid., p. 212.

10. Ibid.

11. Richard De George, "Ethical Responsibilities of Engineers in Large Organizations," *Business and Professional Ethics Journal*, 1:1, (Fall 1981) pp. 1–14.

12. The "Final Test Report" on the Pinto, conducted by the Ford Product Development Office, reported the results of a 1970 rear end, fixed barrier crash test at 21.5 miles per hour. In the test, the fuel tank was punctured by an axle housing bolt and the filler pipe was pulled from the tank. This allowed large amounts of fluid to leak out and produced the conditions for a dangerous fire. See Lee Patrick Strobel, *Reckless Homicide?: Ford's Pinto Trial*, (South Bend, Indiana: And Books, 1980), p. 276.

13. De George, *Business Ethics*, p. 212.

14. De George, "Ethical Responsibilities of Engineers in Large Organizations," p. 6. De George mentions that Francis Olsen clearly had confidence in the safety of the Pinto since he bought one for his daughter. Unlike Olsen, I would want my daughter to be safe in a rear-end crash that took place at a speed between 25 and 30 miles per hour. Rather than proving that the Pinto was adequately safe, I think this merely establishes that people have different expectations with regard to automobiles.

15. De George, *Business Ethics*, p. 212.

16. De George, "Ethical Responsibilities of Engineers in Large Organizations," p. 7.

17. Mark Dowie, "Pinto Madness," *Mother Jones*, September–October 1977, pp. 18–32.

18. Peter Singer. *Practical Ethics*. (Cambridge: Cambridge University Press, 1979) p. 168. The principle is vague enough that it ought to be acceptable to consequentialists, deontologists, and contractualists.

19. Gene James, "Whistle Blowing: Its Moral Justification," p. 336. In my earlier article on whistle blowing, I took a consequentialist approach to this matter. In this paper, I will opt for a deontological view.

20. Even though Gene James takes a human rights approach to whistle blowing, he does not say anything about this problem.

21. This position would not be endorsed by all philosophers, but I accept it with regard to innocent people. A moral paradigm is that my right to well-being does not justify my injuring you and stealing your money even if I am starving. Of course, our rights do justify our harming others in legitimate cases of self-defense. My right to life does justify my harming you or even killing you if it is the only way I can prevent you from killing me.

Part IV

PRODUCT LIABILITY

Introduction: Product Liability

Given the allegations of fuel system design deficiencies in the Pinto and the deaths and injuries from the accidents and resulting fires, the Pinto case is an excellent way to illustrate problems connected to product liability. When someone is injured by a product, they may be able to collect damages from the manufacturer by filing a lawsuit alleging improper conduct by the company, such as negligence or misrepresentation of the product. In these cases, the plaintiff must show that the manufacturer failed to follow legal standards of conduct in producing and marketing a product. The difficulties in proving such cases, and the widespread belief that too many injured consumers were being denied compensation, led to the development of the legal doctrine of strict liability.[1] According to the Restatement (Second) of Torts, Section 402 (a) (1965): "One who sells any product in a defective condition unreasonably dangerous is subject to liability for physical harm thereby caused to the ultimate user or consumer." This approach focuses on the product itself, rather than the conduct of the manufacturer, and presents a lesser burden of proof for the plaintiff. Critics of strict liability claim that it is too easy to sue and that manufacturers are held responsible for conditions over which they have very little control.

In the Pinto case, Ford may or may not have been negligent, but the question under strict liability would be whether the fuel system was defective and unreasonably dangerous. If the car was considered to be defective because of the fuel system problem, victims or their dependents would be entitled to compensation.

The articles in Part IV explore product liability. Fred W. Morgan's "Marketing and Product Liability: A Review and Update" provides an overview of product liability, reviewing case law trends with respect to negligence, warranty, strict liability and, misrepresentation. George G. Brenkert's "Strict Products Liability and Compensatory Justice" argues that strict liability is compatible with the free enterprise system, and that if sellers and manufacturers are not liable in this sense, the free enterprise system is morally deficient. The final selection in Part IV is a summary of the most famous Pinto product liability suit, the one involving Mrs. Lilly Gray and Richard Grimshaw. The original award to Grimshaw of over $127 million in compensatory and punitive damages was a significant landmark in the Pinto case.

NOTE

1. See Frank J. Vandall, *Strict Liability: Legal and Economic Analysis* (New York: Quorum Books, 1989), chapter 2.

FRED W. MORGAN

15

Marketing and Product Liability:
A Review and Update*

The author wishes to acknowledge the helpful comments of Wayne H. Volz, Assistant Professor of Business Law at Wayne State, on an earlier draft of this article.

Product liability developments have been widely discussed but often with differing views regarding their impact on companies. This article reviews this debate from a marketing perspective by analyzing relevant insurance industry data and case law decisions. Conclusions drawn from the analysis as well as their implications for marketing managers are presented.

INTRODUCTION

The controversy over the impact of product liability developments on business practices continues unabated (*Business Week* 1979, 1980, 1981; Johnson 1978). Marketers, like others within the corporation, have demonstrated an interest in product liability, although with

*Reprinted, with editorial changes, by permission of the American Marketing Association from *The Journal of Marketing*, Volume 46, 1982, pp. 69–78.

221

apparent minimal information regarding the extent of the so-called liability problem. Furthermore, little has been written about the marketer's role in preventing the company from being a party to a product liability claim or lawsuit.

This article begins to correct these shortcomings by synthesizing existing data and legal cases relating marketing activities with product liability. First, an overview of the product liability situation in the United States is presented, with an emphasis whenever possible on a marketing perspective. Second, relevant legal cases are cited in order to outline the impact of specific marketing communications and distribution practices in establishing a consumer Plaintiff's lawsuit. Finally, the implications of these trends for marketing practitioners are discussed. By taking several suggested steps, practitioners should be able to minimize their company's product liability vulnerability.

AN OVERVIEW OF THE PRODUCT LIABILITY "PROBLEM"

It is not hard to find conflicting evidence regarding the seriousness of the total product liability problem. For example, while product liability insurance premiums for manufacturers and retailers climbed from $1.3 billion in 1975 to $2.75 billion in 1978 (*Business Week* 1979), these premiums amount to less than 1% of sales dollars for the majority of firms (McKinsey & Company 1977). The average bodily injury settlement rose from $6,800 to $19,500 between 1972 and 1974 (McKinsey & Company 1977), although the average judgment for all product liability claims increased 100% from 1965–69 to 1970–75, not at all an alarming rate considering the length of time and the inflation in health care costs (The Research Group 1977).

Other inconsistent data can be offered, but one point has been clearly established: The product liability problem is a complex one and can be measured by several criteria including insurance premiums, settlements, claims administration costs, legal fees and number of claims filed. Depending on the criteria selected, the extent of the liability problem varies. Most experts seem to agree that the increase in insurance premiums experienced by many firms is an indication that insurance companies had not anticipated the increase in number of filed claims and settlement sizes in the late 1960s and early 1970s. Thus drastic premium increases were enforced in a short period of time, mainly 1974 to 1977, rather than experiencing a gradual increase beginning earlier.

From a marketing perspective, the product liability situation has been even less clearly described. Most product liability insurance is sold as a part of a firm's general liability coverage; therefore, many firms do not have detailed records (*Final Report* 1978), except perhaps for the last two or three years. There is also a time lag between the filing of a liability claim and the eventual settling of the case (Perham 1977) making existing data somewhat outdated. In addition, no data exist that correlate substantive product liability doctrines with the number and size of settlements (Johnson 1978).

Despite the paucity of information, implications for marketers can be extracted from three major studies of the product liability field (Alliance 1980, *Final Report* 1978, Insurance Services 1977), along with related follow-up reports (Gordon Associates 1977, McKinsey & Company 1977, *Selected Papers* 1978, The Research Group 1977, *Uniform Product Liability Law* 1979). Several conclusions of these studies are relevant for marketing practitioners.

Table 1 shows categories of injured persons for both bodily injury and property damage settlements, with the former accounting for more than 85% of total payments to injured parties (Insurance Services 1977). Generally, industrial workers (employees) suffered fewer losses than purchasers or users of consumer products; however, for large loss claims (awards larger than $100,000) two-thirds of the claims were filed by employees (Alliance 1980, "Can Monstrous Product. . ." 1980). Injuries to workers often involve machinery, which can cause very serious disabling injuries (Insurance Services 1977).

Users of products average three (for bodily injury) to four (for property damage) times larger settlements than purchasers of products. Nearly 50% of the people reimbursed for bodily injuries are nonwage earners (Insurance Services 1977). Organizations can suffer property damage losses but not bodily injury. While two-thirds of the parties receiving property damage settlements are individuals, nearly three-fourths of these payments go to organizations. Most expensive machinery that is damaged is likely to belong to corporations or other organizations (Insurance Services 1977).

More than 87% of total product liability payments are based on claims against manufacturers (Insurance Services 1977), compared with 85% for large loss claims (Alliance 1980). Thus the producer of an item is much more likely to be involved in a settlement than a distributor (only 4.6% and 4.1% of total payments on behalf of wholesalers and retailers in the ISO and AAI studies).

Finally, food items generate the most bodily injury claims, while most property damage claims result from automobile related goods

TABLE 1
Status of Injured Persons/Parties

Liability Category	Injured Party	# of Persons with Payment	% of Persons with Payment	% of Total Payment	Average Payment
Bodily injury:	Employee	875	10.6%	42.0%	$97,884
	Purchaser	5,562	67.5	28.7	10,544
	User (not purchaser)	1,441	17.5	22.5	31,836
	Other	364	4.4	6.8	38,016
	Total	8,242	100.0%	100.0%	$24,752
Property damage:	Employee	12	0.2%	0.0%	$ 325
	Purchaser	3,928	78.7	64.3	5,466
	User (not purchaser)	359	7.2	22.8	21,185
	Other	695	3.9	12.9	6,176
	Total	4,994	100.0%	100.0%	$ 6,682

SOURCE: Insurance Services 1977, p. 60, 63.

(auto service and repair, auto parts and tires) (Insurance Services 1977). Automobile parts, prescription drugs, and valves are responsible for most payments for bodily injury claims; however, valves, clothing and miscellaneous services account for the largest per-incident bodily injury settlements (Insurance Services 1977). Increasing product liability costs seem to be oppressive in only a few industries such as industrial machinery, industrial chemicals, automotive components and pharmaceuticals (Alliance 1980, McKinsey & Company 1977).

Several conclusions for marketers can be drawn from this data:

- Industrial goods manufacturers face considerably fewer, but potentially much more damaging, claims/lawsuits for both bodily injury and property damage than consumer goods manufacturers.
- Consumer goods manufacturers should warn users other than purchasers ("bystanders" in a legal context) as well as buyers of products.
- Organizations, primarily corporations, receive much larger but many fewer property damage payments than individuals.
- Manufacturers are much more vulnerable to product liability claims than are resellers (wholesalers and retailers).
- Markets for automobile parts, chemicals, pharmaceuticals, clothing and industrial machinery are the most dangerous from the standpoint of exposure to very large product liability claims.

These conclusions present a general picture of the prevailing product liability situation; however, a more detailed review is required if marketing managers are to understand how specific marketing managers are to understand how specific marketing practices can lead to liability. The next section looks at lawsuits involving marketing activities (or omissions) from the perspective of different product liability theories.

CASE LAW TRENDS

Based on case law decisions, the marketing activities that could result in a company being party to a lawsuit include: (1) statements and actions of salespersons and other sales personnel, (2) print or broadcast advertisements, (3) labeling and written instructions, (4) retailers' actions and (5) wholesalers' actions. Thus the manufacturer's communications mix and distribution system are the critical elements to monitor if marketing-based liability for personal injury or property damage is to be avoided.

The marketing activities that could lead to liability are discussed in the context of the four major theories of product liability: negligence, breach of warranty, strict liability and misrepresentation. Each liability theory is described briefly; a full treatment of technical differences among the theories is beyond the scope of this article.

Negligence

Negligence is generally defined as a violation of the duty to use ordinary care under given circumstances (*American Jurisprudence 2d* 1971). If a person of ordinary prudence would not have performed the act, it is a negligent act. Negligence is, therefore, a breach of duty of reasonable care under the circumstances on the part of the seller (marketer).

The duty to exercise reasonable care extends to all parts of the production and distribution process (Kimble and Lesher 1979). Salespersons can be negligent in the way in which they present a product to a client (*Incollingo* v. *Ewing* 1971, *Love* v. *Wolf* 1967). In *Stevens* v. *Parke, Davis* (1973) salespersons overpromoted a drug product to the extent of causing physicians to pay little attention to warning circulars. When one user of the drug died as a result of a complication described in the warning circular, the manufacturer who did not provide adequate warning was found to be negligent because of its selling tactics.

Advertisements have been found to be actionably negligent acts in several cases (Morgan 1979). Plaintiffs must be able to convince the court that they relied upon the advertisement and that negligence in advertising caused the injury or harm (Hursh and Bailey 1974). Advertisements extolling product safety have led to liability for negligent design (*Texas Bitulithic* v. *Caterpillar* 1962). Specific advertised claims may create certain responsibilities for extra care in manufacturing (*W. H. Elliott* v. *King* 1961). The advertised slogan, "ready-to-serve boned chicken," required the defendant to exercise such care as to permit users to trust with reasonable certainty that bones had been removed from the product (*Bryer* v. *Rath* 1959).

Negligence claims regarding deficient labels have been upheld on behalf of an 18-month-old child (*Jonescue* v. *Jewel* 1974) and two semiliterate laborers (*Dougherty* v. *Hooker* 1976). In *Harrison* v. *Flota* (1978) a worker was severely injured when he inhaled fumes while cleaning up a chemical spill. The court found that the defendant had negligently failed to provide a reasonable and adequate warning label covering the chemical's dangerous properties. The word *prolonged*, as used on the label, was deemed vague; moreover, the label contained no information about how to clean up a spill. The fact that none of the plaintiffs in these cases had read the warning labels did not bar their recovery.

If a manufacturer, as a part of its marketing program, relies on certain retailers to inspect the product or to perform other activities, the manufacturer could be held negligently liable if the retailers are lax. Ford Motor Company was found negligent when one of its dealers failed to replace brake fluid at the appropriate inspection interval, resulting in a serious automobile accident (*Hasson* v. *Ford* 1977). By following prudent inspection procedures, the retailer could have prevented Ford from being held liable because the accident would not have occurred.

Retailers are ordinarily not chargeable for negligence relating to the manufacture of a product (*Product Liability Reporter* 1974). If the retailer is responsible for assembling the product or preparing it for sale to the consumer, the retailer can be found negligent for improper workmanship (*Parisi* v. *Bush* 1949). Retailers have been found negligent for breach of duty to inspect and test the manufacturers' products, even though the manufacturer is reputable and the product defect is not obvious. If retailers should have discovered the defect by exercising reasonable care, given their special product knowledge, they can be found negligent (*Finger* v. *Dobbs* 1978, *Hunt* v. *Ford* 1977).

Retailers have a duty to warn, verbally or through labels or instructions, whenever they have knowledge about a product's dangerous condition and when it appears that the consumer will not discover the danger (*Stapinski* v. *Walsh* 1978, *Westerman* v. *Sears* 1978). The jury questions of whether a warning should have been given and, if given, whether it was sufficient, are difficult ones.

Any institution in the distribution channel can be negligent simply by selling certain products. Examples include selling firearms to minors, drugs to obviously intoxicated persons and gasoline in unlabeled containers (*Product Liability Reporter* 1974).

By labeling a product as their own, retailers shift the burden of liability to themselves from the manufacturers (*Bigham* v. *J. C. Penney* 1978, *Moody* v. *Sears* 1971, *Spiller* v. *Ward* 1974). This status as "imputed manufacturer" (*Restatement* 1965) holds, even if the retailer could not possibly have discovered the defect after taking delivery of the item (Kimble and Lesher 1979).

Wholesalers technically owe duties to inspect, test and warn product users; however, since they neither manufacture the product nor sell it to final consumers, wholesalers are often merely "innocent" redistributors of packaged goods. The wholesaler generally has no obligation to inspect products in sealed packages (*Gobin* v. *Avenue* 1960), especially if the manufacturer is reputable (Kimble and Lesher 1979). As a result, very few cases based on negligence have been brought against wholesalers (Frumer and Friedman 1980).

The wholesaler must warn, however, when its channel position makes it more knowledgeable about the product than the retailer (*Blasing* v. *Hardenburgh* 1975, *Mehochko* v. *Gold Seal* 1966, *Starr* v. *Koppers* 1966). A dynamite wholesaler, dealing with hardware, and implement retailers, was judged negligent for failing to instruct the retailers about proper fuse lengths (*Cooley* v. *Quick* 1974). When one customer of a retailer was severely injured, the wholesaler was found negligent for not checking to see whether the retailers were giving instruction pamphlets and verbal directions to dynamite buyers.

Warranty

In contrast to negligence, a tort action, warranty is a contractual theory of recovery governed by principles of sales (Kimble and Lesher 1979). A warranty is a representation by the manufacturer/seller about the product's qualities or characteristics.

Express warranties are described in detail in the *Uniform Commercial Code* (1972). A central issue in determining the existence of an express warranty is the extent of allowable seller puffing. General statements or affirmations that are nothing more than the seller's opinions about the product do not create an express warranty. Of course, distinguishing between express warranties and puffing is often left to the jury.

An implied warranty may exist as a matter of law even when no express warranty is stated. An implied warranty of merchantability is part of a sales contract, unless explicitly modified or negated, whenever the seller regularly offers the product in question for sale (*Uniform Commercial Code* 1972). Thus the occasional seller, such as a student selling a used book, is excluded from consideration here. This implied warranty means that the item is of average quality and can be used for the purposes for which such a product typically is used. The implied warranty of merchantability is established by the mere fact that a transaction takes place.

By contrast, an implied warranty of fitness arises when the buyer relies on the seller for advice regarding the suitability of the product for the buyer's intended purposes. To recover for breach of an implied warranty of fitness, the buyer must be able to demonstrate this reliance and that the seller can establish an implied warranty of fitness.

Salespersons can readily establish express warranties during conversations with prospects (*A. L. Bell* v. *Harrington* 1975, *Griffin* v. *Wheeler-Leonard* 1976) as well as implied warranties of fitness, if the salesperson makes specific performance promises with regard to the prospect's intended use of the product (*Chemco* v. *DuPont* 1973). In three cases in which cattle were the victims, salespersons' statements about specific levels of milk production and weight gain were considered to be express warranties. When these promises were not met, the livestock owners recovered (*Boehm* v. *Fox* 1973, *D. L. Heil* v. *Standard* 1974, *Shotkoski* v. *Standard* 1975).

Whenever salespersons are clearly overstating the product's capabilities, the statements are likely to be considered puffing. If the salesperson obviously has superior product knowledge compared with the buyer, the salesperson's statements even if somewhat exaggerated are more likely to be interpreted by the courts as warranties (Morgan and Bodecker 1980). Further, total misrepresentation by the salesperson, though done unintentionally, might be taken as a warranty if the buyer is deceived (*American Jurisprutience 2d* 1973).

Advertising may easily be the basis for an express warranty. Consider the following statement from a widely distributed product liability reference (Frumer and Friedman 1980, paragraph 16.04):

Manufacturers constantly extol and represent the quality of their products on labels, on billboards, on radio and T.V., newspapers and magazines, in brochures made available for dealers who are expected to disseminate them to prospective purchasers,...an increasing number of cases are holding or recognizing that under such circumstances a consumer can recover for breach of an express warrenty....

In *Scheuler* v. *Aamco* (1977) the substantial advertising support provided by Aamco to one of its franchised dealers was noted by the court as linking Aamco with a guarantee the dealer gave to its customers. The advertisements also mentioned Aamco's "coast-to-coast ironclad guarantee." Thus the advertisements did not warrant against product failure, but they did establish the tie between Aamco and the written guarantee.

Catalog statements have been interpreted as advertised express warranties when products have failed to perform as stated (*Community*

v. *Dresser* 1977). Occasionally an implied warranty can arise out of advertised statements. Advertising and labels can create certain reasonable expectations in consumer's minds which, if not fulfilled, could lead to breach of implied warranty. When the plaintiff relied on televised advertising about the conditioning and revitalizing effects of a hair treatment, she recovered when her hair became brittle and had to be cut off (*West* v. *Alberto Culver* 1973).

In a labeling case, an implied warranty of fitness was also breached (*Wilson* v. *E-Z Flo* 1972a). The label on a chemical product specified that the product would perform in a certain manner if used according to instructions stated in an accompanying manual. Though noticing that the manual was missing, the retailer sold some of the chemical to the plaintiff, who recovered from the retailer (*Wilson* v. *E-Z Flo* 1972b).

A diagram was determined to be an express warranty to a child that a product could be used safely (*Tirino* v. *Kenner* 1973). The diagram apparently led a seven-year-old boy to apply the product to his face, supposedly causing his face to glow in the dark. The child recovered when the product dripped into his eyes, resulting in considerable irritation.

Usually the express warranty of a manufacturer does not bind the retailer (*Henry* v. *Don Wood* 1974) or wholesaler (*L. A. Green* v. *Williams* 1969) who sells the product when there is no evidence that either reseller has adopted the warranty. But the retailer's conduct may indicate to the court that it has adopted the manufacturer's warranty (*Wilson* v. *E-Z Flo* 1972b). If the manufacturer is at fault, the *Uniform Commercial Code* (1972) allows the retailer to "vouch in" the manufacturer thereby assigning the defense to the latter; likewise, the wholesaler may vouch in the manufacturer.

The same implied warranties of the manufacturer are basically applicable to all nonmanufacturing sellers (Hursh and Bailey 1974) that is, to both retailers and wholesalers. Retailers of food products (*Huebner* v. *Hunter* 1978), beverages (*Demars* v. *Natchitoches* 1977), drugs (*Bichler* v. *Willing* 1977), and cosmetics (*Carpenter* v. *Alberto Culver* 1971) have to exercise greater care regarding implied warranties of fitness or wholesomeness.

Strict Liability

Strict tort liability is a relatively new doctrine and has been associated with the influx of product liability litigation in the U.S. in the past 20 years (*Product Liabiliy Reporter* 1974). Strict liability developed as a response to a complex, consumer oriented economy in which buyers and users acquire products from manufacturers through a series of intermediate sellers.

Strict liability has eliminated some of the burdensome elements of both negligence and warranty actions. On the other hand, strict liability is not absolute liability. The plaintiff must prove that the product was defective when it left the defendant's control and that the product in question caused the plaintiff's injury. Thus strict liability represents a melding of warranty and negligence principles and introduces no concepts that were not already known and applied earlier (Kimble and Lesher 1979).

In a strict liability action, the quality of the product is questioned, not the possible breach of duty of reasonable care by the defendant (Weinstein et al. 1978). The basic statement of strict liability is set forth in *Restatement* (1965, section 402A):

1. One who sells any product in a defective condition unreasonably dangerous to the user or consumer or to his property is subject to liability for physical harm thereby caused to the ultimate user or consumer, or to his property, if
    (a) The seller is engaged in the business of selling such a product, and
    (b) it is expected to and does reach the user or consumer without substantial change in the condition in which it is sold.
2. The rule stated in Subsection (1) applies although
    (a) the seller has exercised all possible care in the preparation and sale of his product, and
    (b) the user and consumer has not bought the product from or entered into any contractual relation with the seller.

Since the quality of the product is the key issue in strict liability pleadings, actions of salespersons are generally irrelevant. In transcripts of strict liability lawsuits, salespersons are occasionally mentioned but only because they may have sold the faulty products to the plaintiffs. Likewise, advertising has been only briefly mentioned in strict liability cases. In one case in which the seller of a defective tire was held strictly liable, the trial court referred to "sustained and vigorous advertising campaigns" (*McCann* v. *Atlas* 1971, p. 704). The judge implied that advertisements increased consumers' expectations regarding product performance. Thus societal legal standards could be altered by advertising programs.

Both statements by salespersons and advertised claims are discussed in greater detail with regard to tort liability in the next section. Section 402B (*Restatement* 1965) contains the rule of strict liability for misrepresentation which, for marketers, is especially relevant for selling and advertising activities.

Labels and printed warnings have been determined to be insufficient, thereby creating defective products in several cases (*Baker v. St. Agnes* 1979, *Bituminous v. Black* 1974, *Nissen v. Terre Haute* 1975, *Ortho v. Chapman* 1979). A lathe operator recovered from the manufacturer of safety glasses when they shattered during use, resulting in an eye injury (*American v. Weidenhamer* 1980). Prominently displayed on the box in which the glasses were delivered were the phrases *safety glasses, Sure Guard* and *surest protection*. A small warning was wrapped around the nosepiece of the glasses stating that they were not unbreakable and that they should be checked for pitting and scratching. Another person had removed this warning tag before giving the glasses to the plaintiff. The court decided that the warning was "dramatically smaller" in terms of print size than the above printed phrases, and the warning was ruled insufficient. Because of this ruling, the fact that the warning had been removed from the plaintiffs glasses by someone else was inconsequential.

Under strict liability the content and meaning of the label and accompanying warnings are examined in a different fashion in comparison with negligence and warranty actions. In a strict liability case the issues are likely to be presence or absence of appropriate labels, the size of print or the location of statements with regard to sales slogans.

Retailers can be brought within the scope of liability under section 402A (*Restatement* 1965), even if they do not deal exclusively or even primarily with the offending products (*Product Liability Reporter* 1974, paragraph 4160; *Sochanski v. Sears* 1979). Several reasons are commonly cited for holding retailers strictly liable: they are engaged in distributing their goods to the public and should therefore be held accountable for faulty goods: often they are the only visible parties to whom injured consumers can turn for redress; and they often play a major role in ensuring that the product is safe or they may pressure manufacturers for this purpose (*Corpus Juris Secondum* 1975). In *Chappius v. Sears* (1977) Sears was found strictly liable for not warning about the possible dangers of using a chipped hammer. The manufacturer from whom Sears purchased and labeled the hammer had also failed to include such a warning and was held liable. The court noted that Sears should have known about this danger because of its size, merchandising skills and power to control the quality of its products.

Courts have been reluctant to hold wholesalers strictly liable in all cases in which they have handled defective products, but under 402A (*Restatement* 1965) and its application, liability could attach even though wholesalers have never transacted with ultimate users of products (*Product Liability Reporter* 1974). A distributor of an aluminum coating machine was strictly liable when a workman using the machine was injured (*Rabadi* v. *Price* 1980). The court even mentioned that the distributor was not the principal defendant and that it was quite unlikely that the jury could conclude that the distributor manufactured the machine.

Conversely, a brokerage firm that arranged the sale of a drug proven to be the cause of death of a child was found not liable (*Lyons* v. *Premo* 1979). The brokerage firm was ruled to have had a passive role in the sale of the product, unlike the drug manufacturers who controlled the product and its quality.

Misrepresentation

The common thread uniting theories of negligence, warranty and strict liability is the defective product. Without a product defect, recovery is not allowed under any of these theories (*Corpus Juris Secondum* 1975). There is, however, the special case of misrepresentation, where the item is manufactured exactly according to nonnegligent standards. Misrepresentation is covered in section 402B of the *Restatement* (1965), which permits a tort recovery:

> One engaged in the business of selling chattels who, by advertising, labels, or otherwise, makes to the public a misrepresentation of material fact concerning the character or quality of a chattel sold by him is subject to liability for physical harm to a consumer of the chattel caused by justifiable reliance upon the misrepresentation, even though
> (a) it is not made fraudulently or negligently, and
> (b) the consumer has not bought the chattel from or entered into any contractual relation with the seller.

Thus liability could attach if someone is injured who relied on false representations, even if they are made honestly based on laboratory or consumer research. The product itself is not defective but unrealistic performance claims were made about it. Misrepresentation under this section can occur without privity of contract or any statutory violation regardless of any dishonesty, bad faith, negligence or other fault (Kimble and Lesher 1979). Section 402B is another example of society's reacting to the influence of marketing practices, especially mass advertising, on consumer purchasing. Despite the ominous implications, the section has rarely been invoked (*Product Liability Reporter* 1974).

The leading case involving statements by sales persons resulting in misrepresentational liability is *Crocker* v. *Winthrop* (1974). Drug salespersons overpromoted a product to physicians and, according to the court, caused physicians to pay little attention to printed warnings about the drug. When one patient died as a result of drug addiction, a side effect that the salespersons specifically mentioned could not occur, the drug manufacturer was liable under section 402B. The salespersons' claims, apparently made in good faith and based on laboratory research, were critical in establishing the liability claim.

Advertising has also been cited as a marketing practice that led to a misrepresentation finding. In *Klages* v. *General* (1976) advertising brochures and other promotional materials contained claims that a Mace spray would totally and instantly subdue an assailant. A motel clerk was seriously injured by a burglar who was not immediately overcome by the spray. The manufacturer of the spray was found liable over its claims that the brochures amounted only to seller's puffing, a common defense in such a case (*Hoffman* v. *Chance* 1972).

In *Winkler* v. *American* (1979) a helmet was depicted on a carton as being used by a motorcyclist. Seeing this carton, an experienced police officer purchased the helmet for use while riding his motorcycle on duty. The helmet was not intended to be used as a motorcycle safety helmet, despite the carton diagrams. The helmet was also available to the general public at sporting goods stores. The court determined that the carton diagram had indeed been viewed by the public and could easily have been interpreted to mean that motorcyclists could safely use the helmet. Misrepresentation under section 402B therefore followed directly.

In *Hauter* v. *Zogarts* (1975) a teenage boy was injured while using a golf-training device. The label on the shipping carton and the cover of the instruction booklet both contained the statement, *Completely safe. Ball will not hit player.* The court viewed this statement as a false yet innocent misrepresentation, not seller's puffery. So either symbols or words can misrepresent the capabilities of a product, leading to manufacturer liability.

Though retailers have been parties to misrepresentation pleadings (*Klages* v. *General* 1976), they have generally been able to secure indemnification from manufacturers. Wholesalers have typically not been involved in misrepresentation lawsuits. It is quite conceivable, however, that both retailers and wholesalers could be held liable for the misrepresentations of their salespersons or of advertised statements.

Being the most recently developed and least used theory of liability in cases involving marketing activities, misrepresentation is still evolving in the courts. At this time, two issues that affect marketing have yet to be resolved. First, misrepresentation has been applied only when statements or disclosures have been alleged to be incorrect or misleading. Whether nondisclosure of relevant information constitutes misrepresentation remains undetermined (Kimble and Lesher 1979). Second, misrepresentation has been charged only in regard to communications to large numbers of product purchasers, not in the case of one or two individuals or nonconsuming buyers (*Product Liability Reporter* 1974). Liability due to marketing communications could readily be expanded if nondisclosures of important data to nonconsumers or to a single user are judged to be misrepresentations.

Conclusions Drawn from Case Law Trends

The cases discussed above illustrate current legal thought regarding the kinds of marketing practices that result in liability for personal injury or property damage because of faulty or improperly handled products. It should be clear from the descriptions of these cases that, for a given set of marketing activities, a company could be sued under several theories of product liability. Since the plaintiff will attempt to establish liability under each theory the firm must be prepared to counter each of the accusations. For example, by refuting a charge of negligent labeling and packaging, the firm has not, as a matter of law, precluded a jury finding of strict liability for inadequate labeling. Every charge must be overcome, if the defendant company is to prevail.

The key cases with which marketing managers should become familiar are cross-referenced in Table 2 according to marketing activity involved and relevant legal theory. By studying these cases, the manager will be in a much stronger position to develop communications and distribution progams that do not implicate the company in product liability actions.

TABLE 2
Product Liability for Marketing Activities under Different Theories of Liability: Selected Cases.

		Legal Theory		
Marketing Activities	**Negligence**	**Warranty**	**Strict Liability**	**Misrepresentation**
Selling	Stevens v. Parke, Davis (1973) Incollingo v.Ewing (1971)	Shotkoski v. Standard (1975) Griffin v. Wheeler-Leonard (1976)	—	Crocker v.Wintnrop (1974)
Advertising	Texas Bitulithic v. Caterpillar (1962) W. H. Eliott v. King (1961)	Scheuler v. Aamco (1977) West v.Alberto Culver (1973)	McCann v. Atlas (1971)	Klages v. General (1976) Hoffman v. Chance (1972)
Labeling and Packaging	Harrison v. Flota (1978) Jonescue v. Jewel (1974)	Tirino v. Kenner (1973) Wiison v. E-Z Flo (1972b)	American v. Weidenhamer (1980) Baker v. St. Agnes (1979)	Winkler v. American (1979) Hauter v. Zogarts (1975)
Retailing	Hasson v. Ford (1977) Moody v. Sears (1971) Stauinski v. Walsh (1978)	Henry v. Don Wood (1974) Huebner v. Hunter (1978)	Chappius v. Sears (1977) Sochanski v. Sears (1979)	—
Wholesaling	Cooley v. Quick (1974) Blasing v. Hardenburgh (1975)	L. A. Green v. Williams (1969)	Lyons v. Premo (1979) Rabadi v. Price (1980)	—

Since every case presents the court with a unique fact situation to consider, generalizations that hold across a strong majority of product liability cases and also lead to specific managerial implications are difficult to state. Nevertheless, given the discussion of the cases above, several broad conclusions can be suggested:

- Companies can be held liable for damages under negligence and warranty pleadings due to marketing communications—statements by salespersons, advertised messages, and packaging and labeling.
- Marketing communications can result in liability due to innocent misrepresentation of facts.
- Since strict liability is based on a product defect, advertising and personal selling activities are generally irrelevant in a strict liability pleading.
- Courts have interpreted defective labels, warnings and packaging as defective products, thereby establishing strict liability actions.
- Distributors—retailers and wholesalers—are generally not liable for the misrepresentations of manufacturers. Distributors' communications to customers can, however, misrepresent the product.
- Distributors are less likely to be found liable for product-related damages than manufacturers because the former are often able to assign the defense to the latter.
- Distributors who brand products as their own are treated as manufacturers, thereby exposing themselves to manufacturers' liability under all theories of liability.
- One channel member's warranty generally does not bind another channel member unless the latter, either explicitly or through its actions, has adopted the warranty.
- The negligent acts of one channel member can result in other channel members being held liable if they should have anticipated the negligent act.

IMPLICATIONS

Marketing managers should keep abreast of product liability trends. To do this, the marketer must keep in close communication with the company's legal counsel and liability insurers. Both court decisions and insurance settlements are vital sources of information. Court decisions reflect current thought regarding the acceptability of business practices and often provide a measure of the cost to corporations of product liability claims. The vast majority of claims,

96% for bodily injury and 97% for property damage (*Insurance Services* 1977) are settled without a court verdict. Marketing managers must also assist their departments in developing a product safety attitude. Since manufacturing and engineering departments tend to be the focus of most product liability claims (*Insurance Services* 1977), marketers may develop a complacent attitude with regard to minimizing liability. This would be unfortunate because many departments within the firm must act responsibly to prevent product liability claims (Chandran and Linneman 1978, Perham 1977).

Liability prevention programs should be written for the entire corporation (Keeton, Owen and Montgomery 1980, Ross and Foley 1979) and the program for the marketing department should be consistent with organizational goals regarding liability prevention. These prevention programs should try to anticipate future problems (Gray et al. 1975). By providing each employee in the marketing department with practical guidelines, product safety will become a legitimate concern within the department.

Finally, consumer education programs should be instituted to narrow the gap between what consumers know and what they should know about product safety (Gray et al. 1975). Marketing activities are especially useful here. Televised advertisements can illustrate visually the safe and correct use of products. Salespersons can perform a reminder function by encouraging buyers to read instructional and safety pamphlets. Retailers can double-check the manufacturers' assembling and packaging procedures. Informed consumers may ultimately be the company's best insurance against product liability due to improper marketing practices.

REFERENCES

A. L. Bell v. *Harrington Manufacturing Company* (1975), 219 S.E.2d 906 (S.Ct. S.C.)

Alliance of American Insurers (1980), *A Survey of Large-Loss Product Liability Claims,* Chicago: Alliance of American Insurers.

American Jurisprudence 2d. Negligence (1971), 57.

American Jurisprudence 2d. Sales (1973), 67.

American Optical Company v. *Weidenhamer* (1980), CCH Prod.Liab.Rep. para. 8670 (C.A.4 Ind.).

Baker v. *St. Agnes Hospital* (1979), CCH Prod.Liab.Rep. para. 8563 (N.Y. Sup.Ct.App.Div.).

Bichler v. *Willing* (1977), 58 App.Div.2d 331, 397 N.Y.2d 57.

Bigham v. *J. C. Penney Co.* (1978), 268 N.W.2d 892, CCH Prod.Liab.Rep. para. 8196 (Minn.).

Bituminous Casualty Corp. v. *Black and Decker Manufacturing Co.* (1974), CCH Prod.Liab.Rep. para. 7445, 518 S.W.2d 868 (Tex.Cir.App.).

Blasing v. *P. R. L. Hardenburgh Co.* (1975), 226 N.W.2d 110, CCH Prod.Liab.Rep. Pra. 7394 (S.Ct. Minn.).

Boehm v. *Fox* (1973), CCH Prod.Liab.Rep. para. 6894 (C.A. 10 Kan.).

Bryer v. *Rath Packing Co.* (1957), 221 Md. 105, 156 A.2d, 442, 77 A.L.R.2d 1.

Business Week (1979), "The Devils in the Product Liability Laws," (February 12), 72–78.

—— (1980), "A Product Liability Bill Has Insurers Uptight," (March 31), 43.

—— (1981), "More Punitive Damage Awards," (January 12), 86.

"Can Monstrous Product Liability Claims Be Contained?" (1980), *Journal of American Insurance*, 56 (Fall), 20–22.

Carpenter v. *Alberto Culver Co.*, 28 Mich.App. 399, 184 N.W.2d 547 (1971).

Chandran, Rajan and Robert Linneman (1978), "Planning to Minimize Product Liability," *Sloan Management Review*, 30 (Fall), 33–45.

Chappius v. *Sears, Roebuck & Co. (1977), 349 So.2d 963 (La.App. 1st Cir.).*

Chemco Industrial Applicators Co. v. *E. I. DuPont de Nemours & Co.* (1973), 366 F.Supp. 278, CCH Prod.Liab.Rep. para 7122 (U.S.D.C. E.D.Mo.).

Community Television Services, Inc. v. *Dresser Industries, Inc.* (1977), 435 F.Supp. 214 (D.C. S.D.), aff'd 586 F.2d 637 (C.A.8 1978).

Cooley v. *Quick Supply Company* (1974), 221 N.W.2d 763 (S.Ct. Ia.).

Corpus Juris Secondum, Supplement, Products Liability (1975), 72.

Crocker v. *Winthrop Laboratories, Division of Sterling Drug, Inc.* (1974), 514 S.W.2d 429 (Tex.).

D. L. Heil v. *Standard Chemical Manufacturing Company* (1974), 223 N.W.2d 37 (S.Ct. Minn.).

Demars v. *Natchitoches Coca-Cola Bottling Co.* (1977), 353 So.2d 433, cert. den. 354 So.2d 1384 (La. 1977).

Dougherty v. *Hooker Chemical Corp.* (1976), 540 F.2d 174 (3rd Cir.).

Final Report (1978), *Interagency Task Force on Product Liability*, U.S. Department of Commerce, Washington, DC: U.S. Government Printing Office.

Finger v. Dobbs (1978), CCH Prod. Liab. Rep. para. 8138 (C.A. Tenn.).

Frumer, Louis R. and Melvin I. Friedman (1980), *Products Liability*, New York: Mathew Bender.

Gobin v. Avenue Food Mart (1960), 178 Cal.App.2d 345, 2 Cal. Rptr. 822.

Gordon Associates, Inc. (1977), *Interagency Task Force on Product Liability; Final Report of the Industry Study*, Springfield, VA: National Technical Information Service.

Gray, Irwin, Albert L. Bases, Charles H. Martin and Alexander Sternberg (1975), *Product Liability: A Management Response*, New York: AMACOM.

Griffin v. Wheeler-Leonard Co., Inc. (1976), 290 N.C. 185, 225 S.E.2d 557.

Harrison v. Flota Mercante Grancolombi, ANA, S.A. (1978), CCH Prod. Liab. Rep. para. 8350 (C.A.5).

Hasson v. Ford Motor Company (1977), 564 P.2d 857, 138 Cal. Rptr. 705.

Hauter v. Zogarts (1975), 14 Cal.3d 104, 120 Cal. Rptr. 681, 534 P.2d 377.

Henry v. Don Wood Volkswagen, Inc. (1974), 562 S.W.2d 483, CCH Prod. Liab. Rep. para. 7364 (C.A. Tenn.).

Hoffman v. A. B. Chance Co. (1972), 339 F.Supp. 1385 (D.C. Pa.).

Huebner v. Hunter Packing Co. (1978), 59 Ill.App.3rd 563, 16 Ill. Dec. 766, 375 N.E.2d 873.

Hunt v. Ford Motor Co. (1977), CCH Prod. Liab. Rep. para. 7929 (C.A. La.).

Hursh, Robert D. and Henry J. Bailey (1974), *American Law of Product Liability*, 2nd edition, Rochester NY: The Lawyers Co-operative Publishing Co.

Incollingo v. Ewing (1971), 444 Pa. 263, 282 A.2d 206.

Insurance Services Ofiice (1977), *Product Liability Closed Claim Survey: A Technical Analysis of Survey Results*, New York: Insurance Services Office.

Johnson, Anita (1978), "Behind the Hype on Product Liability," *The Forum*, 14 (Fall), 317–326.

Jonescue v. Jewel Home Shopping Service (1974), 306 N.E.2d 312.

Keeton, W. Page, David G. Owen and John E. Montgomery (1980), *Products Liability and Safety: Cases and Materials*, Mineola, NY: Foundation Press.

Kimble, William and Robert O. Lesher (1979), *Products Liability*, St. Paul, MN: West Publishing Company.

Klages v. General Ordnance Equipment Corp. (1976), 367 A.2d 304 (Pa.Sup.Ct.).

L. A. Green Seed Co. v. Williams (1976), 246 Ark. 456, 438 S.W.2d 717.

Love v. Wolf (1967), 249 Cal.App.2d 822, 58 Cal.Rptr. 42.

Lyons v. Premo Pharmaceutical Labs, Inc. (1979), CCH Prod.Liab.Rep. para. 8547 (Super.Ct. N.J.).

McCann v. Atlas Supply Company (1971), 325 F.Supp. 701 (D.C. Pa.).

McKinsey & Company, Inc. (1977), *Interagency Task Force on Product Liability; Final Report of the Insurance Study*, Springfield, VA: National Technical Information Service.

Mehochko v. Gold Seal Company (1966), 213 N.E.2d 581 (C.A.5 Ill.).

Moody v. Sears, Roebuck & Co. (1971), 324 F.Supp. 844 (D.C. Ga.).

Morgan, Fred W. (1979), "The Products Liability Consequences of Advertising," *Journal of Advertising*, 8 (Fall), 30–37.

———— and Karl A. Boedecker (1980), "The Role of Personal Selling in Produce Liability Litigation," *Journal of Personal Selling & Sales Management*, 1 (Fall-Winter), 34–40.

Nissen Trampoline co. v. Terre Haute First National Bank (1975), CCH Prod. Liab. Rep. para. 7800, 332 N.E.2d 820 (Ind.App.), rev'd on other grounds, 358 N.E.2d 974 (1976).

Ortho Pharmaceutical Corp. v. Chapman (1979), CCH Prod. Liab. Rep. para. 8450, 388 N.E.2d 541 (Ind.App.).

Parisi v. Carl W. Bush Co. (1949), 67 A.2d 875, 4 N.J.Super. 472.

Perham, John C. (1977), "The Dilemma in Product Liability," *Dun's Review*, 109 (January), 48–50, 76.

Product Liabiliy Reporter (1974), New York: Commerce Clearing House.

Rabadi v. Price Sales & Engineering, Inc. (1980), CCH Prod.Liab.Rep. para. 8620 (D.C. N.Y.).

Restatement (Second) of Torts (1965), American Law Institute.

Ross, Kenneth and Martin J. Foley (1979), *Product Liabiliy of Manufacturers: Prevention and Defense*, NY: Practicing Law Institute.

Scheuler v. Aamco Transmissions, Inc. (1977), 1 Kan.App.2d 525, 571 P.2d 48.

Selected Papers (1978), *Interagency Task Force on Product Liability*, U.S. Department of Commerce, Washington, DC: U.S. Government Printing Office.

Shotkoski v. *Standard Chemical Manufacturing Company* (1975), 237 N.W.2d 92 (Neb.).

Sochanski v. *Sears, Roebuck & Co.* (1979), 477 F.Supp. 320 (E.D. Pa.), CCH Prod. Liab. Rep. para. 8674 (C.A.3 1980).

Spiller v. *Montgomery Ward & Co.* (1974), 294 So.2d 803 (La.).

Stapinski v. *Walsh Construction Co., Inc.* (1978), CCH Prod. Liab. Rep. para. 8341 (C.A. Inc.).

Starr v. *Koppers Company* (1966), 398 S.W.2d 827, CCH Prod. Liab. Rep. para. 5506 (C.A. Tex.).

Stevens v. *Parke, Davis & Co.* (1973), 9 Cal.3d 51, 107 Cal.Rptr. 45, 507 P.2d 653, 94 A.L.R.3d 1059.

Texas Bitulithic Co. v. *Caterpillar Tractor Co.* (1962), 357. S.W.2d 406 (Tex. Civ. App.).

The Research Group, Inc. (1977), *Interagency Task Force on Product Liability; Final Report of the Legal Study.* Springfield, VA: National Technical Information Service.

Tirino v. *Kenner Products Company* (1973), 72 Misc.2d 1094, 341 N.Y.S.2d 61, CCH Prod. Liab. Rep. para. 6950.

Uniform Commercial Code (1972), American Law Institute. "Uniform Product Liability Law" (1979), Interagency Task Force on Product Liability Draft, *Federal Register*, 44 (January 12), 2996–3019.

W. H. Elliott & Sons, Inc. v. *E. & F. King & Co., Inc.* (1961), 291 F.2d 79 (C.A.1).

Weinstein, Alvin S., Aaron D. Twerski, Henry R. Piehler and William A. Donaher (1978), *Products Liability and the Reasonably Safe Product: A Guide for Management, Design, and Marketing*, New York: John Wiley & Sons, Inc.

West v. *Alberto Culver Co.* (1973), 486 F.2d 459 (C.A.10 Colo.).

Westerman v. *Sears, Roebuck & Co.* (1978), CCH Prod. Liab.Rep. para. 8416, 577 F.2d 873 (C.A.5 Fla.).

Wilson v. *E-Z Flo Chem. Co.* (1972a), 13 N.C.App.610, 186 S.E.2d 679.

———— (1972b), 281 N.C. 506, 189 S.E.2d 221.

Winkler v. *American Safety Equipment Corp.* (1979), CCH Prod. Liab. Rep. para. 8601 (C.A. Colo.).

GEORGE G. BRENKERT

16

Strict Products Liability and Compensatory Justice*

I

Strict products liability is the doctrine that the seller of a product has legal responsibilities to compensate the user of that product for injuries suffered because of a defective aspect of the product, even when the seller has not been negligent in permitting that defect to occur.[1] Thus, even though a manufacturer, for example, has reasonably applied the existing techniques of manufacture and has anticipated and cared for nonintended uses of the product, he may still be held liable for injuries a product user suffers if it can be shown that the product was defective when it left the manufacturer's hands.

To say that there is a crisis today concerning this doctrine would be to utter a commonplace which few in the business community would deny. The development of the doctrine of strict products liability,

---

according to most business people, threatens many businesses financially. Furthermore, strict products liability is said to be a morally
questionable doctrine, since the manufacturer or seller has not been
negligent in permitting the injury-causing defect to occur. On the other
hand, victims of defective products complain that they deserve full
compensation for injuries sustained in using a defective product
whether or not the seller is at fault. Medical expenses and time lost
from one's job are costs no individual should have to bear by himself.
It is only fair that the seller share such burdens.

In general, discussions of this crisis focus on the limits to which
a business ought to be held responsible. Much less frequently, discussions of strict products liability consider the underlying question
of whether the doctrine of strict products liability is rationally
justifiable. But unless this question is answered it would seem
premature to seek to determine the limits to which businesses ought
to be held liable in such cases. In the following paper I discuss this
underlying philosophical question and argue that there is a rational
justification for strict products liability which links it to the very
nature of the free enterprise system.

II

. . .To begin with, it is crucial to remember that what we have
to consider is the relationship between an entity doing business and
an individual. The strict liability attributed to business would not
be attributed to an individual who happened to sell some product he
had made to his neighbor or a stranger. If Peter sold an article he
had made to Paul and Paul hurt himself because the article had a
defect which occurred through negligence of Peter's, we would not
normally hold Peter morally responsible to pay for Paul's injuries. . . .

It is different for businesses. They have been held to be legally
and morally obliged to pay the victim for his injuries. Why? What
is the difference? The difference is that when Paul is hurt by a
defective product from corporation X, he is hurt by something
produced in a socioeconomic system purportedly embodying free
enterprise. In other words, among other things:

1. Each business and/or corporation produces articles or services it
sells for profit.
2. Each member of this system competes with other members of the
system in trying to do as well as it can for itself not simply in each
exchange, but through each exchange for its other values and
desires.

3. Competition is to be "open and free, without deception or fraud."
4. Exchanges are voluntary and undertaken when each party believes it can benefit thereby. One party provides the means for another party's ends if the other party will provide the first party the means to its ends.
5. The acquisition and disposition of ownership rights—that is, of private property—is permitted in such exchanges.
6. No market or series of markets constitutes the whole of a society.
7. Law, morality, and government play a role in setting acceptable limits to the nature and kinds of exchange in which people may engage.

What is it about such a system which would justify claims of strict products liability against businesses?. . . In the free enterprise system, each person and/or business is obligated to follow the rules and understandings which define this socioeconomic system. Following the rules is expected to channel competition among individuals and businesses to socially positive results. In providing the means to fulfill the ends of others, one's own ends also get fulfilled.

Though this does not happen in every case, it is supposed to happen most of the time. Those who fail in their competition with others may be the object of charity, but not of other duties. Those who succeed, qua members of this socioeconomic system, do not have moral duties to aid those who fail. Analogously, the team which loses the game may receive our sympathy but the winning team is not obligated to help it to win the next game or even to play it better. Those who violate the rules, however, may be punished or penalized, whether or not the violation was intentional and whether or not it redounded to the benefit of the violator. Thus, a team may be assessed a penalty for something that a team member did unintentionally to a member of the other team but which injured the other team's chances of competition in the game by violating the rules.

This point may be emphasized by another instance involving a game that brings us closer to strict products liability. Imagine that you are playing table tennis with another person in his newly constructed table tennis room. You are both avid table tennis players and the game means a lot to both of you. Suppose that after play has begun, you are suddenly and quite obviously blinded by the light over the table—the light shade has a hole in it which, when it turned in your direction, sent a shaft of light unexpectedly into your eyes. You lose a crucial point as a result. Surely it would be unfair of your opponent to seek to maintain his point because he was faultless—

after all, he had not intended to blind you when he installed that light shade. You would correctly object that he had gained the point unfairly, that you should not have to give up the point lost, and that the light shade should be modified so that the game can continue on a fair basis. It is only fair that the point be played over.

Businesses and their customers in a free enterprise system are also engaged in competition with each other. The competition here, however, is multifaceted as each tries to gain the best agreement he can from the other with regard to the buying and selling of raw materials, products, services, and labor. Such agreements must be voluntary. The competition which leads to them cannot involve coercion. In addition, such competion must be fair and ultimately result in the benefit of the entire society through the operation of the proverbial invisible hand.

Crucial to the notion of fairness of competition are not simply the demands that the competition be open, free, and honest, but also that each person in a society be given an equal opportunity to participate in the system in order to fulfill his or her own particular ends. . . .

. . . Equality of opportunity requires that one not be prevented by arbitrary obstacles from participating (by engaging in a producitve role of some kind or other) in the system of free enterprise, competition, and so on in order to fulfill one's own ends ("reap the benefits"). Accordingly, monopolies are restricted, discriminatory hiring policies have been condemned, and price collusion is forbidden.

However, each person participates in the systen of free enterprise *both* as a worker/producer *and* as a consumer. The two roles interact: if the person could not consume he would not be able to work, and if there were no consumers there would be no work to be done. Even if a particular individual is only what is ordinarily considered a consumer, he or she plays a theoretically significant role in the competitive free enterprise system. The fairness of the system depends upon what access he or she has to information about goods and services on the market, the lack of coercion imposed on that person to buy goods, and the lack of arbitrary restrictions imposed by the market and/or government on his or her behavior.

In short, equality of opportunity is a doctrine with two sides which applies both to producers and to consumers. If, then, a person as a consumer or a producer is injured by a defective product—which is one way his activities might arbitrarily be restricted by the action of (one of the members of) the market system—surely his free and voluntary participation in the system of free enterprise will be seriously affected. Specifically, his equal opportunity to participate in the system in order to fulfill his own ends will be diminished.

Here is where strict products liability enters the picture. In cases of strict liability the manufacturer does not intend for a certain aspect of his product to injure someone. Nevertheless, the person is injured. As a result, he is at a disadvantage both as a consumer and as a producer. He cannot continue to play either role as he might wish. Therefore, he is denied that equality of opportunity which is basic to the economic system in question just as surely as he would be if he were excluded from employment by various unintended consequences of the economic system which nevertheless had racially or sexually prejudicial implications. Accordingly, it is fair for the manufacturer to compensate the person for his losses before proceeding with business as usual. That is, the user of a manufacturer's product may justifiably demand compensation from the manufacturer when its product can be shown to be defective and has injured him and harmed his chances of participation in the system of free enterprise.

Hence, strict liability finds a basis in the notion of equality of opportunity which plays a central role in the notion of a free enterprise system. That is why a business which does not have to pay for the injuries an individual suffers in the use of a defective article made by that business is felt to be unfair to its customers. Its situation is analogous to that of a player's unintentional violation of a game rule which is intended to foster equality of competitive opportunity.

A soccer player, for example, may unintentionally trip an opposing player. He did not mean to do it; perhaps he himself had stumbled. Still, he has to be penalized. If the referee looked the other way, the tripped player would rightfully object that he had been treated unfairly. Similarly, the manufacturer of a product may be held strictly liable for a product of his which injures a person who uses that product. Even if he is faultless, a consequence of his activities is to render the user of his product less capable of equal participation in the socioeconomic system. The manufacturer should be penalized by way of compensating the victim. Thus, the basis upon which manufacturers are held strictly liable is compensatory justice.

In a society which refuses to resort to paternalism or to central direction of the economy and which turns, instead, to competition in order to allocate scarce positions and resources, compensatory justice requires that the competition be fair and losers be protected.[2] Specifically, no one who loses should be left so destitute that he cannot reenter the competition. Furthermore, those who suffer injuries traceable to defective merchandise or services which restrict their participation in the competitive system should also be compensated.

Compensatory justice does not presuppose negligence or evil intentions on the part of those to whom the injuries might ultimately be traced. It is not perplexed or incapacitated by the relative innocence of all parties involved. Rather, it is concerned with correcting the disadvantaged situation an individual experiences due to accidents or failures which occur in the normal working of that competitive system. It is on this basis that other compensatory programs which alleviate the disabilities of various minority groups are founded. Strict products liability is also founded on compensatory justice.

An implication of the preceding argument is that business is not morally obliged to pay, as such, for the physical injury a person suffers. Rather, it must pay for the loss of equal competitive opportunity—even though it usually is the case that it is because of a (physical) injury that there is a loss of equal opportunity. Actual legal cases in which the injury which prevents a person from going about his or her daily activities is emotional or mental, as well as physical, supports this thesis. If a person were neither mentally nor physically harmed, but still rendered less capable of participating competitively because of a defective aspect of a product, there would still be grounds for holding the company liable.

For example, suppose I purchased and used a cosmetic product guaranteed to last a month. When used by most people it is odorless. On me, however, it has a terrible smell. I can stand the smell, but my co-workers and most other people find it intolerable. My employer sends me home from work until it wears off. The product has not harmed me physically or mentally. Still, on the above argument, I would have reason to hold the manufacturer liable. Any cosmetic product with this result is defective. As a consequence my opportunity to participate in the socioeconomic system is curbed. I should be compensated.

III

There is another way of arriving at the same conclusion about the basis of strict products liability. To speak of business or the free enterprise system, it was noted above, is to speak of the voluntary exchanges between producer and customer which take place when each party believes he has an opportunity to benefit. Surely customers and producers may miscalculate their benefits: something they voluntarily agreed to buy or sell may turn out not to be to their benefit. The successful person does not have any moral responsibilities to the unsuccessful person—at least as a member of this economic system. If, however, fraud is the reason one person does not benefit, the system is in principle, undermined. If such fraud were universalized, the system would collapse. Accordingly, the person committing the fraud does have a responsibility to make reparations to the one mistreated.

Consider once again the instance of a person who is harmed by a product he bought or used, a product that can reasonably be said to be defective. Has the nature of the free enterprise system also been undermined or corrupted in this instance? Producer and consumer have exchanged the product but it has not been to their mutual benefit; the manufacturer may have benefited, but the customer has suffered because of the defect. Furthermore, if such exchanges were universalized, the system would also be undone.

Suppose that whenever people bought products from manufacturers the products turned out to be defective and the customers were always injured, even though the manufacturers could not be held negligent. Though one party to such exchanges might benefit, the other party always suffered. If the rationale for this economic system—the reason it was adopted and is defended—were that in the end both parties share the equal opportunity to gain, surely it would collapse with the above consequences. Consequently, as with fraud, an economic system of free enterprise requires that injuries which result from defective products be compensated. The question is: Who is to pay for the compensation?

There are three possibilities. The injured party could pay for his own injuries. However, this is implausible since what is called for is compensation and not merely payment for injuries. If the injured party had simply injured himself, if he had been negligent or careless, then it is plausible that he should pay for his own injuries. No compensation is at stake here. But in the present case the injury stems from the actions of a particular manufacturer who, albeit unwittingly, placed the defective product on the market and stands to gain through its sale.

The rationale of the free enterprise system would be undermined, we have seen, if such actions were universalized, for then the product user's equal opportunity to benefit from the system would be denied. Accordingly, since the rationale and motivation for an individual to be part of this socioeconomic system is his opportunity to gain from participation in it, justice requires that the injured product user receive compensation for his injuries. Since the individual can hardly compensate himself, he must receive compensation from some other source.

Second, some third party—such as government—could compensate the injured person. This is not wholly implausible if one is prepared to modify the structure of the free enterprise system. And, indeed, in the long run this may be the most plausible course of action. However, if one accepts the structure of the free enterprise system, this alternative must be rejected because it permits the interference of government into individual affairs.

Third, we are left with the manufacturer. Suppose a manufacturer's product, even though the manufacturer wasn't negligent always turned out to be defective and injured those using his products. We might sympathize with his plight, but he would either have to stop manufacturing altogether (no one would buy such products) or else compensate the victims for their losses. (Some people might buy and use his products under these conditions.) If he forced people to buy and use his products he would corrupt the free enterprise system. If he did not compensate the injured users, they would not buy and he would not be able to sell his products. Hence, he could partake of the free enterprise system—that is, sell his products—only if he compensated his user/victims. Accordingly, the sale of this hypothetical line of defective products would be voluntarily accepted as just or fair only if compensation were paid the user/victims of such products by the manufacturer.

The same conclusion follows even if we consider a single defective product. The manufacturer put the defective product on the market. Because of his actions others who seek the opportunity to participate on an equal basis in this system in order to benefit therefrom are unable to do so. Thus, a result of his actions, even though unintended, is to undermine the system's character and integrity. Accordingly, when a person is injured in his attempt to participate in this system, he is owed compensation by the manufacturer. The seller of the defective article must not jeopardize the equal opportunity of the product user to benefit from the system. The seller need not guarantee that the buyer/user will benefit from the purchase of the product; after all, the buyer may miscalculate or be careless in the use of a nondefective product. But if he is not careless or has not miscalculated, his opportunity to benefit from the system is illegitimately harmed if he is injured in its use because of the product's defectiveness. He deserves compensation.

It follow's from the arguments in this and the preceding section that strict products liability is not only compatible with the system of free enterprise but that if it were not attributed to the manufacturer the system itself would be morally defective. And the justification for requiring manufacturers to pay compensation when people are injured by defective products is that the demands of compensatory justice are met.[3]

NOTES

1. This characterization strict products liability is adapted from Alvin S. Weinstein et al., *Products Liability and the Reasonably Safe Product* (New York: John Wiley & Sons, 1978), ch. 1. I understand the seller to include the manufacturer, the retailer, distributors, and wholesalers. For the sake of convenience. I will generally refer simply to the manufacturer.

2. I have drawn heavily, in this paragraph, on the fine article by Bernard Boxhill, "The Morality of Reparation," reprinted in *Reverse Discrimination*, ed. Barry R. Gross (Buffalo, New York: Prometheus Books, 1977), pp. 270–278.

3. I would like to thank the following for providing helpful comments on earlier versions of this paper: Betsy Postow, Jerry Phillips, Bruce Fisher, John Hardwig, and Sheldon Cohen.

17

Grimshaw v. Ford Motor Company*

A 1972 Ford Pinto hatchback automobile unexpectedly stalled on a freeway, erupting into flames when it was rear ended by a car proceeding in the same direction. Mrs. Lilly Gray, the driver of the Pinto, suffered fatal burns and 13-year-old Richard Grimshaw, a passenger in the Pinto, suffered severe and permanently disfiguring burns on his face and entire body. Grimshaw and the heirs of Mrs. Gray (Grays) sued Ford Motor Company and others. Following a six-month jury trial, verdicts were returned in favor of plaintiffs against Ford Motor Company. Grimshaw was awarded $2,516,000 compensatory damages and $125 million punitive damages; the Grays were awarded $559,680 in compensatory damages.[1] On Fords' motion for a new trial, Grimshaw was required to remit all but $3½ million of the punitive award as a condition of denial of the motion.

---

* Reprinted with editorial changes by permission of West Publishing Company from *West's California Reporter.*

THE ACCIDENT

In November 1971, the Grays purchased a new 1972 Pinto Hatchback manufactured by Ford in October 1971. The Grays had trouble with the car from the outset. During the first few months of ownership, they had to return the car to the dealer for repairs a number of times. Their car problems included excessive gas and oil consumption, down shifting of the automatic transmission, lack of power, and occasional stalling. It was later learned that the stalling and excessive fuel consumption were caused by a heavy carburetor float.

On May 28, 1972, Mrs. Gray, accompanied by 13-year-old Richard Grimshaw, set out in the Pinto from Anaheim for Barstow to meet Mr. Gray. The Pinto was then six months old and had been driven approximately 3,000 miles. Mrs. Gray stopped in San Bernardino for gasoline, got back onto the freeway (Interstate 15) and proceeded toward her destination at 60–65 miles per hour. As she approached the Route 30 off-ramp where traffic was congested, she moved from the outer fast lane to the middle lane of the freeway. Shortly after this lane change, the Pinto suddenly stalled and coasted to a halt in the middle lane. It was later established that the carburetor float had become so saturated with gasoline that it suddenly sank, opening the float chamber and causing the engine to flood and stall. A car traveling immediately behind the Pinto was able to swerve and pass it but the driver of a 1962 Ford Galaxie was unable to avoid colliding with the Pinto. The Galaxie had been traveling from 50 to 55 miles per hour but before the impact had been braked to a speed of from 28 to 37 miles per hour.

At the moment of impact, the Pinto caught fire and its interior was engulfed in flames. According to plaintiffs' expert, the impact of the Galaxie had driven the Pinto's gas tank forward and caused it to be punctured by the flange or one of the bolts on the differential housing so that fuel sprayed from the punctured tank and entered the passenger compartment through gaps resulting from the separation of the rear wheel well sections from the floor pan. By the time the Pinto came to rest after the collision, both occupants had sustained serious burns. When they emerged from the vehicle, their clothing was almost completely burned off. Mrs. Gray died a few days later of congestive heart failure as a result of the burns. Grimshaw managed to survive but only through heroic medical measures. He has undergone numerous and extensive surgeries and skin grafts and must undergo additional surgeries over the next 10 years. He lost portions of several fingers on his left hand and portions of his left ear, while his face required many skin grafts from various portions of his body. Because Ford does not contest the amount of compensatory damages awarded to Grimshaw and the Grays, no purpose would be served by further description of the injuries suffered by Grimshaw or the damages sustained by the Grays.

NOTE

1. The jury actually awarded Grimshaw $2,841,000 compensatory damages and $125 million punitive damages and the Grays $659,680 compensatory damages. Pursuant to stipulation that sums previously received by plaintiffs from others should be deducted from the amounts awarded by the jury, the judgment was modified to reflect compensatory damages in favor of Grimshaw for $2,516,000 and in favor of the Grays for $559,680.

Part V

THE REGULATION OF BUSINESS

Introduction: The Regulation of Business

The National Highway Traffic Safety Administration first proposed a fuel system integrity standard, designated Standard 301, in 1969. The standard set limits on the amount of fuel that could leak from vehicles after collisions. (A copy of this standard is included in Part I of this book.) In a NHTSA study, it was found that there were about 400,000 cars a year that caught on fire. These fires led to about 3,000 deaths annually. Another study suggested that Standard 301 would save about 40 percent of these lives. When informed of the proposed standard, Ford seems to have tried to delay it and to have begun the testing required to see what would have to be done to comply with it. Their interest in preventing the passage of the bill presumably stemmed from the fact that they would have to modify some of their models, resulting in higher car prices and fewer sales. While all of the automobile companies lobbied against the legislation, Ford had a special interest in doing so. According to NHTSA statistics, Ford made approximately 24 percent of the cars on the road, but accounted for about 42 percent of the fuel tanks ruptured by collisions. Pintos accounted for about 3.5 percent of the cars on the road and approximately 7 percent of the fatal crashes involving fires. Thus, if these statistics were accurate, Ford and the Pinto, in particular, had a bad record on fuel tank safety.

Regulations, like Standard 301, are used by the government to control business. The regulation of business to promote safer products and fair business practices is considered necessary since businesses, which traditionally have been primarily motivated by profit, cannot always be relied on for safety and fairness if left alone. Even proponents of traditional free enterprise capitalism, such as Milton Friedman, believe that some government regulation is necessary to establish guidelines for business competition, but they would keep it to a minimum.

In today's technologically advanced business world, regulation is more important and needs to be more pervasive. Traditionally, many businesses adopted a "buyer beware" attitude, but as products and services have become more complicated, this practice has become less advisable. Prescription drugs represent a good example. Consumers do not have the technological expertise or equipment to test their own pharmaceuticals for safety. Therefore, the government must do it for them by regulating the pharmaceutical industry. Government regulation is an important part of modern capitalism, but the degree to which it is necessary is a controversial matter. The automobile industry was one of the last major industries to fall under serious government regulation. It was not regulated until the Highway Safety Act of 1966, which created the NHTSA. Many corporate leaders in the industry resisted, and continue to oppose, government regulation of their business practices and products.

Part V, the final part of the book, discusses government regulation of business in general, and of the automobile industry in particular. The first selection, "Profits vs. Safety," briefly discusses the matter of automobile safety and profitability with an emphasis on the Ford Pinto. It sets the Pinto controversy in the general framework of the industry's attitude about automobile safety by offering a very limited historical background. The next two articles, Peter Barton Hutt's "Five Moral Imperatives of Government Regulation" and Alasdair MacIntyre's "Regulation: A Substitute for Morality," present a short dialogue about the ethics of government regulation. Hutt offers five moral imperatives that ought to underlie government regulation and thus concludes that regulation ought to be the expression of a particular moral viewpoint. MacIntyre counters by reasoning that, on the contrary, government regulation is a substitute for morality, something that is necessary because we, as a society, have inadequate moral resources. John Fielder's essay "The Ethics and Politics of Automobile Regulation" explores the history, justification, and problems associated with government regulation. He relates this to the introduction of auto regulation in the United States with special emphasis on the role of Ralph Nader. The regulatory climate during the years the Pinto was designed and built provides a valuable insight into the regulatory and business decisions in the Pinto case.

One interesting controversy connected to Standard 301, which is not featured in any of these articles but which deserves mention, is whether it is ethical for automobile companies to lobby against a piece of legislation that would save 3,000 lives a year. The automobile manufacturers would, of course, argue that they had the right to speak up for their economic interests and that regulation can hurt people since it raises the price of cars and may cost some workers their jobs. On the other hand, in the Pinto case, the cost of upgrading the safety of the fuel system was not great, and this fact raises the question of whether any jobs really would have been lost. In general, the conflict often seems to be between consumer safety and profits and jobs. If we look at the debate from the consumer's point of view, we will want more effective government regulation, but if we take the view of management, we will want to protect profits and jobs. Consequently, the issue of government regulation is one of the most interesting and controversial matters connected to business.

FRANCIS CULLEN, WILLIAM MAAKESTAD,
AND GRAY CAVENDER

18

Profits vs. Safety*

In 1965 Ralph Nader published his penetrating and widely discussed book, *Unsafe at Any Speed*. This book called attention to structural defects in GM's Corvair, which caused the vehicle to become uncontrollable and to overturn at high speeds. This would have been an important revelation in itself, but Nader's exposé accomplished much more. Apart from showing the Corvair's defects, Nader challenged his readers to think beyond the dangers inherent in one automobile to the dangers inherent in the nature of corporate decision making. People needed to understand, he argued, that strong, unfettered forces prevailed within big business—including the automobile industry—and led executives to sacrifice human well-being for profits.

This message came at a time when the "confidence gap" was beginning to grow and when mistrust of corporate executives was

---

* Reprinted, with editorial changes, by permission of Anderson Publishing Company from *Corporate Crime Under Attack: The Ford Pinto Case and Beyond* by Francis Cullen, William Maakestad and Gray Cavender. Copyright © 1987 Anderson Publishing Co.

spreading. Thus it fell upon increasingly receptive ears and helped to shape the thinking of citizens and of many elected officials regarding corporate misconduct. A decade after the appearance of *Unsafe at Any Speed*, Nader's message that companies traded lives for profits clearly affected what people would believe about Ford's handling of the Pinto.

Nader began his critique of the motor-vehicle industry by noting that "the automobile has brought death, injury, and the most inestimable sorrow and deprivation to millions of people."[1] This observation raises the question of who is responsible for the "gigantic costs of the highway carnage." According to Nader, the major car manufacturers have invariably had a ready answer: "If only people would take driver education and were not so careless when behind the wheel, then the highway death toll would be minimal." But Nader offered a different interpretation. Attributing accidents to "driver fault," he warned, was merely a case of blaming the victim.[2] As long as the victims of the crashes—the drivers—are held responsible for their own fates, he stated, attention is diverted away from the industry's role in producing cars that are "unsafe at any speed." Such ideology protects corporate interests, but only at the cost of continuing to jeopardize human lives:

> The prevailing view of traffic safety [blaming drivers] is much more a political strategy to defend special interests than it is an empirical program to save lives and prevent injuries. . . . [U]nder existing business values potential safety advances are subordinated to other investments, priorities, preferences, and themes designed to maximize profit.[3]

Nader contended that the push for profits, not poor driving, explains why people are perishing in cars like the Corvair. In offering this explanation Nader was not so naive or dogmatic as to accuse executives of consciously setting out to make dangerous vehicles. Rather, he was asserting that the blind pursuit of profits creates conditions within corporations that are conducive to the production of defective cars. Specifically, he understood that companies place a high priority on two factors that they see as essential to high sales and profit: style and cost. Although nobody wants an unsafe product, conflict inevitably arises when a design feature that would increase safety, such as a rear-end stabilizer or a larger windshield for better vision, makes a car look less attractive or increases its purchase price.[4] As Nader observed, the rewards within companies are given ultimately to those who are prepared to advance corporate sales, not to those who are excessively bothersome about safety. Clearly, then, the organizational context encourages decent, if ambitious, executives to risk cutting corners on safety in hopes of boosting sales and advancing their careers. Nader concluded:

> In the making of the Corvair, there was a breakdown in this flow of both authority and initiative. Initiative would have meant an appeal by the Corvair design engineers to top management to overrule the cost-cutters and stylists whose incursions had placed unsafe constraints on engineering choice. There are, however, deterrents to such action that regularly prompt the design engineer to shirk his professional duty. It is to the keepers of those most sacred totems—cost reduction and style—that corporate status and authority accrue.[5]

These realities made it clear to Nader that the automakers could not be trusted to protect consumer interests. The failure of the industry to police itself demanded that outside regulation be imposed:

> A great problem of contemporary life is how to control the power of economic interests which ignore the harmful effects of their applied science and technology. The automobile tragedy is one of the most serious of these man-made assaults on the human body....The accumulated power of decades of effort by the automobile industry to strengthen its control over car design is reflected today in the difficulty of even beginning to bring it to justice. The time has not come to discipline the automobile for safety; that time came four decades ago.[6]

Again, Nader's words were not without consequence. Fearing that his book might threaten Corvair sales, GM hired detectives to investigate Nader in hopes of discrediting him. Snooping into his background not only failed to reveal any damaging evidence, but when GM's probe became public, it stained the company's reputation. (GM eventually issued a public apology to Nader and paid $425,000 to settle a civil action he had brought on grounds of invasion of privacy.)[7] Ironically, the investigation seemed to confirm Nader's indictment of the auto industry's attenuated morality, and the whole affair helped to turn him into a national figure.

As we know, Nader did not decline this opportunity to promote his agenda and to launch a consumer movement that flourished and that continues today.[8] His influence was felt across corporate America,[9] but he had a special impact on car makers. "Largely as a result of exposés by Ralph Nader," comment Clinard and Yeager, "the auto industry has been the subject of increasing criticism for its lack of ethics, violations of law, and general disregard for the safety of the consumer."[10]

In this light, it is not coincidental that in 1966, the year after the publication of Nader's best-selling book, the U.S. Congress passed the Highway Safety Act, which mandated federal regulation of the automotive industry and led to the creation of an enforcement agency, the National Highway Traffic Safety Administration (NHTSA). Indeed, Brent Fisse and John Braithwaite have observed that "this Act is largely a legacy of *Unsafe at Any Speed*" and of Senate hearings to consider industry regulation, during which GM executives were grilled about prying into Nader's background.[11] As one writer commented in 1966:

> The hearings were a sensation, and did as much as anything to bring on federal safety standards. "It was the Nader thing," said one senator whom I asked how it had all come about. "Everyone was so outraged that a great corporation was out to clobber a guy because he wrote critically about them. At that point, everybody said the hell with them." "When they started looking in Ralph's bedroom," said another Hill man, "we all figured they must really be nervous. We began to believe that Nader was right."[12]

As evidenced by GM's reaction to Nader, consumerism and federal safety regulations were not greeted kindly by the major automotive corporations. Their initial grumblings grew more intense as the industry's control of the market was threatened by a combination of escalating gasoline prices and an influx of inexpensive, fuel-efficient foreign imports. By the beginning of the 1970s, the costs of meeting NHTSA regulatory standards were perceived as a serious danger to the profitability of the American auto industry, and thus had to be resisted. "Safety" had become a dirty word in the headquarters of the big auto manufacturers.

This attitude about safety is illustrated well by conversations drawn from the Watergate tapes. On April 27, 1971, between 11:08 and 11:43 a.m., Henry Ford II and Lee Iacocca (then president of Ford Motor Company) talked with Richard Nixon and John Ehrlichman in the Oval Office. The purpose of this visit was to ask the President to help Ford Motor Company obtain relief from the pressing problems created by the safety standards imposed by the Department of Transportation (which housed NHTSA).[13]

In the first moments of the meeting, President Nixon quickly set the tone, commenting:

> But we can't have a completely safe society or safe highways or safe cars and pollution-free and so forth. Or we could have, go back and live like a bunch of damned animals. Uh, that won't be too good, either. But I also know that using this issue, and, boy this is true. It's true in, in the environmentalists and it's true of the consumerism people. They're a group of people that aren't really one damn bit interested in safety or clean air. What they're interested in is destroying the system. They're enemies of the system. So what I'm trying to say is this: that you can speak to me in terms that I am for the system.

He then continued:

> I try to fight the demagogues, uh, to the extent we can. Uh, I would say this: that I think we have to know that, uh, the tides run very strongly. I mean, you know, the, it's the kick now. You know, the environment kick is in your ads, of course. You're reflecting it. Kids are for it and all the rest, they say. Uh, the safety thing is the kick, 'cause Nader's running around, squealing around about this and that and the other thing. . . .
>
> Now, tell me the problems you've got with, uh, the industry, with the Department of Transportation, and all these things and let me listen.

Soon after these remarks Henry Ford II began to outline his concerns:

> I think the thing that concerns us more than anything else is this total safety problem. And, uh, what we're worried about really, basically, is—this isn't an industry problem—is really the economy of the United States, if you want to get into the broad picture because, uh, we represent the total automotive [unintelligible] supply, industry supplies, dealers, dealer [unintelligible] the whole bit, about one-sixth of G.N.P. Now, if the price of cars goes up because emission requirements is

gonna be in there, even though we, though we've talked about this morning, safety requirements are in there, bumpers are in there. And these things are, and that's leaving out inflation and material costs increases, which are also there.

Nixon responded:

> In other words, it'll, it'll kick up the prices of cars and of all of them, the inexpensive ones and the others too.

Henry Ford:

> We see the price of a Pinto. . .going something like fifty percent in the next three years with inflation part of it, but that's not the big part of it. It's the safety requirements, the emission requirements, the bumper requirements. . .
>
> If these prices get so high that people stop buying cars. . . they're gonna buy more foreign cars; you're going to have balance-of-payment problems.

Nixon:

> Right. I'm convinced.

Lee Iacocca now entered the conversation, focusing on the problems that attended the implementation of safety regulations by the Department of Transportation:

> I'm worried about the, the fact the Department of Transportation, not willfully, but maybe unknowingly, is really getting to us. . .
>
> And I keep saying, "The clock is running and we are wasting money." It, it just kills me to see it starting with Ford. We are becoming a great inefficient producer, and what they're doing to us.
>
> But I think for the basic safety standards, now, the key officials over there—I've talked to 'em now, for two years constantly. . . and they're dedicated—and they say, "Well, we're gonna get on to this, but we've had problems." And they talk about Naderism, and, uh, you know, the. . .the great pressure on them and so forth.

He then focused on the incursions of foreign competitors into American markets:

> And, and, and ya say, "Well, what has this to do with safety?" Well it has one big thing to do with it. They [foreign competitors] are gonna put whatever is demanded by law in this country on at a buck fifty an hour, and we're, we just cracked seven dollars an hour.

Returning to the regulatory issue, Iacocca remarked:

> We are in a downhill slide, the likes of which we have never seen in our business. And the Japs are in the wings ready to eat us up alive. So I'm in a position to be saying to Toms and Volpe [DOT officials], "Would you guys cool it a little bit? You're gonna break us." And they say, "Hold it. People want safety." I say, "Well, they, what do you mean they want safety? We get letters. . .We get about thousands on customer service. You can't get your car fixed. We don't get anything on safety! So again, give us a priority." We cannot carry the load of inflation in wages and safety in a four-year period without breaking our back. It's that simple, and, and that's what we've tried to convey to these people.

Later, Nixon promised to review Ford's situation:

> . . .let me take a look at the whole, uh, John, what I can do here. But the other thing is I want to see what the hell the Department [of Transportation] is doing in the future.

Echoing the Ford officials' reasoning, Nixon then stated:

> I'll have a look at the situation, and I will on the air bag thing and the rest. And, uh, and uh, but, but I think this is an element that had, you see, goes beyond the DOT because it involves America's competitive position, it involves the health of the economy, uh, it involves a lot of things. . .

> I want to find out, I want to find out what the situation is, if cost-effectiveness is the word.

Nixon continued:

> . . .a lot of, what, what it really gets down to is that uh, . . . it,
> it is uh. . . . progress. . . . industrialization, ipso facto, is bad.
> The great life is to have it like when the Indians were here.
> You know how the Indians lived? Dirty, filthy, horrible.
> [Followed by laughs in the room].

At the end of the meeting, Nixon gave Ford the name of a "contact person," but reserved final judgment on matters brought before him:

> Now, John [Ehrlichman] is your contact here. . .

> . . .and, uh, particularly with regard to this, uh, this air bag thing. I, I don't know, I, I may be wrong.

> I will not judge it until I hear the other side.

When juxtaposed with the themes in *Unsafe at Any Speed*, these conversations illuminate the conflict over the appropriate balance of safety and profits that raged as America moved into the seventies. In Nader's view, big companies were callously and recklessly endangering human life in their efforts to maximize profits. Cost-effectiveness, not the Golden Rule was their governing morality. Corporate leaders dismissed such talk as naively or maliciously undermining the nation's economy. Safety was now the fad of those on the political left; if not resisted, it had the potential to cripple industries that were already struggling to fight off foreign competitors.

It was in this context that the Ford Pinto was conceived and produced. Under Lee Iacocca's direction, Ford moved quickly to market the Pinto before Volkswagen and the Japanese manufacturers monopolized small-car sales. Iacocca's formula for success was simple but rigid: the vehicle must weigh under 2,000 pounds and cost under $2,000. "Lee's car," as the Pinto was known at Ford, was rushed through production, taking only twenty-five months as opposed to the normal forty-three.[14] The 1971 model rolled off the production line and into showrooms in September 1970. It cost only $1,919 and weighed in under the 2,000-pound limit.[15]

Though pleased by this success, Ford executives were still concerned about the price of safety. The Pinto had won the initial battle with cost, but faced a war against rising expenditures and vigorous competition. As we have seen, this is one reason why Henry

Ford II and Lee Iacocca traveled to Washington to meet with President Nixon. During this time, too, Ford executives made the decision not to guard against potential fuel-leakage problems caused by the placement of the Pinto's gas tank, which made it vulnerable to puncture in rear-end collisions. In an internal company memo dated April 22, it was recommended that Ford "defer adoption of the flak suit or bladder on all affected cars until 1976 to realize a design cost savings of $20.9 million compared to incorporation in 1974."[16] Whether Ford was reckless in its calculation that improved safety precautions were not worth a substantial reduction in profit would be questioned increasingly in the years ahead.

NOTES

1. Ralph Nader, *Unsafe at Any Speed: The Designed-In Dangers of the American Automobile*. New York: Grossman Publishers, 1965, p. vii.

2. For a discussion of the concept of "blaming the victim," see William Ryan, *Blaming the Victim*. New York: Randon House, 1971.

3. Nader, *Unsafe at Any Speed*, p. 236.

4. The question of whether "safety sells" has remained controversial since Nader's initial writings. For contrasting, though not entirely contrary views, see Marshall B. Clinard and Peter C. Yeager, *Corporate Crime*. New York: The Free Press, 19880, p. 259 and Lee Iacocca with William Novak, *Iacocca: An Autobiography*. New York: Bantam Books, 1984, p. 297.

5. Nader, *Unsafe at Any Speed*, p. 40.

6. *Ibid.*, pp. ix, xi.

After his settlement with GM, Nader decided to use the proceeds (minus legal expenses) for the "continuous legal monitoring of General Motor's activities in the safety, pollution and consumer relations area." See "GM and Nader Settle His Suit Over Snooping," *Wall Street Journal* (August 14, 1970), p. 4. For accounts of GM's reaction to Nader, see J. Patrick Wright, *On a Clear Day You Can See General Motors: John Z. DeLorean's Look Inside the Automotive Giant*. New York: Avon Books, 1979, p. 64. and Brent Fisse and John Braithwaite, *The Impact of Publicity on Corporate Offenders*. Albany: SUNY Press, 1983, pp. 30–33.

8. Thus, in a review of opinion studies, Joseph Nolan concluded that "by 1990, if not before, the notion that companies are responsible for their products in perpetuity will be firmly embedded in the public consciousness— and to an increasing extent, in our laws." See "Business Beware: Early

Warning Signs in the Eighties," *Public Opinion* 4 (April-May 1981), p. 57. See also "Opinion Roundup: Taxes and Regulation," *Public Opinion* 5 (October-November 1982), p. 23; *The Chronicle of Higher Education* (February 1, 1984), p. 14; and Timothy Harper, "Environmental Issues Gaining Importance," *Cincinnati Enquirer* (August 29, 1984), p. A-10.

9. In two samples for example, large proportions (89 and 62.8 percent) of business executives disagreed with the statement that "consumerism or the consumer crusade has not been an important factor in changing business practices and procedures." See Thomas J. Stanley and Larry M. Robinson, "Opinions on Consumer Issues: A Review of Recent Studies of Executives and Consumers," *Journal of Consumer Affairs* 14 (No. 1, 1980), p. 215.

10. Clinard and Yeager, *Corporate Crime*, p. 254.

11. Fisse and Braithwaite, *The Impact of Publicity on Corporate Offenders*, p. 35.

12. Quoted in Fisse and Braithwaite, *The Impact of Publicity on Corporate Offenders*, pp. 35–36.

13. All quotes cited below are taken from "Watergate transcripts" prepared by The National Archives and titled "Part of a Conversation among President Nixon, Lide Anthony Iacocca, Henry Ford II, and John D. Ehrlichman in the Oval Office on April 27, 1971, between 11:08 and 11:43." This information was acquired initially by lawyer Foy Devine for use in a civil suit against Ford conducted in Georgia (*Stubblefield v. Ford Motor Company*).

14. Mark Dowie, "Pinto Madness," *Mother Jones* 2 (September-October, 1977), p. 21.

15. Strobel, *Reckless Homicide?* p. 82. Some accounts have placed the actual weight of the Pinto at 2,030 pounds. See Robert Lacy, *Ford: The Men and the Machine.* Boston: Little, Brown, 1986, p. 575.

16. *Ibid.*, p. 88.

PETER BARTON HUTT

19

Five Moral Imperatives of Government Regulation*

Regulation, in my judgment, is the most difficult function that any government can perform. Our laws, at least in theory, are codifications of the ethical principles by which we have all agreed to live together in society. But regulatory laws often present a stark confrontation between individual freedom and societal safety. That is why our regulatory agencies are under such widespread attack and why we hear so much discussion, although none of it very enlightening, about regulatory reform today.

In dealing with regulation, history has something to teach us. The concept of government regulation, including economic as well as health and safety regulations, is not new. There are references to regulation as far back as there is recorded history. There were hundreds of extraordinarily oppressive regulatory statutes in medieval England and indeed in every other country. Sometimes these laws covered every aspect of a citizen's daily life, not just the questions of

* Reprinted by permission. © The Hastings Center.

health and safety that confront us now. Government regulatory action was not brought on either by railroads or steel or oil; it has been a function of govement for as long as government has existed.

In the United States our regulatory system was largely imported in colonial days from England and other parts of Europe. At first regulatory activity was largely a matter for state and local government because trade was primarily within the state.

The first federal law concerning safety of foods and drugs was passed in 1848—one hundred and thirty years ago. It dealt with imported drugs. Senator Dickenson did not like the bill. He said, "I have no faith in it." In the *Congressional Globe* of June 20, 1848, he said, "The materials would be brought here and the spurious drugs would be manufactured anyway. If we could stop the compounding of these drugs, interdict patients from taking and physicians from prescribing, we might do some good." Does that sound familiar? That could indeed be a statement on the floor of the House or Senate today. Not to be outdone, Senator Dix replied in a way that as far as I can tell is the first expression of the drug lag issue. He immediately referred to the prevailing practice in Great Britain concerning the licensing of drugs and medicine.

We did not have a complete law regulating foods and drugs until the first decade of this century. From 1900 to 1910 Congress enacted most of the basic health and safety laws that governed our society at least up to 1970: the Biologics Act of 1902, the Food and Drugs Act of 1906, the Meat Inspection Act of 1906, and the Insecticides Act of 1910. Those laws were our first environmental laws. They governed not just what people could merchandise, but by denying products to people these laws governed what all of our ancestors could and could not use and do.

We have just finished the second great regulatory surge, which basically occurred between 1970 and 1976 when the Occupational Safety and Health Act was passed, the Environmental Protection Agency and the Consumer Product Safety Commission were created, and all of the new environmental legislation governing clean air, clean water, and toxic substances was set in place. There was more federal regulatory enactment in those seven years than in the previous 194 years.

All of these laws have emerged from our collective sense of a societal ethic. These regulatory statutes have thus expressed fundamental ethical principles for government regulation, particularly in the health and safety field rather than in the economic field. Yet the ethical principles they embody are often in basic conflict with each other. That is why this form of regulation has become so controversial.

Let me describe what I regard as the five moral imperatives of government regulation of health and safety. I will list them and then I will discuss each very briefly.

The first is TO PROTECT THE PUBLIC FROM HARM. That is an easy one. The second is To PRESERVE MAXIMUM INDIVIDUAL FREEDOM OF CHOICE. Now we begin to get into the crunch. The third is TO GUARANTEE MEANINGFUL PUBLIC PARTICIPATION IN THE DECISION-MAKING PROCESS. The fourth is TO PROMOTE CONSISTENT AND DEPENDABLE RULES THAT ARE EQUALLY APPLICABLE TO EVERYONE. And the fifth is TO PROVIDE PROMPT DECISIONS ON ALL OF THE ISSUES THAT ARISE IN A REGULATORY CONTEXT. These represent fundamental credos of our society, yet none, I think we can agree, can be achieved by any regulatory agency today.

The first principle—protection of the public from harm—is the basic rationale for regulation and goes back to the 1848 drug law I mentioned. It can be traced through every congressional debate and every government regulation that has ever been issued. To this day, our statutory law says that FDA must guarantee absolute safety— zero risk—in the United States food supply. There are many other regulatory statutes that say exactly the same thing.

More recently, Congress has changed that language and has said that the government must guarantee no unreasonable risk. Needless to say Congress has never defined an "unreasonable" risk. As we all know, we cannot eliminate all risk; indeed, we cannot eliminate all risk from the food supply. Many of our greatest risks in society stem from our greatest pleasures.

I am indebted to Professor Richard Wilson of Harvard who went to the trouble of calculating from actual accident statistics exactly what the yearly risk of death is in some of the activities we like to do most. A canoeist has a yearly risk of death of 1 in 2,500; rock climbing, 1 in 1,000; and motorcycling, 1 in 550. I must admit I am delighted to say I do not engage in any of those activities. At the Food and Drug Administration I was fond of pointing out that none of our foods and drugs could have that level of risk.

A regulator making judgments about the level of risk that will be permitted, whether it be in recreation or in food and drugs, inevitably alienates those who want to exercise free choice in accepting a greater risk. Health and safety laws in our country transfer the decision of what is an acceptable risk from the individual to the government. Having made that choice for the past 130 years in our society, we now find that we are having second thoughts about it. The public wants scientific decisions from government regulators. But the new regulatory statutes, and indeed some of the old, demand value judgments instead. This, in my judgment, is why the public is rebelling. Having transferred part of their freedom of choice to government, the public is now saying they may want some of it back. What remains to be seen is whether Congress wishes to return any of that freedom or whether we have made an irretrievable decision in giving up much of our freedom of choice to government.

Even when we try to create a no-risk society, government frequently comes up with unintended results. When I was in the Food and Drug Administration, I was concerned about rules that would prohibit any kind of research on the fetus or on children for one reason. The FDA is charged with making certain that all new drugs that come on the market are safe for use by pregnant women and children. If all research is stopped on those two categories of people, then *all* pregnant women in the future and *all* children will be research subjects forever because those new drugs will never have been tested on those specific populations and will never have been shown to be safe and effective for them. The same conflict arises over the debate about recombinant DNA. The people who have argued most for restricting recombinant DNA research are the same people who insist that all our foods and drugs in society should be tested for carcinogenicity and found to be absolutely free from any carcinogenic potential. Yet it is largely through this new form of genetic research that we will be able to determine whether something is or is not a carcinogen and how carcinogenesis works.

Let me turn to the second principle: freedom of choice. To my shock, I have never found a federal regulatory statute that said that the government should pay any attention at all to individual freedom of choice. The laws demand governmental benefit/risk judgments or, in some cases, no-risk judgments. Never once has Congress said that individual freedom of choice has any value whatever in the regulator's decision. That concept is embodied in our Constitution, but as long as Congress says nothing about it in statutory law, it is not surprising that this is often the first principle that disappears in the regulatory crunch.

One can look, for example, at one of my least favorite decisions, namely the one I made when I was at FDA to take sassafras tea off the market because it contained safrole, a natural flavor that is a known animal carcinogen. I am sure that there are people, perhaps some in this room, who believe very deeply that sassafras tea should remain available for those who wish to consume it. The benefit/risk judgment for me was very simple. I neither drink sassafras tea nor know anyone who does. I did not even know it existed until the Bureau of Foods told me about it. Other teas could easily be substituted for it. Obviously sassafras tea was not necessary to the daily diet, and it was promptly banned. Those are the kinds of decisions that are made every day in FDA and in other government agencies. Congress did not tell me, as a government regulator, to pay any attention whatever to the individuals who might wish that they still had sassafras tea to drink.

There are many other examples that could be given. Modern regulations have added up in our society so greatly that all of the individual sassafras tea decisions that are being made every day are gradually reducing our individual freedom. Freedom of choice is still alive and well in Washington; but it is something that Congress will have to pay more attention to if it is not to be drastically reduced in the future.

The third principle is another easy one—public participation. Our country was founded on the democratic principie of participation. During the early years of government regulation this was not a central issue because the government was not regulating very much, its intrusiveness was not very noticeable, and therefore participation was not sought after. But as regulation has grown and *real* restrictions have affected all of us, public participation has become essential to legitimizing the regulatory process. In my opinion, the most important statutes Congress has enacted in the past 100 years are the Freedom of Information Act, the Sunshine Act, and the Advisory Committee Act. Without those the government would be doing its business in private, not in public. They are important in part for appearance's sake as well as for substance, but the potential for actually exposing government stupidity or wrongdoing under those laws is far greater than at any time in our past.

ALASDAIR MACINTYRE

20

Regulation: A Substitute for Morality*

I want to suggest that the kind of regulation which is concerned with the safety or the quality of goods and services is not itself an expression of any particular moral standpoint, but is rather a substitute for morality at just those points in our social fabric where we no longer possess adequate moral resources. I take it to be a very important substitute and the only substitute which we have. Therefore in the end my argument will conclude in favor of certain kinds of regulation. But I start from a very different standpoint from that of Mr. Hutt, whose remarks emphasized the inconsistency of the principles which seem to underlie a good deal of legislation and regulation. I believe that these inconsistencies are no accident.

In all our thinking about and living in a political society we as a culture embrace two systematically inconsistent ways of thinking and living. On the one hand we think of political society in terms of a series of communities—family, workplace, school, the hospital, the

* Reprinted by permission. © The Hastings Center.

local neighborhood—within which we pursue those human goods which are only available to us through common life and action and through which we learn—or at least can learn—that there is no good for me that is not also a good for the community. We discover and identify ourselves in the context of making and remaking various forms of human community. From this point of view we think of the goals of morality as positive. We do indeed need negative rules in order to set limits to what is intolerable behavior in our common life, but we envisage political and moral life predominantly in terms of the positive pursuit of goods for man. Yet at the same time we are also habituated to thinking of human society as an arena in which individuals and groups with rival and competing desires and goals pursue their own private aims and self-satisfactions in such a way that each needs to be protected from the other. We have no systematic way of reconciling these competing standpoints.

Each of these ways of thinking has deep roots in our political culture: the first in the eighteenth-century ideal of a republican people, a people inspired by a common regard for virtue and for community, an ideal which informs much of the founding documents; the second in the individualist vision of society as a device for the protection of individuals, of society as a collection of strangers, each of whom wishes to protect himself or herself and his or her property from government and from each other. Both of these ways of thinking are continuously regenerated in our politics. The first is renewed by the continuous experience of trying to initiate and reinitiate communication and cooperation within the family, the school, and the workplace. The second is renewed by the continual pressures upon us in the market-place where people provide objects for consumption and act as instruments to satisfy the appetites of others. This deep incoherence seems to be at the heart of our political life and consequently of our thinking about regulation.

Let us approach the question of regulation indirectly by examining the ways in which we think about the law. From the standpoint that envisages the goal of political society as the creation and maintenance of communities, we do indeed need a system of public law, but only as a system of last resort. There are indeed actions *so* intolerable that the community cannot permit them to be done without invoking public sanction. Individuals who thus transgress must be identified as answerable for their actions before they can be brought back into the life of the community. Here the law is the *last* resort. In a good community it will be enforced as rarely as possible. There are still areas of our life in which, although to a decreasing degree, we even now do think about the law in this way. We all recognize that once a marriage gets into the hands of the lawyers, it is probably doomed. And there are other areas in human life in which resort to the law is still recognized as the sign that some deeper moral relationship has already broken down. I take this to be the most important fact about contemporary malpractice suits. Malpractice suits do not arise because of greater negligence by the medical profession and only to a small extent because of the greater readiness of patients to challenge doctors, but to a very large extent because of the breakdown in an older relationship of trust between physician and patient. People feel free to resort to law because they no longer envisage the physician-patient relationship as an essentially moral one.

From the competing view of society as the protector of individual interests, law is not a last resort at all. Law is the immediate sanction we invoke in order to protect ourselves from invasion by others. From this point of view law protects our persons and properties and is to be used on the one hand to protect what we have and are already, and on the other hand to be used as an instrument for redistribution and redress when only the state is available to meet the needs of the helpless. The first view depends on an understanding of human relationships as species of friendship when they are in good order. The second takes seriously Plautus's maxim, *homo homini lupus est*, man is a wolf to man; a maxim unfairer to wolves than to men. For, of course, it is true both that human beings are always capable of friendship *and* are always capable of behaving as wolves do in human legends. Each of these notions underlying attitudes to the law is one to which people in certain types of situations naturally resonate.

Unfortunately, there are harmful consequences deriving from this systematic cultural inconsistency in our thinking about the law. When law is thought of in the first way, the primary reason for supporting and identifying with the law is that the law is part of the life of the community to which we belong. If you like, in terms of eighteenth-century republicanism the motive for obeying law is civil virtue. But when the law is thought of in the second way, as a device for the protection of one against another, then fear or self-interest become the dominant motives. We obey the law either because of what the law will do to us if we disobey it, or we obey the law from self-interest. Here I want to advance an empirical thesis, controversial but, so I believe, defensible by an historical analysis. It is that law tends to be effective only insofar and so long as a substantial portion of the community thinks of law in the first way, thinks of it in terms of an identification with the goods of the whole community. When the law is in good working order it is not when everyone is obeying the law from fear, or when everyone is obeying the law from calculated self-interest. It is when obedience to law expresses a genuine allegiance to law. Thus it is precisely when the law is least needed, when it is least invoked, that it is in the best working order. When by contrast there is continuous resort to the law, generally a sign that moral relations have to some large degree broken down. It is a sign that the motives which make us invoke the law are those of fear and self-interest. And when fear and self-interest have to be brought into play, law itself tends to be morally discredited.

This is what has happened in our own society. It has happened because the law has too often been made the instrument of partisan, self -interested purposes. The conversion of law to the service of such purposes perhaps started in the last century with the use of the courts by the large capitalists to aggrandize by transforming the law of property in an individualistic direction. But it was continued in the strategy of reformers and liberals who then tried to make the courts instruments for their purposes. (This is why the question of the political composition of the Supreme Court became important.) Now there is what appears from the liberal standpoint to be a conservative reaction. I do not think it in any coherent sense conservative at all, but rather a reaction by a variety of groups to the period in which liberals used the law as an instrument of political change in favor of themselves and their clients. Such a reaction is sometimes expressed by campaigns for a variety of constitutional amendments, and it is sometimes expressed by attacks upon regulation.

What then are we to say of regulation? When we are concerned with those regulations that deal with the quality and safety of goods and services, we ought to be clear that we need regulation only because human nature is gravely defective when embodied in the modern corporation—regulation, remember, applies primarily to the activities of corporations and only secondarily to the activities of individuals; for corporate America does all that it can to ensure that responsibility is never brought home to individuals.

Let me spell that out. It has been suggested (in one way by Milton Friedman, in other ways by others) that we should abandon a good deal of present law and almost, perhaps all, regulation, and leave individuals free to deal with each other in the delivery of goods and services as market mechanisms permit. Those who may be wronged by what happens will be able to sue in court—to bring civil actions against those who have caused them harm or danger. It is very important to notice that there are two things wrong with this model. One is that those who Milton Friedman proposes should take civil action would often in fact be dead. And those who are not dead will very often have been injured in a way for which no compensation is other than symbolically adequate. Think of the thalidomide case. The recent book on thalidomide, *Suffer the Children*, provides the evidence. What Grünenthal Chemie in Germany and what the Distillers Corporation in Britain were willing to do, as the developers and the licensees for thalidomide, shows very clearly that large corporations are collectively quite willing to undertake courses of action that individuals in the corporation would be deeply shocked by if it was proposed that they as individuals should do what the corporation does. The individuals who staff Grünenthal or Distillers are generally no worse than the rest of us. It is simply the case that in a corporate society one of the ways in which moral relationships have been eroded is by the substitution of corporate for individual responsibility. More than this, a moral and cultural distance is set up between those who receive and those who supply. Grünenthal Chemie and Distillers never themselves had to give thalidomide to a single patient. Thalidomide was administered by physicians and by physicians who had not themselves dealt directly with those in the corporation who had made the decisions about manufacture and research. The moral and physical harm is thus distanced from the actions that caused it. And what is true of thalidomide is also true, for example, of automobiles. I take great encouragement from the action of a jury in Indiana that has sought to bring a homicide charge against the Ford Motor Company for selling Pinto automobiles with gas tanks at the rear in a dangerous location. They will not of course in fact be able to press home criminal charges because they are dealing with a corporation that embodied excuse for irresponsibility. Individual responsibility is an endangered concept because of the combination in our society of corporate power and moral weakness.

The result: regulation is the best we can do. In this I differ from Mr. Hutt; I do not see regulation as an admirable expression of a shared moral code. I see it as a minimal device that has been developed in order to compensate for the grave defects of a culture where the fabric of morality is being torn apart and where government cannot act in the ways that we would want it to if moral community were a real possibility. Regulation is a necessary makeshift. Churchill once said that democracy is the worst form of government except for all the others. Regulation, it seems to me, deserves a similar verdict. One final point: Dr. Gray rightly points out that the reason why institutional review boards had become more effective, why regulation is more effective is that individuals are behaving better. Ten years ago many people would not have acted as conscientiously as they are acting now. And it may be thought that there is a clash between my thesis about the moral defects of our culture and his point about the new moral climate in certain specific contexts. I think not. It has been a characteristic of the last ten years that consciously or unconsciously a response to the moral defects of the culture as a whole has been the remaking of certain kinds of moral community at specific local levels within professions, within institutions, within local communities. Very often this new moral concern emerges in what are at first incoherent and inchoate ways. Nonetheless it is real. And although I would agree with some of the bad things that Professor Barber says about the ways in which we find members of the professions behaving, I think that within the medical profession particularly changes for the better over the last ten years have been dramatic and unpredictably so.

JOHN H. FIELDER

21

The Ethics and Politics of
Automobile Regulation

HISTORY AND THEORY OF REGULATION

Regulation can be undertaken for a variety of reasons, but the major ones concern economic or safety considerations. Economic regulation is designed to control the price of a product or service essential to the public interest, such as electricity or railroad freight service. In situations where the free market does not provide competitive pressure to keep prices down and services readily available, state and federal regulation has been used to fix prices. The clearest examples are public utilities, such as water, electricity, telephone service, and gas. These are essential to public health and well-being and are usually provided by monopolies. Without competitive pressure, unscrupulous suppliers could charge very high rates and exclude many people from these vital resources. Every state regulates the rates and availability of these utilities.

The earliest examples of economic regulation were attempts by agricultural states of the midwest in the nineteenth century to regulate the railroads and grain elevators that were central to their economic life.[1] It is important for the economic health of the region that the rates charged for these essential services be reasonable and nondiscriminatory. While railroads and grain elevators are clearly essential to an agricultural economy, many other businesses have been subject to economic regulation, such as trash hauling and towing companies. Whenever public interest is at stake and abuses from private suppliers are likely, economic regulation will be seen as an option for dealing with the problem.

Another reason for economic regulation is to protect fledgling industries or to prevent ruinous competition. Until relatively recent times, airline fares were regulated by the federal government. There was no economic competition for these services since the rates were fixed by the regulating agency. It was thought that competition among airlines, for example, would prevent the growth of air passenger and airfreight service. While that may have been true in the infancy of the airline industry, by the 1970s there was a consensus that such regulation simply kept prices high and eliminated competition. The *de*regulation movement of the 1980s sought to eliminate economic regulation and return pricing to the free market.

SAFETY REGULATION

Safety regulation is undertaken in response to dangerous technologies where standard market and legal forces do not induce operators to provide adequate safety. The earliest example of federal safety regulation of this kind concerned boiler explosions on steamboats in the middle of the nineteenth century. Operators, in an effort to obtain more speed against rivals, would inadvertently exceed the boiler's pressure limits or deliberately disable its safety valve. Like airline fares in the beginning of the airline industry, competition did not have a beneficial effect on safe operation of steamboat boilers. Conventional free market thinking holds that competition forces operators to provide a safe product in order to attract and keep its customers. Customers want safety and will buy from operators who provide it. Although this is an attractive idea, it is often imperfectly realized in actual situations, such as boiler safety.

An explosion of the steamboat boiler is very dangerous: if you weren't killed by the explosion or the subsequent fire, you stood a good chance of drowning. Contributing to the public interest in this area was the fact that an accident of this kind brings violent death to hundreds of people at once. When the boiler exploded on the steamboat

Moselle in 1838, 151 people died. Like airplane crashes, they clearly demonstrate the danger of this technology.

Responding to the public outcry concerning the *Moselle* accident, Congress passed a weak law, which did little to prevent more explosions. Legal remedies were also ineffective because of the difficulties in proving why the boiler exploded and the reluctance of juries to convict. Finally, when the death toll reached 407 in 1852, Congress established the Steamboat Inspection Service, the first safety regulatory agency. It soon reduced the death rate from boiler explosions and inaugurated the participation of engineering professional societies in establishing technical standards for dangerous technology.[2]

This is a typical pattern in regulation; calls for regulatory solutions to a problem are debated and resisted until a large accident occurs. Only then is there sufficient political will to make significant changes. Cynics refer to this process as "tombstone technology." An adequate number of tombstones are required to prove that the technology requires safety regulation.

THE JUSTIFICATION OF REGULATION

In a society strongly committed to capitalism, free market competition, and individual freedom, regulation is regarded as a last resort, a necessary evil to be undertaken only when it is clear that there are no other remedies for a serious problem. The pattern sketched above in regulating boilers on steamboats is typical of all regulatory reforms. Strong public pressure and clear evidence (hundreds of deaths) are needed to overcome reluctance to interfere in private enterprise. Although we are more willing to turn to regulation today as a solution than we were in the nineteenth century, the burden of proof is on those who propose regulation.[3]

Safety regulation requires a judgment that something is not adequately safe. By definition, safety means "of acceptable risk."[4] Every technology carries with it some risk of harm to people and property. To say that something is not safe is to claim that the risk of harm is not acceptable, but acceptable to whom? The steamboat operators obviously believed the risk was acceptable, and their view prevailed for some time. Clearly a substantial part of the American public felt that hundreds of deaths each year from boiler explosions on steamboats were too many and that steamboats should be made safer. In these matters, what is acceptable is a political decision. Reasonable men and women may disagree about how much safety is required at what cost, but it is ultimately a political process that determines the limits of acceptable risk. The political strength of those who thought the risk unacceptable finally prevailed over the resistance of operators and the general reluctance to regulate. Similar arguments concerning acceptable risk and the desirability of regulation may be found in every area of public life, concerning aircraft, drugs, automobiles, medical devices such as breast implants, household products, toys, sporting equipment, and so on. Virtually every product that poses some risk is a candidate for safety regulation.

THE ORIGINS OF AUTO SAFETY REGULATION

Automobile accidents kill thousands of people every year and injure many more thousands. For a long time, the public regarded this as an acceptable risk that did not require government regulation. This point of view was largely due to the prevailing belief that the primary cause of accidents was improper driving. The major problem of auto safety was "the nut behind the wheel," not the car or the roadway environment. As a General Motors (GM) Vice-President put it, "If the drivers do everything they should, there wouldn't be accidents, would there?"[5] From this perspective, highway safety was mainly a matter of individual behavior and the appropriate means for improvement were education, training, law enforcement, and exhortations to drive safely. The entire safety establishment, which was heavily influenced by the auto industry, promoted this view of the problem and its solutions. Safety meant "safe behavior by drivers."

Part of the persuasive force of this prevailing outlook was its emphasis on individual freedom and responsibility. In a society where these are strong cultural values, explanations of problems that invoke these values have a presumption of validity. In addition, the automobile has long been a symbol of independence and individuality in American life. Regulating automobiles appeared to be an attack on our most cherished social values.

For these and other reasons, autos had largely escaped regulation that was characteristic of other forms of transportation. According to Elizabeth Drew, the auto industry was complacent:

And back in Detroit, the giant $25 billion-a-year auto industry nestled comfortably in its corporate cocoon, content in the knowledge that this was the pride of private enterprise, the backbone of the American economy (accounting for nearly one-sixth of it), and the only major transportation industry so free of government regulation.[6]

This comfortable "corporate cocoon" ended in 1966, when President Lyndon Johnson signed two pieces of legislation, the National Traffic and Motor Vehicle Safety Act and the Highway Safety Act, which gave sweeping authority to the government regulators. Before discussing these two acts, it is useful to see how the industry went from unregulated complacency to widely regulated.

THE SHIFT TO AUTO REGULATION

There are several major factors that contributed to this revolutionary result. First, a number of scholars had challenged the prevailing view that highway safety was mainly a problem of bad driving. Researchers like Hugh DeHaven, an aviation enthusiast, called attention to the role of seat belts and crash mitigation engineering. This latter approach emphasized better vehicle design to lessen the effects of the "second collision," when the driver collides with the inside of the car. DeHaven and other pointed out that accidents were inevitable, and that manufacturers should design cars—like airplanes—with this in mind.

This alternative to the prevailing view of safety as a matter of individual responsibility had some effect on industry thinking, for in 1956 Ford offered many safety features on its new cars, which it featured prominently in its advertising. Public reaction to the new emphasis on safety was generally positive, but GM

did not respond favorably to the safety campaign. There were reports of "snide insinuations about safety," the use of anti-seat belt propaganda, and outright pressure on Ford executives by their GM counterparts to "lay off" safety.[7]

In addition, the Chevrolet Division of GM took a commanding lead over Ford by emphasizing styling and performance based on a new V-8 engine. Ford management responded by deemphasizing safety and focusing more on styling and horsepower. When sales at Ford fell that year, many in the industry concluded that "safety doesn't sell." That conclusion was—and is—disputed, but Ford's experience with auto safety was hardly encouraging.

In addition to scholars and engineers, people in politics began to take up the cause of safer cars. Senator Abraham Ribicoff chaired hearings on auto safety in 1965 and revealed that "the President's own Traffic Safety Commission was staffed by individuals who were not on the federal payroll but on the payroll of automobile manufacturers. Suddenly a whiff of scandal was in the air."[8] Daniel Patrick Moynihan, chair of the New York State Traffic Policy Committee in the late 1950s, attacked the prevailing view of auto safety and called attention to the lack of consideration given to engineering design in making safer cars. When he became Assistant Secretary of Labor in the Kennedy administration he hired a young lawyer named Ralph Nader in 1964. Nader burst into public awareness with the publication of his book, *Unsafe at Any Speed: The Designed-in Dangers of the American Automobile*, in 1965.[9] Nader's forceful prose, moral outrage, and careful attention to facts won extensive praise for his work. Although it focused on the design defects of the Chevrolet Corvair, it also attacked the industry for neglecting design safety. More than anything else, Nader's book shifted public thinking about auto safety from the driver to the car.

Moynihan and Nader were joined by other supporters in Congress and lobbied for auto safety legislation. During the Ribicoff hearings, General Motors President James Roche admitted that his company earned $1.7 *billion* in profits in 1964, but spent only $1.25 *million* on safety. While the political pressure was increasing, there was still much opposition. What put the campaign for regulation over the top was the revelation that GM had hired private detectives to investigate Ralph Nader after his book appeared. At first they were trying to discredit him by looking for financial ties to the many lawsuits filed by Corvair owners. But when nothing emerged, GM investigators went further and delved into his private life, hoping to find damaging evidence to use against him. Again finding nothing improper, they apparently tried to create incidents. Nader reported being approached by women and bothered by late-night phone calls. Friends and neighbors were asked about his sex life, if he was anti-Semitic or belonged to left-wing political groups. Just after his testimony in Congress, Capitol police arrested two men who were following Nader. Not a shred of wrongdoing or improper behavior on Nader's part was ever discovered by these investigations.

Intense public outrage followed these disclosures. It is hard to imagine how GM could have helped the cause of regulation more than by their arrogant and ethically improper investigation of Nader, particularly his private life. The auto industry was now the villain, and although GM President Roche apologized to Nader in Congressional testimony, the damage was done. The auto industry lost all credibility in their arguments against regulation, and the bill proposed by the Johnson administration was strengthened by Congress. From this point on, the industry gave up the fight against regulation and sought to shape its content.

AUTOMOBILE REGULATION

The National Traffic and Motor Vehicle Safety Act was enacted to establish safety requirements for all motor vehicles. The Highway Safety Act's purpose was to develop comprehensive programs of traffic safety. Both acts were administered by the National Highway Traffic Safety Administration (NHTSA), which was housed in the new Department of Transportation.

NHTSA had a broad mandate, to "meet the need for automobile safety" and to protect the public against "unreasonable risks."[10] Under its legislative authority, NHTSA has issued safety standards for items such as seat belts, the design of interior knobs and controls, rear-view mirrors, energy-absorbing steering wheels, door latches, fuel standards, and windshields. NHTSA's Standard 301 (Part I) is an NHTSA regulation setting out the allowable amount of fuel that can be lost after an accident.

The Vehicle Safety Act required that NHTSA issue initial rules by January 31, 1967. Although the budget for the agency was not finalized until November 15, 1966, NHTSA still managed to establish 20 rules for the deadline. Not surprisingly, the standards they set had already been extensively discussed before the legislation, and thus consisted of practices that were either standard in most domestic cars or reflected the best of current auto industry standards.[11]

The empire struck back when these initial standards were issued, charging that the regulations were costly and/or impossible to implement. This response was typical of the auto industry's reaction toward regulation. John Rae describes it thus:

> First, industry spokesmen denied that the problem existed; they then conceded that it did exist but asserted that it had no solution; finally they conceded that it could be solved but that the solutions would be very expensive, difficult to apply, and would require a long time to develop.[12]

NHTSA revised some of its rules in response to industry criticisms. A new public debate ensued about whether the agency had surrendered to the auto industry. Ralph Nader was highly critical of the agency and William Steiglitz, head of MHTSA's rule making division and a longtime advocate of engineering safety, resigned in protest.

William Haddon, a physician whose book, *Accident Research*[13] emphasized scientific rigor in safety studies, was the first NHTSA administrator, and established the role of scientific data in rule making. He wanted standards that were based on scientifically valid evidence about safety. Attempts to set standards based on scientific evidence ran into serious difficulties, for often the data needed were incomplete or not available. Many of the agency's most important proposals were withdrawn because of industry objections to their scientific basis. By requiring a high degree of scientific certainty for its proposals, the agency had guaranteed that rule making would be a long and laborious process, one that was open to obstruction by manufacturers.

On addition, NHTSA adopted a component-specific approach in its regulation. That is, instead of developing a general visibility criterion that manufacturers could meet, NHTSA elected to establish standards for headlights, taillights, windshield wipers, and rear view mirrors. This was done for two reasons; first, most existing standards and studies were equipment-specific and, therefore provided whatever scientific evidence that was available, and second, this approach reflected the language of the Act that standards must be reasonable.[14] As a result, rule making became a debate between NHTSA and the manufacturers on questions of production feasibility for dozens of components.

REGULATION AND THE PINTO

Although most of the initial regulations consisted of standards already in place for most cars or that were the best of current industry practices, implementing them did impose costs on Ford and other manufacturers. Redesign was often required to meet NHTSA standards. Manufacturers not only challenged NHTSA regulations, but also sought regulatory relief. Ford senior executives were seeking such relief in a 1971 meeting with President Nixon. Preserved on the Watergate tapes, this meeting reveals the automakers' concerns about rising costs in the face of increasing competition from foreign cars. Henry Ford II claimed that

> We see the price of a Pinto. . . going something like fifty percent in the next three years with inflation part of it, but that's not

the big part of it. It's the safety requirements, the emission requirements, the bumper requirements. . .

If these prices get so high that people stop buying cars. . .they're gonna buy more foreign cars; you're going to have balance-of-payment problems.[15]

A sympathetic Nixon promised to do what he could to help.

Over at NHTSA, because of its emphasis on scientific validation and component-based regulation, the agency was

[m]ired in regulatory trench warfare with the industry; starved for revenues, personnel, and facilities; under constant attack by putative public interest friends; flanked by protean bureaucratic bedfellows; and trapped, in part, by its own sense of professionalism, in a staggeringly laborious regulatory approach...[16]

"Profits vs. Safety" (chapter 18) provides a fuller discussion of this issue.

Standard 301, for example, which deals with fuel spill standards in accidents, was proposed in 1969 but the first parts were not implemented until 1975, and other sections did not become applicable until later. Thus from a legal standpoint the Pintos built during that period appear to have met the existing regulatory standards for fuel safety.

The delays in implementing Standard 301 followed the pattern described above; its approval in 1976 had much to do with the Pinto scandal and the public outcry it generated. To meet Standard 301 for the 1977 Pinto, Ford attached a plastic guard to the gas tank to prevent it from rupturing when pushed into the differential in rear-end crashes, and modified the filler pipe to make it more secure. Had these standards been adopted more rapidly, there would have been fewer deaths and injuries, and no Pinto case or books about it.

PROBLEMS WITH REGULATION

Regulation is a far from perfect solution to problems of auto safety. For one thing, regulating technology is not easy. Here is a list of conditions for optimal regulation, compiled by Stephen Unger:

1. The technology must be reasonably stable and well understood.
2. There must be an effective political consensus that regulation should take place.

3. A set of clear, sensible, and enforceable rules must be formulated.
4. Adequate funds must be allocated for the work necessary (including research) to generate and enforce the regulations.
5. The regulatory agency should have as its *sole* function the regulation of the industry in the public interest. It should *not* have other, sometimes conflicting, goals such as promoting the rapid growth of the industry.
6. Agency personnel, at all levels, should be competent, honest, and free to pursue the goals of the agency without conflicts of interest or political pressure.[17]

Unger notes that "no regulatory agency has ever operated with all these conditions fully satisfied," but they provide a useful standard for assessment.

Looking at the first requirement, auto regulation has an advantage over, say, aircraft, because the technology is more mature and therefore contains fewer surprises. Also, automotive technology does not operate under such extremes of temperature, pressure, and force as aircraft, which requires exotic metals and high production accuracy. It is not so much the technology that is a problem in auto regulation as it is NHTSA's component-specific approach which is open to extensive debate concerning production feasibility.

As we have seen, events in the 1950s and 1960s traced the growing political consensus that auto safety regulation was not only desirable but necessary, important for Unger's second criterion. With a strong political mandate, the regulatory agency had the power to make the regulations it believed were appropriate. Developing and enforcing regulations is a political process, no matter how much independence is officially granted to the regulating agency. Regulated industries have political power which they exercise through all branches of government. They have supporters in Congress and the executive branch, and they have the resources to seek legal solutions to their problems. This is particularly true of the auto industry because of its size and centrality to the American economy. Despite its overwhelming legislative defeat in 1966, the auto industry has been successful in delaying and modifying NHTSA's rules, of which Standard 301 is a good example.

Regulated industries will attempt to influence the regulatory process to their advantage as part of the political dimension of regulation. As one scholar notes,

...anticompetitive or strategic use of regulation is pervasive. There is a lot of wealth at stake, and managers would be remiss in their fiduciary responsibilities if they ignored profits available through (legal) manipulation of governmental processes. The decision to invest resources in lobbying to prevent the entry of rivals, to form a regulatory cartel, or to impose costs on existing rivals does not differ materially from other decisions managers make on a daily basis.[18]

For example, in the 1970s GM argued for a more stringent mileage standard than was actually implemented. They knew that the effect of a higher requirement would fall much more heavily on Chrysler and American Motors. Their competitors would have to spend more to meet the higher standard than GM, thus giving GM a competitive advantage. This is a clear example of strategic use of regulation, i.e., using the regulatory process to gain advantage over rivals. Because regulations do not affect all producers equally, companies often support regulations that give them an advantage. Ford's and Iococca's discussion with President Nixon is another kind of lobbying designed to keep costs down and sales up. They wanted Nixon to put pressure on the Department of Transportation to reduce the burden of safety regulation.

Unger's third criterion, "clear, sensible, and enforceable rules" hides an important problem. One of the great difficulties of regulation concerns striking the balance between safety and the burdens imposed upon the industry. Safety is not free; it requires additional engineering design, inspection, added manufacturing techniques, and money invested in research to meet safety requirements. It raises the cost of goods and services to consumers and thus is a brake on economic activity. Regulators must decide how much safety to require at what price to producers and consumers. Unless one is thoroughly familiar with the complex tradeoffs such decisions involve, it is easy to criticize the results as too favorable to industry or to the public. Trade associations and consumer groups compete for public attention in promoting their versions of regulatory decisions. Usually a case can be made on both sides, leaving all but the insiders confused about the merits of the case.

Unger's call for clear and sensible regulations appears uncontroversial, but it seems to overlook the political dimension of regulation. Different groups will have different views of the relative weight given to safety and to the burdens placed on the industry. What counts as an acceptable tradeoff is both a political and technical decision.

Thus what one side regards as a sensible rule may be unreasonable to another. This is particularly true from the point of view of the regulated industry, whose economic fortunes will be strongly affected by regulatory decisions.

Unger's fourth requirement is adequate funding for regulatory agencies. This is a vulnerable spot for regulatory agencies, for if the executive branch cuts their funding the result is less regulation, regardless of the regulations on the books. The Reagan administration, which was ideologically committed to reducing regulation, used this method to reduce the effectiveness of the Environmental Protection Agency (EPA) and the FAA.[19] Consumer groups may file lawsuits to force adequate funding, but this is a difficult process, since there is, necessarily, much legal leeway in how a regulatory agency carries out its legislative mandate. Funding regulatory agencies is simply another way in which the political issues in regulation appear.

Unger makes much of his fifth criterion, the need for regulatory agencies to have a single function, or at least, no conflicting functions. The primary example he has in mind is the FAA, whose charter requires it both protect the flying public (safety) and promote the industry. This conflict was a significant factor in the handling of design problems in the DC-10 aircraft.[20] But even if these requirements were eliminated, the central issue, balancing public and private interests, would remain for any regulatory agency. Somewhere, the government must decide how much safety to require at what cost to producers and to consumers. There is no objective formula for this decision; one must make a judgment based upon weighing the various factors involved. Obviously these are going to be affected by one's philosophical view of the public interest as well as an assessment of the real burdens a regulation will impose on all parties. Clearly reasonable men and women may disagree at a variety of points in this process.

It is for these reasons that I believe Unger's final requirement, that regulators be free to pursue their work "free of political pressures" is unrealistic and misleading. This requirement is one that is imbedded in the traditional theory of regulation, the idea that impartial regulators, independent of outside influence, can reach an objectively fair decision. It is an engineering model of regulation, one that makes more sense when applied to boiler codes than to more complex decisions about mileage standards or fuel leakage limits. It treats regulatory decisions as *technical* determinations rather than complex weighings of different social values.

While this [traditional] theory [of regulation] admits that the initial decision whether a given industry should be regulated is largely prudential, it assumes that once the decision is made the regulatory process itself can proceed on an entirely objective basis.[21]

Unger's view of regulation illegitimately separates political and technical judgments, implying that sufficiently independent regulators with concern for the public interest will be able to reach objective conclusions. A important corollary of this view is that when regulation fails, it is likely the result of either incompetence or political and ethical corruption.

If regulation involves the weighing of various public and private interests, the best one can hope for is a rough social consensus about how these interests are to be balanced. Important philosophical differences concerning the importance of these interests and their effects upon the well-being of society are to be expected, as well as change over time. Different administrations espousing different political conceptions will appoint regulators who reflect their views. The result of these differences will be hard to judge, since much depends upon circumstances beyond the control of regulators. The attempt to impose a particular view of regulation on various federal agencies may result in actions that clearly violate the social consensus, or it may create a new sense of what is possible and desirable.

REGULATION AND LEGAL LIABILITY

In the 1960s courts also took up the issue of auto safety in lawsuits against manufacturers. In the case of *Larsen v. General Motors Corporation* (391 F.2d 495, 8th Cir. 1968) the court held that manufacturers have the legal obligation to foresee the kinds of accidents their cars are likely to have and to provide a reasonable degree of safety to its occupants. This is the doctrine that cars must be *crashworthy*, capable of providing a reasonable degree of protection to the occupants in foreseeable crashes. Thus the courts followed Congress in rejecting the idea that accidents are primarily caused by improper driving and insisting that manufacturers take responsibility to mitigate harm caused by crashes.

What is a crashworthy car? If a car meets all the regulatory safety requirements of NHTSA, is it, from a legal standpoint, crashworthy? Strict liability (see Part IV) holds a manufacturer responsible for damages caused by a product which is defective and unreasonably dangerous to the user. Can a manufacturer claim that because all NHTSA regulations were met that a car is *not* "defective and unreasonably dangerous to the user"? If a manufacturer meets all regulations, should it be immune from lawsuits alleging that its product was defective? The general legal rule is that meeting applicable regulations is not an absolute defense to liability. Courts have held that since regulations may be clearly inadequate, resulting in wrongful injury to consumers, the manufacturer may have an obligation to do more than the regulations require to produce a safe product.[22]

It is easy to imagine a weak regulatory agency dominated by industry which refuses to create adequate safety regulations. Allowing immunity from liability if all regulations were met would, in this kind of situation, unjustly deny injured consumers the right to compensation for their injuries. In this approach, courts recognize the weaknesses of the regulatory system described above and refuse to allow manufacturers to hide behind regulatory requirements which unreasonably endanger consumers.

REGULATION AND THE HONOR SYSTEM

A popular conception of regulatory oversight conceives regulators as continually present during product design, testing, and manufacturing, always on the lookout for violations of regulations. Regulators would always be looking over the shoulders of those regulated, making sure that safety regulations are met. If this were the case, we would be much more confident that our autos and airplanes would be safe. However, the reality is quite different.

If regulation took place in this way, two very serious consequences would occur. First, it would be very expensive. The number of regulators needed would be enormous for a single large industry like automobiles. Multiply this through the economy, including drugs, medical devices, airplanes, trucks, railroads, foods, cosmetics—it would take an army of inspectors.

Second, the presence of so many regulators in the workplace would be intrusive. Every industry has many trade secrets, special procedures, and manufacturing techniques that they have developed to give them a competitive edge. Having a lot of people around who are not part of the organization would increase the risk that such information would make its way to their competitors. This conception of regulation would be a significant change in the privacy accorded to regulated organizations.

In order to respond to both of these issues, the regulatory system that we have developed is one that relies heavily on industry personnel to conduct tests, make inspections, and determine that regulatory requirements are met. Regulators receive documents attesting to these activities, and the bulk of their actions consist in reviewing these documents. While there are inspections and direct involvement of regulators, this is a relatively small part of the process.

Regulatory compliance is, to a large degree, an honor system, dependent upon the ethics of people in the regulated industry. Despite appearances of the fox guarding the chickens, this arrangement works surprisingly well for autos, aircraft, food, drugs, and medical devices. While it would be wrong to discount the ethical concerns of business managers in regulated industries, no small part of the success of regulation is the threat of lawsuits and the dangers of public exposure of wrongdoing. Amending Samuel Johnson's remark that the prospect of being hanged "concentrates a man's mind wonderfully," the awareness of the severe damage to Ford and its reputation by the Pinto case tends to concentrate the minds of those who make automobiles.

CONCLUSION

It is tempting to cast the story of the Pinto, NHTSA, and the belated adoption of Standard 301 as a classic case of a regulatory agency being captured by the industry. But as we have seen, this hardly does justice to the plurality of interests, issues, history, and personalities that constitute the process of regulation. Thinking of the regulatory process using a technical model, as Unger does, more easily lends itself to the capture theory of what has gone wrong. On this view, it is easy to believe that good regulations are delayed or not adopted because their adversaries defeated them for their economic reasons. While this is certainly true in many cases, a better approach is one that frankly acknowledges the political dimension of safety regulation, accepting the moral ambiguity and pluralism of political life as well as its strengths and weaknesses.

NOTES

1. Kenneth M. Sayre, Ellen L. Maher, Peri E. Arnold, Kenneth E. Goodpaster Robert E. Rodes, and James B. Stewart, *Regulation, Values and*

the Public Interest, (Notre Dame, IN: The Philosophic Institute of the University of Notre Dame, 1980), p. 8.

2. Stephen H. Unger, *Controlling Technology: Ethics and the Responsible Engineer*, (New York: Holt Rinehart and Winston, 1982), p. 101–2.

3. For example, changes in aircraft safety regulation typically follow serious crashes which finally prove that a problem exists and regulation is needed. See John H. Fielder and Douglas Birsch, *The DC-10: A Case Study in Ethics, Technology and Society*, (Albany, NY: State, University of New York Press, 1992), p. 272–3.

4. William Lowrance, *Of Acceptable Risk*, (Los Altos, CA: William Kaufman, Inc., 1986).

5. Quoted in John D. Graham, *Auto Safety: Assessing America's Performance*, (Dover, MA: Auburn House Publishing Co., 1989), p. 18.

6. Quoted in "The Birth of Federal Regulation" in Graham, *Auto Safety*, p. 27. I have leaned heavily on Graham's book for information on auto regulation.

7. Joel W. Eastman, *Styling vs. Safety: The American Automobile and the Development of Automotive Safety, 1900–1966*, (Lanham, MD: University Press of America, 1984), p. 231.

8. Jerry L. Mashaw and David L. Harfst, *The Struggle for Auto Safety*, (Cambridge, MA: Harvard University Press, 1990), p. 51.

9. New York: Grossman Publishers, 1966.

10. Ibid., p. 68.

11. Ibid., p. 70.

12. John Rae, *The American Automobile Industry*, (Boston, MA: Twayne Publishers, 1984), p. 134.

13. William Haddon, E. Suchman, and D. Klein, eds., *Accident Research 4–5 (1964)*.

14. Mashaw and Harfst, *Struggle for Auto Safety*, p. 75.

15. Quoted in Francis T. Cullen, William J. Maakestad, and Gray Cavender, *Corporate Crime Under Attack*, (Cincinnati, Ohio: Anderson Publishing Co., 1987), p. 157.

16. Mashaw and Harfst, *Struggle for Auto Safety*, p. 83.

17. Unger, *Controlling Technology*, p. 103.

18. Robert E. McCormick, "A Review of the Economics of Regulation: The Political Process," in *Regulation and the Reagan Era: Politics, Bureaucracy and the Public Interest*, edited by, Roger E. Meiners and Bruce Yandle (San Francisco: The Independent Institute, 1989), p. 29.

19. A General Accounting Office report, reprinted in Fielder and Birsch, *DC-10 Case*, shows the reduction in funds allotted to the FAA in the Reagan years (p. 39).

20. See Fielder and Birsch, *DC-10 Case*, p. 286.

21. Sayre et al., *Regulation, Values, and the Public Interest*, p. 13.

22. See Alvin S. Weinstein, Aaron D Twerski, Henry R. Piehler, and William A. Donaher, *Products Liability and the Reasonably Safe Product: A Guide for Management, Design, and Marketing*, (NY: John Wiley and Sons, 1978), p. 7–8.

Appendix
Abbreviated Ford Pinto Chronology

1967—Ford Motor Company decided to build a subcompact car in the United States. Design and development began. Lee Iacocca was instrumental in the project.

1969—The NHTSA first proposed Standard 301. Ford conducted crash tests to see if subcompacts modified to have Pinto-type fuel systems would meet Standard 301. The results showed the gas leakage exceeded the standard.

September 1970—The Ford Pinto went on sale.

October 1970—A production model Pinto was crashed backward into a fixed barrier at 21 mph. A bolt on the differential housing punctured the gasoline tank and the filler pipe is dislodged. Similar results were achieved in several other crash tests.

December 1970—Ford engineers tested a rubber "bladder" inside a Pinto gas tank to see if it would upgrade the safety of the fuel system. The "bladder" was successful in rear-end, fixed-barrier crashes of 20 and 26 mph.

April 1971—Ford executives wrote a memo recommending that neither the "bladder" nor a gasoline tank "flak vest" be adopted until 1976 in order to save the company $20.9 million.

September 1976—The part of Standard 301 applicable to rear-end collisions went into effect. Cars were not to leak more than an ounce of fuel a minute after being impacted by a barrier moving at 30 mph. The 1977 Pinto, modified with a plastic shield between the differential housing and the tank, an improved filler pipe, and an improved bumper, met the standard.

September 1977—"Pinto Madness" by Mark Dowie appeared in *Mother Jones.*

February 1978—Richard Grimshaw, a victim of a Pinto rear-end crash and fire, was awarded over $127 million dollars in a product liability suit. The award was later reduced on appeal.

March 1978—Pinto owners in Alabama and California filed class-action suits, demanding that Ford recall all Pintos built from 1971 through 1976 and modify their fuel systems. NHTSA notified Ford that the 1977 Ford Pinto did not pass a 30 mph front-end barrier test. This led to the recall of of about 300,000 Pintos.

May 1978—The NHTSA announced that it had made an initial determination that a safety defect existed in the fuel systems of 1971–1976 Ford Pintos. Public hearings were scheduled for mid-June. The agency had studied 38 cases of Pintos involved in rear-end collisions that had resulted in fires. There had been 27 fatalities and 24 incidents of nonfatal burns in these cases.

June 1978—Ford announced the recall of its 1.5 million Pintos and similar subcompacts "to end public concern." It replaced the filler pipe and added two polyethylene shields to help protect the tank. The cost was estimated by Ford at 20 million dollars after taxes.

July 1978—Lee Iacocca was fired by Ford. Whether this was directly connected to the Pinto case is unknown.

August 1978—The three Ulrich girls were burned to death in their Pinto following a rear-end collision in Indiana.

September 1978—Ford Motor Company was indicted for three felony counts of reckless homicide by a Grand Jury in Indiana (maximum penalty $10,000 fine for each count if convicted).

January 1980—The trial began.

March 1980—Ford was found innocent on all charges. Ford had to be found guilty of recklessly manufacturing a lethal vehicle and of keeping it on the road despite obvious danger. The prosecution tried to show that Ford had not fixed the car because it was not cost effective. Ford lawyers seem to have convinced the jury that the Ulrich girl's car was stopped when it was hit by a van and therefore their deaths were not a result of reckless homicide.

July 1980—The last Ford Pinto rolled off the assembly line. Ford had manufactured about 3 million of these cars.

August 1980—Ford reached an out-of-court settlement with the Ulrich family to avoid a civil suit. The family reportedly received a total settlement of $22,500. The low figure is because Indiana law severely restricts compensation to surviving families.

Sources—The *Chicago Tribune*, October 13, 1979 and Lee Strobel, *Reckless Homicide?: Ford's Pinto Trial* (South Bend, Indiana: And Books, 1980).

Bibliography

Beauchamp, Tom L. and Norman E. Bowie, eds., *Ethical Theory and Business* (Englewood Cliffs, NJ: Prentice Hall, 1993)

Bowie, Norman E., ed., *Ethical Issues in Government* (Philadelphia: Temple University Press, 1981)

Chamberlain, Neil W., *The Limits of Corporate Responsibility* (New York: Basic Books, 1973)

Childs, Marquis W. and Douglass Cater, *Ethics in a Business Society* (New York: Harper & Bros., 1954)

Clinard, Marshall B., *Corporate Ethics and Crime: The Role of Middle Management* (Beverly Hills: Sage Publications, 1983)

Clinard, Marshall and Peter D. Yeager, *Corporate Crime* (New York: Free Press, 1980)

Cullen, Francis T., William J. Maakestad, and Gray Cavender, *Corporate Crime Under Attack: The Ford Pinto Case and Beyond* (Cincinnati Ohio: Anderson Publishing Company, 1987)

DeGeorge, Richard T., *Business Ethics*, 3rd ed. (New York: Macmillian Publishing Company, 1990)

DesJardins, Joseph R. and John J. McCall, eds., *Contemporary Issues in Business Ethics*, 2nd ed. (Belmont, California: Wadsworth Publishing Company, 1990)

Eastman, Joel W., *Styling vs. Safety—The American Automobile Industry and The Development of Automobile Safety*, 1900–1966. (New York: University Press of America, 1984)

Eisner, Marc Allen, *Regulatory Politics in Transition* (Baltimore: The Johns Hopkins University Press, 1993)

Ezorsky, Gertrude, *Moral Rights in the Workplace* (Albany: State University of New York Press, 1987)

Fisse, Brent and John Braithwaite, *The Impact of Publicity on Corporate Offenders* (Albany, NY: State University of New York Press, 1983)

Frank, Nancy and Michael Lomness, *Controlling Corporate Illegality: The Regulatory Justice System* (Cincinnati Ohio: Anderson Pub. Co., 1988)

French, Peter A., *Collective and Corporate Responsibility* (New York: Columbia University Press, 1984)

Frumer, Louis R. and Melvin I. Friedman, *Products Liability* (New York: Matthew Bender, 1980)

Glazer, Myron Peretz and Penina Migdal Glazer, *The Whistle Blowers: Exposing Corruption in Government and Industry* (New York: Basic Books, 1989)

Graham, John D., *Auto Safety: Assessing America's Performance* (Dover, MA: Auburn House Publishing Company, 1989)

Halberstam, David, *The Reckoning* (New York: William and Morrow and Company, Inc., 1986)

Hirschman, Albert O., *Exit, Voice, and Loyalty* (Cambridge Mass: Harvard University Press, 1970)

Hoffman, W. Michael and Jennifer Mills Moore, *Business Ethics* (New York: McGraw-Hill, 1990)

Jackall, Robert, *Moral Mazes* (New York: Oxford University Press, 1988)

Kannon, N. P., Kathy K. Rebibo, and Donna L. Ellis, *Downsizing Detroit— The Future of the U.S. Automobile Industry* (New York: Praeger Publishers, 1982)

Kimble, William and Robert O. Lesher, *Products Liability* (St. Paul, MN: West Publishing Company, 1979)

Layard, Richard, ed., *Cost-Benefit Analysis* (New York: Penguin Books, 1972)

Lombardi, Louis G., *Moral Analysis: Foundations, Guides and Applications.* (Albany, NY: State University of New York Press, 1988)

Machan, Tibor R., and Bruce M. Johnson, eds., *Rights and Regulation: Ethical, Political and Economic Issues* (Cambridge MA: Ballinger Pub. Co., 1983)

Mashaw, Jerry L. and David L. Harfst, *The Struggle for Auto Safety* (Cambridge, MA: Harvard University Press, 1990)

Mitnick, Barry M., *The Political Economy of Regulation* (New York: Colombia University Press, 1980)

Nader, Ralph, *Unsafe at Any Speed: The Designed-In Dangers of the American Automobile* (New York: Grossman Publishers, 1965)

Nader, Ralph, Peter J. Petkas, and Kate Blackwell, *Whistle Blowing* (New York: Grossman Publishers, 1972)

Noble, David, *America By Design: Science,Technology and the Rise of Corporate Capitalism* (New York: Alfred A. Knopf, 1977)

Owen, Bruce M. and A. Breautigam, *The Regulation Game* (Cambridge MA: Ballinger, 1978)

Papandreou, Andreas G., *Paternalistic Capitalism* (Minneapolis: University of Minnesota Press, 1972)

Perrow, Charles, *Complex Organizations*, 2nd ed. (Glenview, Illinois: Scott, Foresman and Co., 1979)

Peters, Charles and Taylor Branch, *Blowing the Whistle: Dissent in the Public Interest* (New York: Praeger Publishers, 1972)

Peters, Tom and Nancy Austin, *A Passion for Excellence: The Leadership Difference* (New York: Random House, 1985)

Peters, Thomas J. and Robert H. Waterman Jr., *In Search of Excellence: Lessons from America's Best-Run Companies* (New York: Harper & Row, 1982)

Rae, John, *The American Automobile: A Brief History* (Chicago: University of Chicago Press, 1965)

Rothschild, Emma, *Paradise Lost—The Decline of the Auto-Industrial Age* (New York: Random House, 1973)

Samuels, Warren J. and Arthur S. Miller, *Corporations and Society: Power and Responsibility* (New York: Greenwood Press, 1987)

Sayre, Kenneth M., *Regulation, Values and the Public Interest* (Notre Dame, IN: The University of Notre Dame Press, 1980)

Silk, Leonard and David Vogel, *Ethics and Profits* (New York: Simon and Schuster, 1976)

Singer, Peter, *Practical Ethics* (Cambridge: Cambridge University Press, 1979)

Stone, Christopher D., *Where the Law Ends: The Social Control of Corporate Behavior* (New York: Harper & Row, 1975)

Strobel, Lee Patrick, *Reckless Homicide?: Ford's Pinto Trial* (South Bend, IN: And Books, 1980)

Tuleja, Tad, *Beyond the Bottom Line* (New York: Penguin Books, 1985)

Unger, Stephen H., *Controlling Technology: Ethics and the Responsible Engineer* (New York: Holt Rinehart and Winston, 1982)

Velasquez, Manuel G., *Business Ethics—Concepts and Cases* (Englewood Cliffs, NJ: Prentice Hall Inc., 1982)

Westin, Alan, ed., *Whistle-blowing!* (New York: McGraw-Hill, 1981)

Westin, Alan F. and Stephen Salisbury, *Individual Rights in the Corporation: A Reader on Employee Rights* (New York: Pantheon Books, 1980)

White, Lawrence, *The Automobile Industry Since 1945* (Cambridge Mass: Harvard University Press, 1971)

Index